SWINDON COLLEGE

LEARNING RESOURCE CENTRE

Warren Kidd & Gerry Czerniawski

Successful
Teaching 14-19

Theory, Practice and Reflection

SAGE

Los Angeles | London | New Delhi
Singapore | Washington DC

© Warren Kidd and Gerry Czerniawski 2010

Apart from any fair dealing for the purposes of research or
private study, or criticism or review, as permitted under the
Copyright, Designs and Patents Act, 1988, this publication may
be reproduced, stored or transmitted in any form, or by any
means, only with the prior permission in writing of the
publishers, or in the case of reprographic reproduction, in
accordance with the terms of licences issued by the Copyright
Licensing Agency. Enquiries concerning reproduction outside
those terms should be sent to the publishers.

SAGE Publications Ltd
1 Oliver's Yard
55 City Road
London EC1Y 1SP

SAGE Publications Inc.
2455 Teller Road
Thousand Oaks, California 91320

SAGE Publications India Pvt Ltd
B 1/I 1 Mohan Cooperative Industrial Area
Mathura Road
New Delhi 110 044

SAGE Publications Asia-Pacific Pte Ltd
33 Pekin Street #02-01
Far East Square
Singapore 048763

Library of Congress Control Number: 2009933780

British Library Cataloguing in Publication data

A catalogue record for this book is available from
the British Library

ISBN 978-1-84860-712-5
ISBN 978-1-84860-713-2 (pbk)

Typeset by C&M Digitals (P) Ltd, Chennai, India
Printed in Great Britain by TJ International, Padstow, Cornwall
Printed on paper from sustainable resources

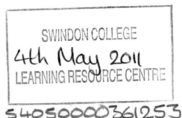
SWINDON COLLEGE
4th May 2011
LEARNING RESOURCE CENTRE

54050000361253

Mixed Sources
Product group from well-managed
forests and other controlled sources
www.fsc.org Cert no. SGS-COC-2482
© 1996 Forest Stewardship Council
FSC

54050000 361253

18th APRIL 2011

Gerry dedicates this book to Jen.

Warren dedicates this book to his son Freddie.

CONTENTS

ABOUT THE AUTHORS

Warren Kidd is Senior Lecturer in Post-Compulsory Education and Training (PCET) at the Cass School of Education, University of East London (UEL). He is the Programme Leader for the part-time PCET PGCE/Cert Ed. provision. Previously, he taught both sociology and psychology for 14 years in secondary schools and sixth form colleges in Surrey, Kent and London. Along with Gerry, Warren is an experienced author of sociology textbooks aimed at the A-Level market. For the past nine years, Warren has worked in the multicultural, urban environment of Newham in east London in the Post-Compulsory sector as a teacher of sociology, social science manager of a large sixth form college and as a cross-college manager responsible for Teaching and Learning. In 2007 he completed managing a 'highly commended' Beacon Award action research project in transferable teaching skills. He was the teaching and learning development manager of a large, diverse sixth form college, and was an Advanced Teaching Practitioner.

Gerry Czerniawski is Senior Lecturer in Secondary Social Science and Humanities Education at the Cass School of Education, University of East London (UEL). He has passionately worked in the multicultural environment in the London Borough of Newham for over 10 years teaching humanities, sociology and business studies at secondary and post-16 levels before gradually moving into teaching within Higher Education in both the political sciences and education (The Open University, University of Northampton, London Metropolitan University and London University's Institute of Education). An established author and teacher trainer, Gerry still teaches part-time in a comprehensive school in Hertfordshire.

ACKNOWLEDGEMENTS

We would like to thank our colleagues in the Cass School of Education and our trainee teachers who have been the inspiration for this book. Gerry would like to acknowledge Pat McNeil for his wisdom and guidance, John Hickman for his relentlessly high standards and expectations of what a good teacher is, and Peta Jarmey for the 'scaffolding' of his early journey into teacher education. Warren would like to acknowledge Jean Murray, Nina Weiss and Rania Hafez for their enthusiasm and support with changing professional identities and roles. Finally, both authors would like to thank all the readers who have looked at and commented on previous drafts of the manuscript as well as Jude Bowen and Amy Jarrold at Sage for the opportunity to write this text, and for their continued support and guidance.

HOW TO USE THIS BOOK

Undertaking a teacher training course is both challenging and rewarding. It is a fabulous profession to join, and one full of many diverse learning experiences – for yourself and your learners. The teacher education course you are enrolled on is no different. For some, it will be the hardest period of your life. The transition you are about to make is enormous and the skills you are about to develop will fundamentally change both your professional and private personas. This book aims to support those working within the 14–19 age range – covering secondary schools, school sixth forms and further education colleges.

The subtitle for this book is 'theory, practice and reflection' and these are the essential elements of any teacher training course and all subsequent professional practice. All three interrelate. As a professional-in-the-making you are required to reflect upon your teaching, adopt theory as a means through which to see and make sense of the world of the classroom around you, and choose between theories at appropriate moments on the basis of the type of practice you are doing.

As a teacher of learners, we recognise that you are also a learner yourself. This is true of all teachers. We see this book as part training manual, part introduction to academic debates around education and teaching and learning, and part teaching techniques, hints and tips. We hope that these elements enable you to complete your teacher training course, while at the same time develop as a practitioner.

We have divided this book into five sections.

Section 1 'Educational Policy' looks at your developing professional role and the background to recent educational change and reform.

Section 2 'Professional Skills' introduces you to the habits of good teachers and good teaching. This section ends with chapters that consider what good teaching is and what your teaching placement and practice will be like.

Section 3 'Theory' looks at academic and research debates, literature and evidence surrounding effective teaching. We also introduce you to aspects of the sociology of education and the literature on teaching and learning styles.

Section 4 'Practice', takes you through the mechanics of your practical placement and classroom-based elements of your training. We look at mentoring; understanding your placement institution; planning and preparation. Chapters in this section of the book also provide ideas for you to try in your classroom. It is important to recognise that good teaching is experimental and reflective – it is about trying new things and seeing what works both for yourself and also for your learners. We will look, in turn, at questioning, skills development, group work, starts and ends of lessons, resource creation and 'e-learning'.

Section 5 'Reflection', ties the various sections of the book together and presents issues and debates that you might take forward into your first year in the profession. In light of the government's plans for teaching to become a Master's (M)-level profession, we also present a chapter on academic debates looking at the M-level issues that many teacher training courses provide.

Features

Good teaching is about good communication. We feel the same could be said for good writing. To enable you to get the most from this book, we have adopted the following features. They are designed to aid your reading of the text and to help you choose more easily which ideas to try and when.

 'Objectives': each chapter starts with learning objectives. We do this as we are very conscious that a great deal of effective teaching involves clear instruction and communication to the audience so that the learner understands at all times where s/he is.

 'M-level thinking': from time to time you will see this icon running through the text of the book. This is so that you, the reader, can see the importance of these themes running through the text as a whole. These ideas are then taken up in the final section, in Chapter 19. It is a consideration and awareness of these vital and contemporary debates that will really raise the levels of your critical awareness and evaluative writing.

 'Discussion points': these enable us, the authors of this book, to really speak directly to you about our own experiences of teaching and learning to teach.

 'Case studies': we use this feature as a means through which we can allow the story to shine through of various practitioners that we have met in our working lives as practitioners ourselves, managers and teacher educators.

*** **'Ease of use'**: a large part of this book is made up of practical ideas. The majority of these are contained in the chapters in Section 4, 'Practice'. We recognise that teaching is both academic and practical – it is both informed by wider academic discourse and yet at the same time has a feel of a 'craft' about it as practitioners are in their classrooms teaching their learners. We have rated out of five stars each teaching tip and idea for its 'ease of use' by the teacher. For each of the ideas and techniques we present in Section 4 of the book, we ask ourselves the question, does the successfulness of the learning being generated outweigh the practical and logistical considerations of planning and preparation? In a sense, this is a 'cooking book' approach to lesson preparation – how long does it take and what ingredients are needed? How can you, as the teacher, create something from the elements you draw together?

'References': we keep our references and guide to further reading to a minimum, but urge you to invest some time reading around the debates contained within this book. Good teaching is about the interplay and interface between the academic literature and how this impacts upon the classroom experience of the learner. See the suggested further reading for useful next steps in your professional learning.

Entering into teaching – becoming a classroom craftsperson and understanding the theories and research behind your practice – is a demanding and challenging endeavour. It is one that we have really valued and one that has completely changed how we viewed the world of work, young people and our own learning, and we sincerely hope you discover these things too.

We hope you enjoy this book and hope you enjoy your new career and professional role.

Warren Kidd
Gerry Czerniawski

SECTION 1

EDUCATIONAL POLICY

CHAPTER 1

WHY TEACH?

Objectives

By the end of this chapter the reader will be able to:

1. understand some of the key debates in forming a professional teacher identity;
2. recognise the importance of educational theory to better understand classroom practice;
3. understand the meaning of the term 'reflective practitioner';
4. see the importance of the interconnection of theory, practice and reflection for developing effective teaching skills;
5. recognise some important educational research on the nature of effective teaching.

Training to be a teacher

Learning to teach is both rewarding and challenging. In fact, the reward is intensified by the challenging nature of the role and of the profession. For a number of years now, teacher education has spoken of the importance of being a 'reflective practitioner' as an essential part of adopting a professional teaching role. As we shall also see, notions of 'professionalism' are very important for the trainee teacher as s/he starts out. In one's attempt to be a 'good' or an 'effective' teacher we look briefly here at the forces that shape and affect teachers and teaching, and we look at the rewards of the role. We would like to paint a picture of teaching as a complex social encounter, buttressed by wider social forces and yet, at the same time, a reflective process making teachers as much learners as those they teach.

Teacher training, or to use its other term, initial teacher education, is a tricky process to try and pin down. It is not one thing, but an interesting mixture of many different skills, disciplines and experiences. This tells you something very significant about what it means to be a teacher. On your course and through this book you will be introduced to a wide range of ideas, tools, techniques and tips drawing from a wide range of disciplines: politics, sociology, psychology and education studies itself. Teacher education is academic, and yet also practical. Teaching is as much to do with the physical activity of managing a class as it is the creative endeavour of preparing good quality resources. The teaching experience is also based upon developing an extensive and effective range of emotional and interpersonal skills; what we call the 'affective' domain of learning.

Perhaps more importantly, this is the time to fully immerse yourself in the possibilities and options that are available to you as a new teacher. It is a time for mistakes, experimentation and reflection. It is a time to build a solid base upon which to establish your future professional role.

Breaking through all the misunderstanding

It is almost impossible to get away from 'education, education, education' in our modern society. It is the source of frequent news items; almost constant and continuous media debate, 'spin' and policy-making. Every few years the government of the time announces the next great educational reform. Every summer the media lays siege to examination boards in an attempt to establish once and for all, are qualifications getting easier or not? It is equally impossible not to meet someone who has an opinion about education, or at least, in a more narrow sense, an opinion about schooling and teachers and teaching. We have all been to school – we all have experiences (good and bad). That makes us all an expert in our own way.

And yet, nothing could be further from the truth. So much is spoken about teachers and teaching, so much media attention is seemingly given to the profession, and yet most of us as adults are completely unaware of what schools, colleges and teaching are really like. Schools and colleges are still closed worlds. It would be a mistake to base our impressions on education on either our own limited experiences as a learner or on media-saturated accounts of moral panics and partial viewpoints.

'Everyone remembers a good teacher'

From the start we need to be clear that it is essential to separate ourselves as a learner or, at least, how we might (mis)remember learning, from ourselves as a professional teacher-in-the-making. Learning to teach is a strange mixture of many different skills and types of knowledge – it is practical, theoretical and reflective. Learning to teach means we need to juggle our own experiences and observations with the evidence we see in front of us. We need to use educational theories and research as a lens through which to help us focus our attention on what we are doing, why we are doing it, and whether or not it is working.

Sometimes teaching is highly pragmatic – things just seem to work. On other occasions, theory and research can be used to point you in useful directions; to shape and mould your practice in some specific way. Teaching is both a craft and an intellectual endeavour. It is practical, physical and changes over time, and yet, at the same time, to teach well requires not just an understanding of current educational theory but an awareness of how these theories aid and shape the practical 'hands-on' work that we do with learners in classrooms and other learning environments. We call this 'evidence-based practice'; practically observed outcomes of your own teaching understood through the lens of theory and models. To teach well, you will need to become part craftsperson, part pragmatist and opportunist, and part sociologist, psychologist and actor!

Teaching is an immensely rich and rewarding profession. It is also very hard to communicate to trainee teachers at the start of their professional formation just how rewarding, exciting, challenging, tiring and life-changing the profession can be. As the adverts claim, 'everyone remembers a good teacher'. This is certainly true, and one of the greatest rewards of the profession. What is not so clear-cut, however, is just what it is that makes a 'good teacher' 'good'.

What is a 'good teacher'?

Some teachers are 'good' because the support they offer learners makes them feel able and comfortable to learn and take risks learning where otherwise they might not; some good teachers inspire through the force of their personality, offering a charismatic persona for learners to respond to in an excited and interested way; some good teachers 'simply' put in the hours, time and effort to ensure that all their learners are as well equipped as possible to meet the challenges of examinations, growing up, the world of work and constant change. We hope through your journey as a trainee teacher you come to know the experience of being a good teacher, and in your changing professional identity and role, that you come to know the new you a little better. You can be sure of one thing – the experience of teacher training will change you as much as your teaching will change the lives of those you support in the classroom.

In many respects, the whole of this book is about becoming a 'good teacher'. Earlier we have noted that good teachers unify theory, practice and reflection. They link these essential elements together in order to identify what works and to know why it does.

Ruddock (1985) warns us against slipping into comfortable 'habit'. She argues that good teaching is experimental. If we allow our practice to slip into habit – to become unthinking and uncritical – we are in danger of losing sight of why something works; we are then a very short step away from being unable to identify the need for change, ever teaching in the same pattern and routine, separated from understanding the needs of our learners. Ruddock describes this process as a 'hegemony of habit' – we allow our teaching to become taken for granted. It becomes cemented into habit and eventually we are unable to break free.

Learners themselves are as much aware of good teaching as we are, sometimes more so. Consider these descriptions of a 'good teacher' by eight-year-old learners:

> A good teacher … is kind, is generous, listens to you, encourages you, has faith in you, keeps confidence, likes teaching children, likes teaching their subject, takes time to explain things, helps you when you're stuck, tells you how you are doing, allows you to have your say, doesn't give up on you, cares for your opinion, makes you feel clever, treats people equally, stands up for you, makes allowances, tells the truth, is forgiving. (Hay McBer, 2000: 2)

It is difficult to disagree with the importance of these sentiments. What is interesting, however, is that this collection of statements can be broken down into three subsections.

- Good teaching is emotionally supportive of learners and based upon successful interpersonal skills and relationships.
- Good teaching is based upon your clarity as an effective communicator and in how you engage with learners.
- Good teaching is expressed through your enjoyment and pleasure of the support of the learning of others.

At times you will find learning to teach hard. Maybe even harder than you once found learning to learn.

When you start to access the research literature, and for your reading of the rest of this book, you will quickly come across two very important terms.

The first is 'teaching and learning'. A mouthful to keep saying, but it is important to be sensitive to the fact that by saying teaching and learning we are making an important statement – that teaching cannot exist without learning having taken place. This is simply the only measurement of 'good teaching' that it is possible to have. This simple observation has massive implications for what we do and how we judge ourselves.

The second key term is pedagogy. The term 'pedagogy' is of great importance for the rest of this book and for the rest of your professional life. By pedagogy we mean thinking and theorising about how learners learn, with a view that this then shapes the teaching and learning strategies, tools and techniques we adopt. Strictly speaking, pedagogy means the study of how children learn, with 'andragogy' being used for how adults learn. In education studies and initial teacher education the term pedagogy tends to be favoured, and also used as a catch-all term to describe the methods you adopt to engage learners and to maximise learning.

Discussion point

When I was learning to teach I really don't think I realised at the time the absolute importance of the idea that teaching and learning are so connected – to the point that the learning is more important than the teaching. This is hard – when we start we think so much about ourselves – and feel so much on show; exposed to a group of people. The idea that our behaviour in class is simply a vehicle to engage the learning behaviour of others is difficult to come to terms with – but once you do, it really shapes your planning and your classroom practice.

How might this observation help you to think about your own assumptions about teaching?

Can teachers 'make a difference'?

It is important to recognise that teaching is a 'social situation'. By this we mean that it takes place within a social context – it is open to bombardment by wider social forces. The doors of an educational institution might be closed, but they are open to the effects of class, gender, ethnicity, location, globalisation, policy and the trends and fashions of the media.

As a society, we often hold education up as both one of our most valuable assets and at the same time, one of our most valuable tools for social change. While this is true, education is but a part of a much wider complex society and in turn, part of a much wider global stage. Education alone cannot compensate for the ills of society. And yet it sometimes feels as if teachers hold the weight of the rest of the society upon their shoulders.

Although education is shaped by some powerful social forces, it is still possible for us to identify teaching that is 'trend-breaking': practice that enables learners to

M-level thinking: Situatedness

All social activity (of which education and classroom practice is but a part) is what some social scientists call 'situated'. This means that we can only understand the activity by thinking about where it occurs and about how the roles and relationships between those involved are constructed. Within education, the variables that affect classroom practice (inside and outside the school or college) are hotly contested. How might these variables affect teaching and learning or locate it in relation to the environment it occurs within?

obtain higher than would otherwise be indicated by national and regional trends in attainment according to social factors such as class, gender and ethnicity.

Who are you? What do you wish to become?

Within all this complex array of pressures, forces and theories, at some point you need to recognise the role of choice in becoming a professional teacher. You need to adopt a style that you think 'works' – one that suits your own image of your 'self' and one that gets the intended outcomes with the learners you work with. You need to make decisions and choices regarding what sort of teacher you become. You need to choose what sources you will use for inspiration in making this journey and these changes.

There are a number of sources you might turn to, to model for you what is a good teacher – this book being a start. There is the wider research literature, the supportive relationship with your tutors and mentor(s) and other colleagues. You need to seek different approaches and styles of classroom teaching and the wider teacher role, as acted out by those you meet around you. You need to question and reflect upon everything that you see: do things work? How can you tell? Why do things work? What is the factor making something successful?

Reflective practice and reflective practitioners

 M-level thinking: The reflective practitioner

This term refers to the way in which professionals, by virtue of their professional roles, reflect upon what they do and engage with theory to make sense of their experience. There is a debate surrounding the extent to which teachers are and can be reflective and the extent to which reflection can change practice or not. Why do you think reflection might be a really powerful tool for teachers?

We feel that embarking on teacher training is a massive and exciting undertaking and one that warrants reflection:

- Reflection is a key process through which we make events 'meaningful' and therein construct our understanding of them.
- Reflection allows for the individual involved to 'step back' and think about action and practice.
- Reflection – with a view to improving practice – is one of the key characteristics of becoming and being a professional.
- Reflection enables us to make sense of theory which at times might seem distanced and abstracted from our own experiences.

Teacher training is a lifelong process. It is a journey through which pre-service trainees are able to begin to construct a professional identity and through which in-service teachers are able to further reinforce and shape their already existing identity.

Teaching is both reflective and also reflexive: it needs those involved (that is, teachers themselves) to think about their own actions and to think about their own identity and role.

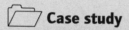 **Case study**

A great deal of 'becoming a teacher' is about how the role feels, how the label 'teacher' fits comfortably within your own self-image and how learners are able to respond to this. Consider this example: Robert completed his teacher training two years ago. Through the duration of his initial teacher education he found classroom management really hard and at times confidence-destroying. He had a strong personality and was usually a 'larger than life' figure, yet found it very difficult to adopt the authority role within his own classroom. On a couple of occasions he almost left his training incomplete, thinking that maybe teaching was not for him. His tutors tried to reassure Robert that many trainees have difficulties with classroom management and that this was a common experience for new teachers. Happily, two years into his first post, Robert is now a very competent, successful and well-liked teacher who commands respect with ease. On reflection, Robert recognises that his original problems with classroom management were largely due to the artificiality of the 'student/trainee teacher role'; once he had his 'own class' and was 'there before the learners' at the very start of the year, he found it much easier to adopt with confidence an authority role and, by his own admission, 'believed in it' himself a little more. He no longer felt like a 'fake' teacher but as a fully established member of staff, albeit with much more still to learn. Now he really feels like a teacher and this identification with the role has made a genuine difference to his practice.

It has long been recognised that for effective teaching to take place, teachers need to unite both theory and practice – they are two sides of the same coin. Practice uninformed by theory is never going to be critical and will be blinkered – it will be always kept in the dark – whereas theory uninformed by practice will be pointless and merely abstract. Uniting theory and practice is essential for sound reflective thinking – being able to see the connections between what you do, how you feel about it, how you evaluate it and what research and theory also tells you. The unification of theory and practice is referred to as 'praxis'. Attempts to link the two result in a far greater outcome than simply having theory and practice separate from each other.

We have used the term 'reflective practitioner' in teacher education to refer to the ways in which good teachers, as part of their professionalism, reflect upon what they do with a view to making their practice more informed and ultimately improved. This term, developed by Schön (1983), is seen to be at the very heart of being a professional.

Teacher professionalism, and initial teacher education programmes, are what we might call a 'community of practice' (Lave and Wenger, 1991). By this we mean that such training courses seek to induct the participants into a shared set of values and to help all involved feel a sense of belonging to a mutually supportive group.

Consider this quotation:

> Reflective practice is thus always a joint activity to some extent. It is linked to and influenced by the reflective working of others and is influenced by a whole set of informal and formal reflective interactions … In a variety of formal and informal roles, such as leaders, managers, mentors and coaches, others can influence an individual's reflection. The everyday professional interactions with fellow colleagues can facilitate mutual reflection or co-reflection. Professional dialogue of this kind can enhance creativity because it can bring together different perspectives. Teachers' experience of the practice of others is also likely to shape their reflections. (James, 2007: 34)

In the light of the above, we want you to develop the habit of always evaluating, reflecting and thinking about your teaching, but we also want you to develop the habit of talking with others about your work and your practice. We feel that there is a hugely important role for your colleagues and peers to play in helping you to think about your teaching and that this mutual dialogue is absolutely essential in becoming a professional.

Becoming a 'professional'

 M-level thinking: Professionalism

The notion of being a 'professional' and what is a 'profession' is a highly contested issue. It is a role that we undertake that is based upon a specialist and formal set of knowledge that is used by a community to reflect, self-regulate and meet particular standards in the field they have 'expert' status over. The degree to which the teaching profession is, in fact, a 'profession' in these terms is open to criticism and debate. With the increasing openness of learning, listening to the learner's voice, outside inspection from Ofsted (the Office for Standards in Education) and other UK equivalents, for example, Estyn (Her Majesty's Inspectorate of Education and Training) in Wales, increased teacher practitioner research into 'what works' and attempts to make schools accountable to market and parental choice, we might begin to question to what extent is teaching a profession that regulates its own specialist knowledge? Why do you think teaching is such a 'hot political issue' that it needs to be regulated from the outside?

When entering a new 'profession' there is a period of time where you adopt a role of 'trainee' or 'professional-in-the-making' – this is a fluid and ongoing construction – time to think about yourself and your development. However, to continue to develop as a teacher, you need to retain, as we have argued above, this commitment to reflective practice. What we are talking about here, and at various other places in this book, is building your professional role. It is important to understand that role and identity are not the same thing, but affect each other. By 'identity' we mean how you think about yourself and what you think others think about you. You will probably have a range of aspects to your identity – and these will change over time. By 'role' we mean the norms and standards of behaviour that you 'act out' in specific contexts.

The professional teacher role is complex and contested. By 'professional' it is often meant an organised body of people who have acquired specialised and systematic knowledge that puts them in a separate social standing from others who do not possess this specialised knowledge. Doctors are an excellent example of this. Further, professionals are seen to belong to a community of practice, sharing knowledge and insight, and who regulate their own practice. They are also seen to be trusted by those they serve. This makes teaching as a profession problematic and raises some questions:

- Is it the case that teachers really regulate themselves within their own community? After all, inspections come from the outside and despite the hard work for all those involved, inspections often seem to teachers to be a process 'done to them'.
- Is it the case that teacher knowledge is specialist? If so, then what exactly is this knowledge – is it the pedagogy or is it the subject-specific knowledge of the disciplines they teach, or both?
- Finally, is it the case that the media and society at large trusts teachers – and should they? Parents and learners have a right to be involved in the education process and commitments to these two groups erode the distance between the teacher and the learner.

Much good teaching is based upon the erosion of the gap between teacher and learner. So, are teachers professionals? Many teachers feel alienated by educational theory and the production of research-based knowledge. At the same time, much 'evidence-based practice' is pragmatic at the expense of any reference to the wider research community (Winch, 2007). Many have noted that there is a wide gulf between the knowledge of researchers and the policies of policy-makers the two being 'foreign territories' to each other (Saunders, 2007). Having said this, there is now a ground-swell of practitioner led evidence based practice slowly taking hold through the 'profession' (see Hopkins, 2002; Petty, 2006).

Forde et al. (2006) argue that teaching is a profession but one that has undergone massive changes since educational policy in the mid to late 1980s. The effects of these changes has been to erode teacher professional identity, making it complex and contradictory. Forde et al. suggest that it is time for teachers to 'reclaim' these identities – and that this can only be achieved through systematic reflection, professional development and engagement with research which in turn validates their own knowledge of their classroom experiences.

Welcome to the 'rollercoaster'

Your journey as a professional-in-the-making will have both ups and downs. This is to be expected. It is an emotional, academic, physical and practical journey. You will need to really draw upon the support of those around you – your tutors, peers, colleagues and mentor. But it is important to remember that we have all been there at one time or another. The way to get the most out of your training, your course, your teaching and your learners, is to put the most that you can in. The most meaningful way that you can make sense of your training in this thing called 'education, education, education' is through 'reflection, reflection, reflection'.

All of this confused picture paints a highly complex world to the new entrant. It is a world waiting to be both discovered and claimed by those new to it. Training to be a teacher is more than being in the classroom, and more than developing some tricks here and there (useful, though, that the tricks are). New entrants need to understand the wider position of education in society and the wider effects of social forces on learners. They need to develop a repertoire of 'what works' and root their understanding of what works in both practical and research-based knowledge. All the while, new teachers need to get comfortable with their new role and comfortable with being in the classroom.

In later chapters of this book we look at all these issues in turn, uniting the claims of educational theory and research with practical tools we have found useful, and urging you, the reader, to reflect upon what you are doing and why you are doing it.

Chapter links →

Themes and ideas explored in this chapter link to corresponding ideas in Chapters 5, 6 and 20.

Suggested further reading 📖

Moore, A. (2004) *The Good Teacher. Dominant Discourses in Teaching and Teacher Education*. Oxford: Routledge.

Schön, D.A. (1983) *The Reflective Practitioner. How Professionals Think in Action*. New York: Basic Books.

References

Forde, C., McMahon, M., McPhee, A. and Patrick, F. (2006) *Professional Development, Reflection and Enquiry*. London: Sage.

Hay McBer (2000) *Research into Teacher Effectiveness: A Model of Teacher Effectiveness*. London: DfEE/The Stationery Office.

Hopkins, D. (2002) *A Teacher's Guide to Classroom Research*. 3rd edition. Maidenhead: Open University Press.

James, C. (2007) 'Collaborative practice: the basis of good educational work', *Management in Education*, 21(4): 32–37.

Lave, J. and Wenger, E. (1991) *Situated Learning: Legitimate Peripheral Participation*. Cambridge: Cambridge University Press.

Moore, A. (2004) *The Good Teacher: Dominant Discourses in Teaching and Teacher Education*. Oxford: Routledge.

Petty, G. (2006) *Evidence-Based Teaching: A Practical Approach*. Cheltenham: Nelson Thornes.

Ruddock, J. (1985) 'Teacher research and research based teacher education', *Journal of Education for Teaching*, 11(3): 281–9.

Saunders, L. (ed.) (2007) *Educational Research and Policy-Making: Exploring the Border Country between Research and Policy*. Oxford: Routledge.

Schön, D.A. (1983) *The Reflective Practitioner: How Professionals Think in Action*. New York: Basic Books.

Winch, C. (2007) 'On being a teacher', in J.Dillon and M.Maguire (eds), *Becoming A Teacher: Issues in Secondary Teaching*. Maidenhead: Open University Press.

CHAPTER 2

UNDERSTANDING SECONDARY EDUCATION

Objectives

By the end of this chapter the reader will be able to:

1. summarise post-war educational policies affecting the secondary and post-compulsory sectors;
2. identify the pattern of secondary educational change since the Second World War;
3. understand the marketisation of education and its effects on becoming a teacher;
4. comprehend the impact of New Labour education policy on teaching;
5. understand the re-occurring themes that are a feature of recent educational reform and policy.

Understanding educational reform

In this book we emphasise the importance for emerging teachers to reflect, and be reflective about, the many processes of becoming a teacher. Understanding the wider context in which 'becoming a teacher' is constructed is particularly important when considering the ever-changing educational landscape that successive governments introduce to the teaching profession. By understanding the background to and history of recent educational change you will be in a better position to see how your professional work fits into education processes and society as a whole. This 'policy busyness' that emerging teachers are catapulted into, can, to some extent, be clarified by talking to more experienced colleagues. It is a confusing world of governmental decisions, White and Green Papers and political ideology and spin. However in this chapter we provide a framework for understanding some of the more critical reforms in education spanning over half a century. By focusing on educational provision and key educational policies that have shaped the meaning of education, teaching and learning, this chapter paves the way for an examination of the tensions, dilemmas, ambiguities and debates within the education system as well as explaining some of its key features.

Education in Britain continues to be a 'political football' as successive governments struggle to balance the conflicting interests of parents, learners, teachers, religious institutions and the economy. Governments juggle these competing interests in their desire to satisfy the electorate and the expectations of business in an increasingly competitive and globalising economy. Within this, there is much to celebrate, despite what impressions you might obtain from the media:

- Newly qualified British teachers are the most successful generation of teachers to date (Baker, 2007; TDA, 2006).
- Levels of numeracy and literacy are rising, as are the percentages of young people going to university. Tony Blair, during his premiership, promised that over the next few years 50 per cent of all young people will leave school and attend universities – there is little reason to believe that his successors will be any less committed to this goal.
- More young people today pass their public school examinations (GCSEs and A levels) than ever before.

But there is also much to criticise.

- Universities and employers complain that British teenagers are not fully equipped with the skills required to enter both sectors. Just under a quarter of a million 16-year-olds drop out of education and training altogether.
- English teenagers lie third bottom (just above Turkey and Mexico) in a list of the top 30 industrialised countries' participation rates for 15–19-year-olds in further education (Wylie, 2006).

〰️ M-level thinking: Crisis of masculinity

Changes in traditional patterns of employment and the continued rise of female educational achievement at primary, secondary and tertiary levels have created, it is argued, conditions in which some male teenagers are alienated by school curricula and that this accounts for their underperformance. To what extent do you agree with these explanations?

- A 'crisis of masculinity' in many British schools refers to the fact that many boys are under-achieving in examinations in relation to their female counterparts in all phases of education.
- Finally, many commentators (for example, David Gillborn) argue that British schools continue to marginalise some members of ethnic minorities, most notably, Afro-Caribbean male learners.

For some, educational reform plays an essential role in developing social order and preparing young people for future employment. For others, the reforms taking place in the UK are both a form of cultural and social engineering and an attempt to re-create a fantasy education based upon the myths of national identity (Ball, 1994).

M-level thinking: The role of education

Academics argue about what purpose education fulfils, although few dispute the relationships between education and the economy. More contentious and therefore fascinating to research are the variety of ways education constructs national identities. In what ways can the formal and 'hidden' curricula artificially construct a national identity?

Greater understanding of educational reform can help emerging teachers reflect on the many changes they will encounter as they progress from fledgling practitioners to experienced colleagues.

Education in post-war Britain

1944 Education Act

Both the 1944 Education Act in England and Wales and the 1947 Act in Northern Ireland came at a time when Europe was suffering from the atrocities of the Second World War. Many Europeans had experienced war at first hand and in many cases were disillusioned with the policies and the politicians that had allowed such a war to take place. The years 1939 to 1945 had witnessed widespread destruction, mass killing and human suffering on an enormous level. Policy-makers and the general public in many Western European societies wanted a new and better society to replace the one that had been partially responsible for the Second World War. Both Labour and Conservative parties were committed to the principles of the welfare state, full employment and a mixed economy. The Education Act needs to be seen in this light because of the powerful role education has within society – particularly in relation to the economy.

Aims:

1. The 1944 Education Act aimed to offer an equal chance to develop the talents and abilities of all learners.
2. The Act created a balance of responsibility (and tension) for the new education system between central government, local government and schools.
3. The free system of compulsory state education was to be completely reorganised into primary education (nursery, infant and junior education) to the age of 11, secondary education from the ages of 11 to 15, and then post-compulsory education, that is, a free choice that could take children into further and/or higher education at university level.

These were exciting and ambitious aims. However, the way in which these aims were to be achieved has been viewed by many educationalists as highly contentious. A psychometric or IQ (intelligence quotient) test was given to children in their last year of primary school. The test would be used to measure 'intelligence' and was commonly known as the '11-plus examination'. It would be used to 'determine' which type of secondary school in the 'tripartite system' these children would attend once they had completed their primary education. The tripartite system of education was set up as a result of the 1944 Education Act. 'Tri' referred to three types of schools that children, at that time, could attend: grammar schools, secondary moderns and the technical schools.

- The grammar school accepted what it considered to be academically bright learners who had done well in the 11-plus examination. Such schools taught a wide range of academic subjects including Latin and, in some cases, Greek. These schools entered their learners for public examinations (O and A levels) which were needed for any learner that wished to attend university. Twenty per cent of the population at that time attended these schools.
- The secondary modern accepted most other learners. Such children would not have performed as well in the 11-plus examination as those who went on to grammar schools and, as a result, they would receive a basic education with a more practical emphasis. Up to the 1960s there was very little opportunity for public examinations to be taken in such schools, meaning that the opportunity to go to university was effectively ruled out if you went to such a school.

 Discussion point

As new models for schooling get introduced, it isn't always the case that the old ones completely disappear. Many counties in the UK still have grammar school systems and offer both an 11-plus and a 14-plus. All this diversity reveals a confusing landscape. Some commentators refer to the UK education system as 'postmodern' due to all this diversity, change and local and regional variation. What difficulties can you identify in trying to compare educational systems in Britain?

- Technical schools only accepted about 5 per cent of learners in the country at that time. Such schools were designed for learners that excelled in technical subjects and consequently emphasised vocational skills and knowledge.

Despite its ambitious and exciting aims, there were three significant problems with the tripartite system of education.

1. The problem with IQ tests as a form of assessment is that they can be culturally biased in favour of middle-class learners. This meant that the majority of grammar school learners came from the middle classes. Far from providing an equal education for all, the tripartite system reflected the existing social divisions in society.
2. 'Parity of esteem' (the idea that one school should be considered to have the same 'status' as another) did not exist between these three types of school. Parents, teachers and learners saw the grammar school as superior to the other types of school. This could mean that some parents, some teachers and some learners could see themselves as failures if they were involved in any school that was not a grammar school.
3. Despite the aims of the 1944 Education Act to provide better education for all, the tripartite system did not include those learners whose parents or guardians paid for their education, that is, independent or private school education. At that time, seven per cent of the population of school children attended such schools.

The introduction of comprehensive schools

The conservative Prime Minister Harold Macmillan's famous catchphrase 'You've never had it so good; symbolised the rising standards of the 1960s in comparison to the relative austerity of the 1950s. The demands for greater public expenditure on education, fuelled by sections within the Labour Party, teaching unions and leading academics were informed, in part by emerging educational disciplines and a common desire for a more egalitarian society. In 1965, keen to promote social reform through education the then Labour government, led by Harold Wilson, requested that all local education authorities run secondary education along comprehensive lines. Comprehensive schools were set up to provide one type of school for all types of learner, inclusive of all types of ability regardless of gender, class or ethnicity. This meant that there was also no requirement for an entrance examination, 11-plus result or interview. Learners were placed in streams or sets based on ability.

Evaluating the success of comprehensive schools is difficult for two reasons. First, due to the nature of British politics and what is effectively a two-party system, what one political party works hard to set up, the other party can work equally hard to change, modify or destroy when it gains power. Traditionally the Conservative Party has favoured the tripartite system while the 'old' Labour Party supported the idea of a fully comprehensive system. Until the Blair government came into power in 1997, the Conservative Party largely dominated post-war politics in England and Wales.

Consequently, they worked hard to destroy or attack any idea that comprehensive schools could be a success. Secondly, the idea of any 'comprehensive' system is that it works in the same way for a large group of people. However, in the case of comprehensive schools, they took their learners from what are referred to as catchment areas, that is, learners had to live in the immediate area around the school. That means that it is very difficult to compare, for example, a comprehensive school in an inner-city area to one in the leafy green suburbs.

There are four further difficulties in trying to measure how well comprehensive schools have performed in the past:

1. With a small minority of relatively well-off children attending private schools it is impossible to know how well comprehensive schools might have performed had these children attended them.
2. Measuring how well a school performs depends on what you are actually measuring, for example, examination results, the ability to take children from very low ability to a significantly higher ability, or the creation of an emotionally warm supportive and caring environment.
3. Although comprehensive schools were extremely popular, there were always a significant number of grammar schools around to 'attract' high-achieving learners. Had the grammar schools not been there, these learners would have attended the comprehensive schools and boosted the schools' overall examination pass rates.
4. Some comprehensives broke down many of the barriers between class, gender and race, however, a school's ability to do this is partially dependent on the locality of the school. A comprehensive in a predominantly white, middle-class area, for example, might not include learners from different ethnic backgrounds if they do not live in the catchment area.

The popular complaint, voiced by parents, that comprehensive schools lowered standards for high-achieving learners was used by the Conservative Party as an excuse to attack and restrict the number of comprehensive schools that existed. 'Progressive' and 'child-centred' approaches associated with much educational thinking of the 1960s were seen as partially to blame for growing discipline problems but comprehensive schools took disproportionate blame for the moral panic about education. By the 1970s the focus of blame was to turn to the teaching profession.

 Discussion point

Many schools (more so than colleges) continue to stream and set learners. Despite the problems identified above, this is often a clearly thought-through approach to dealing with issues of 'differentiation' – the attempt to meet the different needs of different learners by targeting relevant support. To what extent do you agree with setting and streaming as a differentiation strategy?

'New' vocationalism

Vocational training refers to any type of training that is preparing people for the world of work. In many countries in Europe throughout most of the twentieth century, vocationalism was very much part of the school curriculum. However, in many parts of the UK in the 1960s, vocational training was viewed by governments as something that should be tackled in the workplace rather than in school. 'New vocationalism' referred to the change in the view by the government that vocational training should take place in schools and colleges. This form of vocationalism emerged in Britain in the late 1970s and, amid much debate, is still being developed within schools and colleges across Britain today (see Chapters 3 and 4). During the 1970s the British economy (as well as many other European economies) went into recession. British politicians were concerned about the rising levels of unemployment that this created and, in particular, rising youth unemployment. In 1976, at Ruskin College, Oxford, the then Labour British Prime Minister James Callaghan blamed teachers for the lack of skills that young people possessed. Schools, he argued, should improve vocational training and education to meet the requirements of industry.

Organisations and policies associated with 'new vocationalism'

- The Manpower Services Commission became the main agency in developing youth training in the 1970s.
- In 1978 the Youth Opportunities Programme was introduced to offer young people six months of work experience and 'off the job' training.
- In 1983 the Youth Training Scheme was introduced to offer school leavers a year of training in a variety of different occupations.
- In 1986 the National Council for Vocational Qualifications was set up to offer a nationally recognised system of qualifications.
- General National Vocational Qualifications (GNVQs) were quickly introduced as alternative ways for young people to gain qualifications that were work orientated.
- With Curriculum 2000 (see below) came the introduction of Advanced Vocational Certificates of Education (AVCEs) which were to replace GNVQs and offer a qualification equivalent to two A levels.

The introduction of 'new vocationalism' can be criticised in four ways:

1. It might be argued that it was poor economic management by the British government that was responsible for unemployment rather than the lack of skills of young people.

2. On many vocational training programmes young people were used as cheap labour rather than being trained in the workplace to learn new and valuable skills.
3. Stephens et al. (2001) argues that in Britain there has always been class snobbery between those that are 'trained' and those that are 'educated'. This partially accounts for why, in the UK, many people see A levels as being socially more acceptable than the vocational qualifications.
4. Pring (1990) ironically refers to a 'New Tripartism' consisting of those with A levels, those with vocational qualifications and those who have received some sort of youth training. The lower status held by vocational qualifications can be correlated with class, occupation and pay.

 Discussion point

Many teachers teach a combination of what we might refer to as 'academic' and 'vocational' subjects, and schools are increasingly looking at vocational choices at Key Stage 3 to enhance their curriculum offer. In fact, the very notion of choice is something introduced to education in the UK from the New Right policies we are discussing here. The new Diplomas (see Chapter 4) will further increase the 'vocational' offer made by schools. To what extent do you believe 'vocational' education can successfully be taught in the school or college environment?

The marketisation of education

M-level thinking: The marketisation of education

Should we really think about schools in the same way as we think about other businesses, for example, supermarkets? While some of you might believe that this is the way that schools should be run, others might argue that public services like health and education should not be run along the competitive business principles that increasingly inform education systems.

New Right ideas, developed in the UK at the end of the 1970s, took a distinctive view on education. The term 'New Right' specifically refers to a strand of Conservatism influenced by former Conservative Prime Minister Margaret Thatcher. These policies included the deregulation of business, the weakening of trade unions, the disman-tling of sections of the welfare state and the privatisation of nationalised industries. Underpinning these policies were two complementary ideologies.

1. The first was a neo-liberal belief in the free market economy, freedom of choice for consumers and minimal state interference with that market.
2. The second was a neo-conservative belief in traditional values.

These two ideologies have brought about a major change in the way that we conceive the nature of schooling and education today. Hargreaves (1989) has referred to this development as a change to 'Kentucky Fried Schooling'. The New Right ideology behind the marketisation of education involves the belief that competition at all lev-els should provide a higher standard of education. The idea was that the market should allocate resources where required. Paradoxically however, while talking the language of the 'free' market, Conservative central government increased its control over all public services including education.

The 1988 Education Reform Act (ERA) encapsulated much of the ideologies of the New Right agenda for education. The ERA did not apply to Northern Ireland and Scotland, both of which have their own separate curriculum arrangements (see below). Schools in England and Wales, however, were to move away from being run by the local authorities to a more market-style system based on the 'language' of the commercial world of business. This had a number of implications:

*   Schools, rather than local education authorities (LEAs) were to manage their own budgets.
*   Schools had to provide freedom of choice for the 'consumer', that is, the parents of the children they were trying to attract.
*   Schools had to be cost-effective as well as market themselves with an image that would attract new consumers.
*   Schools would compete with each other in the chase for new consumers, that is, published league tables would provide parents with the information required for them to make their choices.
*   For each learner attending a school, that school would gain a specific sum of money from the government.

The assumption behind running education systems along business principles is that if schools compete with each other, costs will be brought down while the standard of education will rise. These ideas are still inherent in education systems throughout much of the UK today.

There are a number of problems with this way of thinking. It has been argued that reforms that reflect marketised ideas concerning education can only benefit middle-class families who know how to work the system to their advantage. David Gillborn (2001) has also shown that when schools start to compete for high positions in league tables, many learners get marginalised, that is, will not be accepted in some of the more high-achieving schools. In many cases this means that disproportionate numbers of working-class and ethnic minority learners are to be found in schools lower down the league tables. Equality of education cannot be provided under a system that assumes little inequality. Middle-class schools in middle-class areas do not face the same problems as working-class schools in predominantly working-class areas. However, they have gained more money as a result of their higher position in the league tables.

New Labour and 'Education, Education, Education'

When Tony Blair triumphantly took 'New Labour' into government after 18 years of Conservative rule, he did it with the election manifesto that included 'Education, Education, Education' as his battle cry. At the time evidence from international studies on learner achievement highlighted areas of weakness in primary school delivery of literacy and numeracy, sparking an unprecedented intervention by the government in teaching methodology. In their attempt to harness swing-voters New Labour was quick to adopt many existing conservative policies on education. Baseline assessment was introduced in all parts of the UK. This meant that the assessment of 4–5-year-olds in reading, writing and personal and social skills took place. The introduction of a National Strategy for Literacy and Numeracy swiftly followed and non-statutory frameworks for English and Mathematics were introduced in 2001, followed in 2002 by similar frameworks for the teaching of science, information and communication technology and the foundation subjects. Another Conservative idea adopted by New Labour was the introduction of 'academies'. A private sponsor is given control of these types of school, which may be an existing or a newly built institution. The remainder of the capital and running costs are met by the state in the usual way for UK state schools. Controversy exists over these schools because of the fear that private investment will skew the content of the curriculum. That said, both New Labour and Conservative parties are committed to the expansion of these schools.

Communitarianism

The policies of New Labour have been described by some commentators as 'communitarian' in approach. This concept is associated with modern-day American social democratic ideas expressed clearly in the book *Spirit of Community* by sociologist Etzioni (1993). He argues that while individual rights and individual aspirations need to be valued and protected, a moral reinvigoration of 'community' needs to take place to further cement social networks. This new 'spirit of community' should be based upon recognising our collective responsibilities and what works best in the 'public interest'. These views take what they see as the

(Continued)

(Continued)

decay of the collective value of social networks and try to rebuild them as a means to solving social problems such as poverty, crime, anti-social behaviour and poor education. In this view, education would be both renewed by a stronger community, and is itself the source of a strong community. These views often mark out the polices and ideologies of New Labour as a 'third way', meaning not the previous policies of the Conservative New Right, and not the old policies of the Labour Party prior to its revisioning as a 'New' Labour.

New Labour has also been responsible for a new 'discourse of specialisation' (Brisard et al., 2006) as secondary schools were encouraged to develop a profile in a particular area of the curriculum with learners being selected, in part, through their aptitude in their particular specialist subject, for example, languages, humanities or sports.

Curriculum 2000

'Curriculum 2000', named after the year the policy came into force, was the biggest reorganisation of post-16 education since the 1950s and introduced AS and A2 levels (the equivalent to a full A level), which replaced the existing A level system. Sir Ron Dearing, the former head of the School Curriculum and Assessment Authority (SCAA), was appointed in 1993 by the then Conservative government in London to review the provision of post-16 education in England and Wales. He was already highly critical of the level of testing and the highly prescriptive National Curriculum (that is, one that told teachers exactly how to teach the subjects listed by government). He was also critical of the level of educational provision for 16–19-year-olds. The report suggested that learners should take on a larger common component of core subjects along with grading that no longer separated the 'academic' from the 'vocational', that is, that both academic and vocational subjects should be graded using the same grading scale of A–E. As a result of the Dearing Report in 1998, it was found that while learners in France and Germany experienced 30 hours of 'taught' time per week, sixth-formers in England studying A levels were taught between 15 and 18 hours per week. European learners were also seen to study a much broader range of subjects than learners in England and Wales, who specialised very early on in a narrow range of subjects. In response to the Dearing Report's findings, the aim of Curriculum 2000 was to broaden the curriculum for 16–19-year-olds to include a mixture of arts and sciences, vocational and academic subjects, and to increase the skills awareness that industry required in mathematics, and information communication technology (ICT).

Curriculum 2000 can be criticised in three ways:

1. For many less able learners, the increased work pressure along with the reduced amount of teaching time available in the AS year meant that certain learners suffered from rising stress levels.
2. Teachers had less time to teach their subject areas. The final term became a term of examination rather than teaching.
3. With a greater share of working-class and ethnic minority learners being chan-nelled by teachers into taking the Advanced Vocational Certificates in Education route, the system would increase rather than narrow the divide between classes and between the majority and ethnic minorities.

Under New Labour, curriculum reform continues to be at the heart of educational policy making and in Chapter 4 we explore the significant reform process taking place in 14–19 education (see the end of this chapter for specific regional differences in curriculum design and implantation). The Qualification and Curriculum Authority (QCA) in England and the Qualifications, Curriculum and Assessment Authority for Wales (ACCAC) are the statutory bodies responsible for the reviews of curriculum and assessment arrangements in each country. In 2009 the QCA changed its name to the Qualifications and Curriculum Development Agency (QCDA). The statutory National Curriculum for 5–16-year-olds is divided into four key stages (KS1–4) covering the age ranges of: 5–7 (The 'Foundation Phase' in Wales covering a wider age range of 3–7), 7–11, 11–14 and 14–16 respectively. In England the core subjects are mathematics, English and science and the foundation subjects are technology, history, ICT, geography, music, art and physical education (modern foreign languages at KS3). Religious education and sex education are legal requirements within any school's curriculum provision. In England, Wales and Northern Ireland most learners will sit their General Certificates in Secondary Education (GCSEs) covering a range of academic and vocational subjects. In 2008 new government Diplomas (see Chapter 4) were introduced offering a wider range of qualifications that encompass both the academic and vocational under the guise of 'applied learning'. In all three countries short GCSE courses are available as are entry-level qualifications for learners performing below GCSE standards.

A lot has changed since the creation of the 1944 Education Act. Now that you have read most of this chapter you will realise that far from providing equal opportunities of education to all, British education continues to treat different types of learners dif-ferently despite the many reforms that have taken place. You will also realise that the teaching profession is constantly being shaped and reshaped by economic, political and social agendas. Preparing young people for that world of work via formal educa-tion is a complex and challenging process, particularly where the concept of a job for life no longer exists. We continue to look at this theme in the next chapter on lifelong learning. While there are many similarities in the education systems of the four coun-tries that make up Britain, there are also some tantalising differences. As reflective teachers we can all learn as much from these differences as we can from the similar-ities. In remaining open to difference, teaching becomes the rewarding, exciting, chal-lenging and life-changing profession that we so firmly believe it is.

Similarity and difference: Scotland, Northern Ireland and Wales

Scotland

Scottish secondary schools are currently non-selective and comprehensive. Of the 381 schools in the public sector 61 offer Gaelic-medium education (Brisard et al., 2006). Scotland has embraced comprehensive education. The transition from selective schooling to comprehensive education took place between 1965 and 1975 and this led to an increase in average attainment of all learners.

Scotland, unlike its English, Welsh and Northern Irish counterparts, does not possess a National Curriculum, having preferred to set out guidelines on what should be taught in the 5–14 age range. In marked difference to the other three countries in the UK Scotland does not separate schooling into primary and secondary experiences but rather provides and emphasises seamless continuity in education over this age range. In 2005 the Scottish Executive launched *A Curriculum for Excellence* which is attempting to streamline curriculum delivery in schools while enabling relative school and teacher autonomy in shaping the curriculum. Up till the age of 14 learners are offered curriculum areas in mathematics, language, environmental studies, expressive arts, physical education (PE), religious and moral education (RME) and health education. Learners aged 14 and over will study seven to eight subjects from mathematics, English, history, computing, geography, modern studies, science, modern foreign languages (MFL), art and design, PE, technology, RME, music, drama, social and personal development. Each curricular area for the 5–14 age ranges has a set of assessment outcomes that learners are expected to satisfy which are then subdivided into attainment targets with 'A' being the lowest and 'F' being the highest. Learners are allowed to progress from one target to the next at their own rate, with assessment taking place when the learner is considered to be ready. In their last year of compulsory education learners take the national Scottish qualification. Known as the Standard Grade the qualification is assessed both internally and externally and exists at foundation, general and credit levels.

Northern Ireland

Secondary education in Northern Ireland is selective. Of its 235 secondary schools, 69 are grammar and 159 are secondary intermediate. Education in Northern Ireland has historically developed along religious segregation lines and there has been a tradition of segregation both by ability and gender with many schools in the region single-sexed (Brisard et al., 2006). However the Department of Education (DENI) has encouraged initiatives to reduce religious segregation and, following the re-establishment of the Northern Ireland Assembly in 2007, it is difficult to state with certainty how education will change in the region. Following in the direction of England and Wales, a compulsory school curriculum was introduced in Northern

Ireland in 1990 with responsibility for assessment procedures resting today with the Northern Ireland Council for Curriculum Examinations and Assessment (CCEA).

In September 2004 a new curriculum framework was introduced emphasising life and employment skills. The Northern Ireland compulsory curriculum is similar to its English counterpart. Four key stages exist with slightly different age ranges (KS1 = age ranges 4–8; KS2 = 8–11; KS3 = 11–14; KS4 = 14–16). Compulsory subjects include religious education, English, mathematics, science and technology, creative and expressive studies and language studies. From KS1 cross-curricular themes include education for mutual understanding, cultural heritage, health education and information technology. From KS3 these themes include: economic awareness and careers education. Similar to the English and Welsh scenarios, learners are assessed at the end of each key stage (that is, at the ages of 8, 11 and 14).

Wales

As we have hinted at during this chapter, Wales in most cases has followed Westminster's lead in terms of educational provision but with some subtle differences. Most secondary schools in Wales are comprehensive. Of the 224 schools in the public sector 54 are Welsh medium schools (Brisard, et al., 2006). In most cases Wales has followed England in post-war educational reform and much of this chapter is therefore relevant to those teachers training in Wales. Core subjects in Welsh schools are mathematics, ICT, science and Welsh. The foundation subjects include history, music, geography, technology, art and physical education, and at KS3 this includes modern foreign languages. As in England, learners are assessed through standard assessment tasks (SATs) at KS1–4 however the KS1 assessments are by teacher assessment only. Wales is recognised as having an innovative early years curriculum, and has led the way to some degree for play-based learning and learning outdoors.

Chapter links →

Themes and ideas explored in this chapter link to corresponding ideas in Chapters 3, 4 and 12.

Suggested further reading 📖

Ball, S.J. (2008) *The Education Debate*. Bristol: Policy Press.

Olssen, M., Codd, J. and O'Neill, A. (2004) *Education Policy – Globalisation, Citizenship and Democracy*. London: Sage.

References

Baker, M. (2007) 2nd Annual 14–19 Diploma Conference – Introductory Speech given at Hotel Russell, London, 20 September 2007.

Ball, S.J. (1994) *Educational Reform – a Critical and Post-structural Approach*. Buckingham: Open University Press.

Brisard, E., Menter, I. and Smith, I. (2006) *Convergence or Divergence? Initial Teacher Education in Scotland and England*. Edinburgh: Dunedin Academic Press.

Etzioni, A. (1993) *The Spirit of Community: Rights, Responsibilities and the Communitarian Agenda*. New York: Crown.

Gillborn, D. (2001) 'Raising standards or rationing education? racism and social justice in policy and practice', *Support for Learning*, 16(3): 105–111.

Hargreaves, A. (1989) 'Teaching quality: a sociological analysis' in B. Cosin, M. Flude and M. Hales (eds), *School, Work and Equality*. Buckingham: Open University Press.

Pring, R. (1990) *The New Curriculum*. London: Cassell.

Stephens, P., Egil Tonnessen, F. and Kyriacou, C. (2001) *'Teacher Training and Teacher Education in England and Norway: Competent Managers and Reflective Carers'*. Paper presented at the annual International seminar, Department of Educational Studies, University of York, 16 June 2001.

Teacher Development Agency (TDA) (2006) 'Career switchers choose teaching', news release, 26 May.

Wylie, T. (2006) Speech given at the Annual 14–19 Diplomas Conference, *Planning and Delivering the Universal Entitlement*, Hotel Russell, London.

CHAPTER 3

UNDERSTANDING LIFELONG LEARNING AND POST-COMPULSORY EDUCATION

Objectives

By the end of this chapter the reader will be able to:

1. define the terms lifelong learning and post-compulsory education;
2. understand the diversity and variety across the lifelong learning sector;
3. understand the workplace reform of further education;
4. understand the rate, pace and pattern of policy change in the lifelong learning sector;
5. evaluate the impact that the forces of globalisation have had on lifelong learning policy-making.

Post-compulsory education and reform

The educational provision referred to here as 'post-compulsory education' is characterised by one single key feature: it is highly diverse. Even the variety of terms used to describe the same sector illustrates this: we might refer to it as 'post-compulsory education and training' (known as PCET), 'further education' (FE), 'lifelong learning' or even 'adult education'. In this chapter we use the terms FE and PCET interchangeably and try wherever possible to use the term most associated with the literature, arguments and debates being covered at that time. At the end of this chapter we consider the notion of 'lifelong learning' in more detail.

In some senses we have all these different terms because the sector is a combination of different services aimed at different groups of learners – there are both similarities and differences within the sector as a whole. These differences give rise to different institutions with different patterns of work: sixth form colleges (SFCs) are attended by 16–19-year-olds and now 14–19-year-olds due to the Diplomas and the wider 14–19 agendas, whereas further education colleges are attended by all ages post-school leaving age. This makes the institutional ethos quite different – making SFCs more 'school-like' in ethos and FE colleges often responsible for a large adult provision with the implications that this involves, for example, childcare responsibilities for learners, employability programmes, access courses back into education and evening classes.

Post-compulsory education therefore, can occur in a variety of contexts across a variety of institutions and meet the needs of a variety of learners. It covers everything beyond the school, from the 16-year-old attending college and the work-based apprentice going to college one day a week for a short period of time, to adults returning to education after a long period of absence. This education and learning covers school and college partnerships, FE college teaching, adult education classes and, even, museum and prison education. This means that learners within this 'post-compulsory' sector might variously be described as pupils, students, learners, adults, independent learners, apprentices, employees, clients and trainees.

Staff working within the PCET sector themselves, might not technically or philosophically even see and define themselves as 'teachers'. They might be instructors, technicians, trainers, facilitators, tutors or teachers. And those that are employed to 'teach' might prefer to describe their work as 'lecturing'.

Within all this variation there are attempts to put in place structure from central government. Across the UK there are what we refer to as 'Sector Skills Councils' (SSCs), each of which monitor the interests and stakeholders of different sets of businesses. There are 25 of these in all and their remit is to work on developing skills, workforce participation in education, learning for life and all input into discussions about the reform of the credit and qualifications national framework. They draw up the national occupational standards that vocational qualifications and 14–19 curriculum changes need to address. The body known as Lifelong Learning UK (LLUK), responsible for the monitoring of teacher education in the PCET sector, is also one of the 25 SSCs. This body (and its sister organization, Standards Verification UK [SVUK]) set and maintain the professional standards that PCET teacher training is awarded against.

All of this is a huge area of education and in many respects training to teach in the PCET sector is different from that of initial teacher education in secondary schools:

- Trainees undertaking work in this sector are obliged to obtain the 'licence to practice' award know as 'Preparing to Teach in the Lifelong Learning Sector' (PTLLS), and technically this should take place before they are allowed to teach classes while on placement.
- Qualified teacher status (QTS) is not awarded at the end of a PGCE PCET programme – thus PCET trainees are not qualified to work in secondary schools (despite the fact that many such schools have sixth forms which clearly teach 'post-16' qualifications).
- Qualified teacher learning and skills (QTLS) is awarded after employment and following a period referred to as 'professional formation'.
- Post-compulsory education and training sector teachers do not join the Graduate Teacher Training Registry (GTTR) but rather join the Institute for Learning (IfL) which awards the QTLS.
- Teachers in the sector are obliged to register with the IfL and to record a minimum of 30 hours continuing professional development (CPD) with the IfL per year.

 Discussion point

There seems to be a contradiction between the restructuring of teacher education and the consequences these have for employment and the restructuring of the 14–19 agenda (see Chapter 4). On the one hand, 14- and 15-year-olds now can attend college in partnership with their existing school provision (and this has in some cases been occurring for some time), and yet on the other, teacher training is firmly divided into 'secondary' and 'post-compulsory' with their own separate professional bodies and CPD requirements. Consider teaching 14–16-year-olds at a college rather than at a school – in what ways do you think this might be the same and yet also different?

 Discussion point

While all education institutions differ in some respects with regard to their ethos and atmosphere, leadership and structure, it is still possible to discern some very real differences between the 'feeling' of school sixth forms, sixth form colleges and further education colleges. In practice they are very different and this makes working within them a different experience. It is important to recognise just how significant the impact of the institution is on the teaching and learning that takes place within its walls and how that in turn affects the working lives, professional roles and identities of the workforce. When you next visit an educational institution, consider how they communicate their ethos to you. What does it tell you?

Due to the increasing diversity and change in this area of educational provision, Edwards and Usher (2006) describe the post-compulsory sector (or, in their words, the lifelong learning sector) as being an example of the 'postmodern condition'. They argue: 'Lifelong learning is implicated in this postmodern condition which…is opening up (as well as closing down) ambivalent spaces for learning' (Edwards and Usher, 2006: 58). What this means is that post-compulsory education in the UK is diverse and continuously changing. This change might open up possibilities and opportunities and yet at the same time it means a period of anxiety and unsettlement for those working and learning in the sector.

 M-level thinking: The postmodern condition and education

Is education 'postmodern' and what does this highly loaded term mean? The idea of a postmodern condition has been popular within social scientific debate since the 1970s and the rise of what variously has been described as the 'global age', 'the information society', 'the post-industrial society' and the 'post-welfare society'. It means that there has been such rapid and overwhelming change in the very fabric of social life and its structural organisation that things will never be the same again. These changes are seen to break the contemporary world from the past in a fundamental way – hence the idea of being postmodern. In such an age, global forces shape and dictate the complexity of interconnections between nation states. Media and communications technologies change the shape of lifestyles, leisure and ultimately culture and identity. When applied to education (and here to post-compulsory education) policy change is seen to respond to global changes in the commodification of knowledge as the new product of the economy, hence politicians' concerns with skills and competition being the basis for educational reforms. In what ways do schools and colleges demonstrate that they are shaped by the forces of globalisation?

A key feature of this 'postmodern condition' is an overwhelming speed and pace of change. This change results in a situation where policies change structures well before the final outcomes of previous policies can be felt and understood. Within the change, within the new, the old still peeks through, increasing diversity and variety with each successive policy initiative.

M-level thinking: 'Policy epidemic'

Levin (1998) speaks of a 'policy epidemic' in education: a flood of almost unstoppable polices concerning reform and change, the pace of which deconstructs and reshapes education in an unstable fashion. We might suggest that this is true of both UK education systems and qualifications frameworks, but especially true of post-16 learning since the New Labour government of 1997. Why do you think there is such policy change generated around education in the UK?

In the words of Dunleavy and O'Leary (1987), the UK educational system is seen to be characterised by a 'hyperactivism' of policy. Ball (2008) suggests that this pace of change in the reform of education is a key characteristic of New Labour ideology. For example, Ball cites Tony Blair's speech writer saying, 'modern politics is all about momentum. Stagnate, drift, wobble, and the media or, if strong enough, the opposition, will pounce' (Hyman, in Ball, 2008: 2). Tomlinson (2005) suggests that what is key about the educational reforms and polices since the first New Right government of 1979 is the remarkable continuity between policies of the New Right and the New Labour government that replaced them in 1997: both are characterised by a discourse that emphasises the global dimension to change, the need for a new skills agenda within the PCET/FE sector and the need to reform post-16 qualifications to meet the 'demands of industry'. Tomlinson sees the path of all this change as an increasing centralisation of the lifelong learning sector and she argues it is underpinned by a desire to reform welfare provision, in the face of an 'overload' of welfare, by returning as many people to work via training as possible.

One way to think about the context of such massive change and reform is to draw upon the idea of a 'risk society' to help us explain the policy context and global political climates that these reforms respond to. Beck (1992) refers to the rise of a risk society as being a consequence of the wider process of the postmodernisation of the world. In a risk society, culture, policy and political discourse become concerned with the recognition and avoidance of global ills and harms. Policy becomes responsive and reactive to perceived global forces that are in turn seen to threaten social stability and economic well-being. Bartlett (2003) suggests that the New Labour response to the rise of a risk society is to develop post-compulsory education policies that are concerned with the themes and principles of widening participation, building community, social inclusion and partnership. We can see these as key themes within the broad 'third way' approach of New Labour and, again, they are a recognition, within policy-making, ideological thinking and media discourse, of the importance of global forces.

The FE workplace reform

The traditional image of the FE sector has been one described originally by Venables (1967) as a 'dual-professionalism'. What is meant by this is the fact that the teaching workforce in the FE sector can be seen, largely, as two different workforces. There are the academic teachers and lecturers who are largely degree educated, the majority (but not all) having undergone a teacher training qualification. On the other side of the professional identity divide, are those teachers in the FE sector who come from industry to teach a highly specialised and vocational set of skills for learners undertaking vocational and work-based learning. Further, this second set of professionals have themselves their own 'dual-professionalism' since they see themselves as occupying both a teacher professional identity as well as their vocational occupational identity.

In many respects the strength of the sector is that the teaching workforce does attract people who have very valuable occupational and vocational experiences. But the concern has been that the workforce is not united and that the 'sector' as such, is not a unified whole. Some commentators have gone further and argued that through the late 1980s and mid-1990s the FE sector has been suffering from both a crisis of confidence and a crisis of identity. In the light of these concerns, we now see the introduction of perhaps the most wide-sweeping workplace reform of FE than ever before.

The FE workplace reform is a consequence of the changes laid out in the Department for Education and Skills (DfES) 2006 White Paper *Further Education: Raising Skills, Improving Life Chances* and the subsequent Department for Innovation, Universities and Skills (DIUS) paper in 2007 *World Class Skills: Implementing the Leitch Review of Skills in England*. These changes have taken effect within the English sector since 1 September 2007 and are intimately bound up with the establishment and role of both Lifelong Learning UK covering all four countries within the UK, and the Institute for Learning within the sector as a whole. These changes include:

- new regulations for the training of teachers in the PCET/FE sector along with new professional standards placing professional values at their heart;
- the creation of a new qualifications framework for initial teacher education in the sector including PTLLS and the establishment of the (QTLS) status for those occupying a 'full teaching role';
- the creation of a secondary status for those with instructor roles less than that of a 'full teacher' who now need to gain Associate Teacher Learning and Skills (ATLS);
- all teachers of English for speakers of other languages (ESOL) and literacy and numeracy are further required to obtain an additional specialist qualification;
- all teachers to complete a period of 'professional formation' after initial teacher education and training;
- all teachers employed in the sector to register with the IfL;
- all teachers to complete a minimum 30 hours CPD per year and to maintain a record of this commitment;
- introduction of new 'principals' qualifications' required for all newly appointed principals and all those seeking this career route, as awarded by the Centre for Excellence in Leadership (CEL);
- establishment of a new qualifications and credit framework (QCF) which emphasises transferable credits and units that travel between institutions with the learners and can be 'cashed in';
- all leaner achievements to be recorded on a national learner achievement record (LAR) and accessible by learners, institutions of education and employers;

- specialist teacher status in new 'skills for life' provision. Teachers of these skills areas to have separate and additional teacher training.

These reforms are seen as an attempt to professionalise the previously 'dual' or divided workforce in the sector, or at least, to re-professionalise the sector. The reforms can be seen as parallel with the changes taking place in secondary teacher training for CPD and the Teaching and Learning Masters programmes. They are all part of a wider process of the increased professionalisation of the teaching profession and the increased role played by both governmental and charitable bodies in the monitoring and regulating of teacher education and training.

Changing patterns of lifelong learning

Increasingly we have been speaking less of 'adult education' or of 'post-compulsory education', and more of lifelong learning. As Field notes:

> Lifelong learning is a beautifully simple idea. It is obvious that people learn throughout their lives ... And while learning clearly has some connection with what goes on in schools and colleges, it is not limited to the planned instruction that these great institutions deliver ... [there is] growing evidence of a broad and general acceptance that a one-off dose of school and college will not serve to get you through life's many challenges and opportunities. (Field, 2006: 1)

Lifelong learning could be either formal or informal – it could be in the workplace or the school. It could be an evening class 'just for fun'; it could mean attendance at a training course or a seminar held at a library or community centre. The concept refers to the notion that learning itself is continuous. It does not stop after 'school' and nor should it. To indicate its breadth and depth, the work of Lifelong Learning UK – the organisation charged with the remit to monitor and support lifelong learning in England, Northern Ireland, Scotland and Wales – identifies five aspects or 'areas' to its work covered by the broad 'lifelong' remit. These are:

1. Community learning.
2. Further education.
3. Higher education.
4. Libraries.
5. Work-based learning.

Lifelong learning is huge in scope and itself a big business. For example, LLUK estimate that the lifelong workforce in the whole of the UK consists of between 1 and 1.2 million individuals:

- 283,094 staff in community learning and development;
- 272,970 staff in further education;

- 340,000 staff in higher education;
- 52,007 staff in libraries, archives and information services;
- 136,625 staff in work-based learning.

The breakdown of this workforce for England alone, is at least 800,000 individuals:

- 167,924 staff in community learning and development;
- 246,000 staff in further education;
- 307,587 staff in higher education;
- 44,300 staff in libraries, archives and information services;
- 30,000 staff in work based learning (www.LLUK.org).

The idea of lifelong learning, in terms of its origins in government policy, is often closely linked to the idea of a knowledge economy (and its needs) and to the wider forces of globalisation and the effects they might have on education. A knowledge economy refers to the global (but Western and European) situation where economic production or activity is not based in the manufacture of a product or the delivery of service, but knowledge itself is the commodity of production. Knowledge itself is a resource, a commodity.

Notions of lifelong learning and associated debates and educational reforms currently run all through Western Europe. In 2000 the European Commission published their Memorandum on lifelong learning, which has been a key influence on UK debates and policy agendas and reforms. The Memorandum suggests that lifelong learning is a global priority to ensure citizenship and participation in community in society and in developing skilled workforces that are able to adapt to change and to diversity. In this document, the Commission suggested six key 'messages' for policy-makers to ensure that lifelong learning is a priority:

1. The need for member nations to focus upon the development of new basic skills in the rise of a knowledge society.
2. The need to raise levels of investment in human resources.
3. The need to focus attention on teacher training and educational provision within lifelong learning sectors to ensure the highest possible standards.
4. The importance of 'valuing learning' in all its forms, and the supporting of learning to enable it to take place, both formal and informal.
5. The provision of accessible information about learning opportunities made available to all.
6. Ensuring that lifelong learning provision is as close as possible in proximity to the learners who need to access it.

Ball (2008) notes that the rhetoric and discourse of government policy often contextualises itself with claims that education needs to serve the economy. Governments across Europe position changes to the lifelong learning sector as necessary in the light of supposed global forces and the competition resulting from global markets. This 'skills agenda' is seen to be a necessary response to workplace reform in a changing global world. The world of work is seen as different, the workforce of today and the future will need to be different, and so education needs to respond to forces beyond the respective nation states and their individual education systems. Ball says that, 'the meaning of education and what it means "to be educated" are changed and a new kind of flexible, lifelong learner is articulated by policy in relation to the knowledge economy' (Ball, 2008: 39).

What does all this mean for the learner? How does the flexibility for qualifications and skills affect us? Will there be increased opportunity or will the quality of education decline as market forces take over? A number of educational thinkers speak of a process of the 'marketisation of education' (see pages 21–22) – the increasing 'erosion' of educational standards and quality serve political ideologies about the needs for global economic competition. On the one hand, Falk (1999) notes that the very notion of lifelong learning creates new ways to talk and think about education. It allows us to see education as open-ended, as flexible and it offers a framework for political debate and policy that increases opportunities for learners. However, both Falk and, later, Ball warn of a rather sinister potential consequence of this 'flexibility' and 'personalisation' of education: in a world where we as learners are having to keep up, update and add new skills to our portfolio, responsibility for learning and education is thrown onto the learner and away from the state. As in previous eras and with previous educational reforms, the problems of social disadvantage reinforcing cycles of education, deprivation and underperformance still might continue to limit and ghettoise whole groups of potential learners. In a world where we are all trying to keep up in the race towards flexibility and the global competitive edge, some might just be left behind.

Similarity and difference: Scotland, Northern Ireland and Wales

Lifelong Learning UK, one of the 25 sector skills councils, has a remit that encompasses and unites regional difference between the four countries in the UK – England, Scotland, Northern Ireland and Wales – despite their differences in educational systems and qualification frameworks, especially between Scotland and the rest of the UK.

Scotland

According to figures provided by LLUK, the lifelong learning workforce in Scotland is estimated to comprise over 155,500 individuals:

* 10,935 staff in community learning and development;
* 12,330 staff in 43 further education institutions;
* 52,091 staff in 21 higher education institutions;

- 5,205 staff in libraries, archives and information services;
- 75,000 staff in work-based learning (www.LLUK.org).

In addition to the size of the workforce, according to the May 2007 document *More Choices, More Chances* (Scottish Executive, 2007) produced by the Scottish Government, there are approximately 32,000 young people in Scotland who are not in education, employment or training. It is estimated that around 24,000 young people need additional support to be able to move into learning or employment. The policy implications of *More Choices, More Chances* highlights action points for Scottish work and education policy over the next decade, targeting this 'lost' group of young people.

The policy strategies and reforms to come from *More Choices, More Chances* attempt to target young people both pre-16 and post-16. It recognises the need for the Scottish education system to provide financial support for post-16 learners and routes for young people to return to education once they have left. It also recognises the importance of ensuring that all pre-16 learners have 'a place to go' and a clear and recognised pathway into training or education post-16.

Northern Ireland

According to LLUK, the lifelong learning workforce in the Northern Ireland is estimated to consist of at least 16,200 individuals:

- 3,907 staff in community learning and development;
- 6,357 staff in further education;
- 6,747 staff in higher education;
- 380 staff in libraries, archives and information services;
- 1,625 staff in work-based learning (www.LLUK.org).

The 1998 Green Paper *The Learning Age* (DfEE, 1998), outlined a set of proposals, designed to:

- make lifelong learning a 'normal' and expected part of a general learning culture;
- raise the level of skills of the population to meet new global demands;
- allow all to develop new skills and new leaning opportunities in the light of massive social, technological and economic change.

Following on from this, the UK-wide 1999 report *Lifelong Learning – A New Learning Culture for All* (DANI, 1999) is perhaps the best statement on lifelong learning as applied to the Northern Ireland context. This document speaks of the 'new demands' placed upon society and upon the workforce due to a changing world and a need to engage with the raising of basic skills among the young and adults as well as increased opportunities for engagement in learning for all.

Wales

According to LLUK, the lifelong learning workforce in the Wales is estimated to consist of approximately 70,000:

* 4,123 staff in community learning and development;
* 9,122 staff in 23 further education institutions;
* 24,528 staff in 12 higher education institutions;
* 2,122 staff in libraries, archives and information services;
* 30,000 staff in work-based learning (www.LLUK.org).

The 2001 Welsh Assembly Government paper *The Learning Country: Vision into Action* (NAFWC, 2001) provides a clear statement on lifelong learning – seeing it as essential for the new economic and global challenges that Wales faces in the years to come. The policy attempts to provide access to lifelong learning through, initially, the expansion and review of FE sector provision: in particular, through a credit-based qualification system with flexible and transferable frameworks across and between educational institutions and types of qualifications. In addition, the policy document seeks to provide new forms of financial support for learners, apprentices, and trainees to encourage learning opportunities to be taken up.

The Learning Country set out a 10-year strategy, due for review in 2010, looking at ways to improve the life-chances of the Welsh population through the use of lifelong learning and training as a mechanism to develop financial well-being and employment, as well as a highly skilled population. This need was couched, in the document, in terms of the need for a changing workforce to meet the changes of a 'technological revolution' across the globe as a whole.

A great deal of this work, in creating flexible routes to learn and train, has been focused upon the development of an integrated qualifications framework and the widening of apprenticeship and traineeship opportunities. The development of a Welsh baccalaureate alongside measures to reform National Traineeships and Modern Apprenticeships and the creation of a modular, credit system for vocational and academic qualifications, is all set to integrate the education system and the world of work into a unified, yet flexible, whole.

The Welsh Assembly Government in the 2005 strategy document *Words Talk, Numbers Count* (NAFWC, 2007) makes the point that in order to think about and target lifelong learning, important preparatory work still needs to be done with young learners to ensure that by the time they are adults they have the necessary skills needed to engage with a flexible learning culture. Specifically, the Department for Children, Education, Lifelong Learning and Skills contributes to the Welsh Assembly Government's vision of a lifelong learning culture in the 2004 document *Making the Connections* (NAFWC, 2004). This strategy highlights the need to integrate lifelong learning to the provision of both adult learning and pre-16 education, to ensure flexible learning opportunities are provided and accessible for all through an integration, at a governmental and departmental level, of all these key services.

Chapter links →

Themes and ideas explored in this chapter link to corresponding ideas in Chapters 2, 4 and 12.

Suggested further reading 📖

Tummons, J. (2007) *Becoming a Professional Tutor in the Lifelong Learning Sector*. Exeter: Learning Matters.

References

Ball, S. (2008) *The Education Debate*. Bristol: Polity Press.

Bartlett, S. (2003) 'Education for lifelong learning', in S. Bartlett and D. Burton (eds), *Education Studies: Essential Issues*. London: Sage.

Beck, U. (1992) *Risk Society. Towards a New Modernity*. London: Sage.

Coffield, F., Edward, S., Finlay, I., Hodgson, A., Spours, K. and Steer, R. (2008) *Improving Learning, Skills and Inclusion: The Impact of Policy on Post-compulsory Education*. London: Routledge.

DANI (1999) *Lifelong Learning – A New Learning Culture for All*. http://www.delni.gov.uk/acfbb7f. pdf (last accessed September 2009).

Department for Education and Employment (DfEE) (1998) *The Learning Age: A Renaissance for a New Britain*. Crown Copyright. http://www.lifelonglearning.co.uk/greenpaper/index.htm (last accessed September 2009).

Department for Education and Skills (DfES) (2006) *Further Education: Raising Skills, Improving Life Chances*, White Paper 2006 HMSO Crown Copyright DfES.

Department for Innovation, Universities and Skills (DIUS) (2007) *World Class Skills: Implementing the Leitch Review of Skills in England*. HMSO Crown Copyright.

Dunleavy, P. and O'Leary, B. (1987) *Theories of the State*. London: Macmillan.

Edwards, R. and Usher, R. (2006) 'A troubled space of possibilities: lifelong learning and the post-modern', in P. Sutherland and J. Crowther (eds), *Lifelong Learning: Concepts and Contexts*. London: Routledge.

Falk, C. (1999) *Sentencing Learners to Life: Retrofitting the Academy for the Information Age, Theory, Technology and Culture*, 22 (1–2) http://www.ctheory.com/

Field, J. (2006) *Lifelong Learning and the New Educational Order*. London: Trentham Books.

Levin, B. (1998) 'An epidemic of education policy: what can we learn for each other?', *Comparative Education*, 34(2): 131–41.

NAFWC The Welsh Assembly – Department for Education, Lifelong Learning and Skills (2001) *The Learning Country: Vision into Action*. http://wales.gov.uk/dcells/ (last accessed September 2009).

NAFWC The Welsh Assembly – Department for Education, Lifelong Learning and Skills (2004) *Making the Connections*.

NAFWC The Welsh Assembly – Department for Education, Lifelong Learning and Skills (2007) *Words Talk, Numbers Count*. http://wales.gov.uk/dcells/ (last accessed September 2009).

Scottish Executive (2007) *More Choices, More Chances: A Strategy to Reduce the Proportion of Young People not in Education, Employment or Training in Scotland*. Edinburgh: Crown Copyright.

Tomlinson, S. (2005) *Education in a Post-Welfare Society*, 2nd edn. Maidenhead: Open University Press.

Venables, E. (1967) *The Young Worker at College: A Study of a Local Tech*. London: Faber and Faber.

CHAPTER 4

UNDERSTANDING THE 14–19 AGENDA

Objectives

By the end of this chapter the reader will be able to:

1. understand why reforms to the 14–19 curricula are necessary;
2. evaluate the government's Diploma qualifications;
3. comprehend reforms to both GCSEs and A levels;
4. understand how the International Baccalaureate fits into the qualifications framework.

What does curriculum change mean for teachers?

This is an extraordinary time to be training for a career as a professional teacher. This chapter explains how the educational landscape is transforming for all those working within the 14–19 sector. Whether this transformation is evolutionary or revolutionary we will leave it to you to decide once you have considered the arguments and evidence. Either way 2013 is the year that the statutory 14–19 entitlement comes in and is also a year when the compulsory leaving is extended to 17-year-olds. If that were not enough, 2013 is also the year that the government has decided to review all 14–19 qualifications.

This chapter will help unpack the long- and short-term implications of these changes for you as a teacher. This is important because to be awarded QTS for Key Stages 4 and 5 you need to be able to show awareness of the progression through 14–19 phases in school, colleges and work-based settings. For those of you seeking QTLS and working within what we used to refer to as the 'FE sector', you will be increasingly working with younger aged children both on day release into your institution and maybe even visiting local secondary schools to work in collaboration and partnership. As you can see, this means the landscape of so-called post-compulsory education has truly changed!

Though this chapter is called 'Understanding the 14–19 agenda' it might equally be called the '11–19 agenda'. Any assessment structure that is introduced to 14-year-olds in schools will have a ripple-down effect on teachers teaching pupils in the years below because they will be preparing those pupils for subject choices, examinations and, ultimately, employment and HE options. Like it or not, examinations structure the way that you teach and the way you assess. But being a teacher is more than just about teaching. It is about the way you must also be able to be a conduit of information from a variety of institutions that include schools, sixth form colleges, FE colleges, work-based learning providers, independent learning providers and universities. Parents and the pupils and learners you teach will seek information from you about different routes and opportunities to maximise their life changes. Two statistics are worth noting before reading this chapter any further. Both should make you stop and think about the pathways that currently exist in the institution where you seek employment. First, while the media bombards the public with the fact that many more learners are getting grade As in all their subjects, this actually only accounts for approximately 5 per cent of the entire age group. Secondly, fewer than half of all learners achieve GCSEs in English and mathematics (McNeil, 2008). Both sets of statistics inform the reformation of 14–19 education that this chapter is all about.

Reforming the 14-19 curriculum

Since the 1980s, British governments have attempted to reform the provision of 14–19 education through a variety of initiatives. There has been a gradual acceptance of the need to treat 14–19 as a unified phase rather than the traditional '11–16' and '16–18' conceptions of secondary and tertiary education that have dominated structures since the end of the Second World War. The Dearing Review in 1996 forcefully argued for drawing together of the 14–16 and 16–19 learning experience. This report argued for replacement of GCSEs and A levels with a single Diploma qualification. However, it was not until January 2003, that New Labour (under the leadership of Tony Blair) announced that a complete overhaul of the education system would be taking place of 14–19 education. There were many reasons why reform of the system had to take place:

- 16–19 participation rates of young people in British education and training compared with other advanced industrialised countries has been embarrassingly low for a decade (Britain being twenty-seventh out of the top 30 industrialised counties, with a 68 per cent retention rate; this compared to a European average of 86 per cent).

- The British labour market has traditionally followed its American cousins in its voluntarist approach to employment policy. This means that there can be little incentive for some young people to stay on in education. They can be easily pulled into relatively unskilled labour where, even though wages are low in comparison to more skilled employees, a living can be made. This can be an attractive option for many young people who feel alienated by secondary education. This is not the case in many European labour markets, which are more regulated and where a licence to practise is required thereby forcing young people to get qualifications before they seek employment.

- The affluence that emerged during the 1990s is not homogenous. Hodgson and Spours (2008) note that the social polarisation that exists in many parts of Britain has meant that many groups of young people and their parents have lost touch with the importance of education; both preferring the immediate gratification of employment opportunities compared to the deferred gratification but increased expense of further and higher education.

- While many countries in Europe hold the status of vocational subjects on a par with academic subjects, there is a relative lack of parity of esteem between vocational and academic subjects in Britain. This can be problematic for some British parents who view education as providing social advantage. Their choice of school, examination and employment is a pathway to that advantage. But this can mean that parents choose educational pathways for their children that might be unsuitable for them.

∿ M-level thinking: Narrowing the ∿ academic/vocational divide

For decades politicians have attempted to provide parity of esteem between vocational and academic pathways in education and training. The reforms in the DfES (2005 White Paper), *14–19 Education and Skills*, have focused mainly on the vocational. There is a danger, however, that if vocational education at post-16 level requires lower entry requirements (for example, pupils with fewer than five GCSEs A* to C), this will effect the status of level 3 vocational qualifications and consequently parent and pupil choice and their acceptance of these pathways. In what ways do you think parity of esteem between the academic and the vocational can be addressed?

- Wylie (2006) notes that the qualification and assessment system that exists in secondary school alienates many young people from a curriculum that was constructed in 1988 (see Chapter 2). Not only are British teenagers assessed formally more than in any other country in the world, but many children find the transition from primary education to secondary confusing and alienating, leading many to 'vote with their feet' and walk into low-skilled, low-status jobs. This in turn can create a cycle of low expectations as some of these young people become young parents.

In 2005 we saw the government's White Paper on 14–19 educational provision that promised to transform the educational landscape and bring an end to the marginalisation that many young people experience in British schools.

The White Paper, *14–19 Education and Skills* (DfES, 2005)

In 2003, at the behest of the Blair government, the Working Group on 14–19 Reform was set up following widespread concern over A-level examination results from the previous summer, when results were downgraded and confidence in the current 14–19 system was undermined. On 18 October 2004, the working group – headed by Mike Tomlinson – published its final report, referred to as the 'Tomlinson Report', recommending a radical shake-up of secondary education in England. Recommendations were made to:

- raise participation and achievement – by tackling the educational causes of disengagement and underachievement and low post-16 participation;
- get the basics right – ensuring that young people achieve specified levels in functional mathematics, literacy and communication and ICT, and are equipped with the knowledge, skills and attributes needed to succeed in adult life, further learning and employment;
- strengthen vocational routes – improving the quality and status of vocational programmes delivered by schools, colleges and training providers, setting out the features of high-quality provision and identifying a clear role for employers;
- provide greater stretch and challenge – ensuring opportunities for greater breadth and depth of learning. This will help employers and universities to differentiate more effectively between top performers. Stretch and challenge at all levels will encourage young people to think for themselves and be innovative and creative about their learning;
- reduce the assessment burden for learners, teachers, institutions and the system as a whole by reducing the number of times learners are examined; extending the role of teacher assessment and changing assessment in A levels in order to improve the quality of teaching and learning;
- make the system more transparent and easier to understand by rationalising 14–19 curriculum and qualifications within a diploma framework, where progression routes and the value of qualifications are clear (DfE, 2004).

The White Paper *14–19 Education and Skills* (DfES, 2005) was both a response to Mike Tomlinson's working group report in 2004 and governmental concerns over international economic performance. The aims of the White Paper were to:

- increase post-16 participation rates from 75 per cent to 90 per cent by 2015;
- ensure that levels of English and mathematics are of a sufficient level to serve the needs of employers, further and higher education;

- raise the status and participation rates in vocational education and training;
- stretch young people at all levels of education and training;
- re-engage those young people 'disaffected' from education and training.

The response to the government paper was far from overwhelmingly positive and there were many who felt that the White Paper had only 'cherry picked' elements of the Tomlinson Report rather than being wholly faithful to Tomlinson's dream. However, despite many criticisms, the 14–19 reforms have attempted to achieve:

- parity of esteem between vocational and academic qualifications;
- provision of choice through a variety of academic and vocational pathways to broaden the curriculum choice for pupils;
- the development of a three-pronged framework of qualifications that embraces work-based learning, academic and vocational studies;
- the increase of post-16 participation rates, which remain some of the lowest in the industrialised nations.

The target for post-16 participation rates has been set at 90 per cent (Abbot and Huddleston, 2007). Targets are similarly ambitious for apprenticeships, with 500,000 being set for 2020 (Leitch, 2006). Central to the government's vision is the desire to ensure that programmes of learning lead to clear destinations for learners rather than the 'snakes and ladders' arrangements whereby learners are often prevented from pursuing different pathways once they have embarked on a particular route (Abbot and Huddleston, 2007).

The National Qualifications Framework

Trying to make sense of all of the qualifications available (and then try to explain them to confused parents and pupils) can be a nightmare. The National Qualifications Framework (NQF) brings within its sphere all occupational, academic and vocational pathways. The framework allocates all qualifications within it an NQF level. This ideally gives parents, pupils, teachers and employers an indication of the parity of qualification across different pathways, for example, an NVQ level 2 should contain within it similar demands on learners to GCSE A* to C. We say, 'ideally' as the variety and types of qualification that exist are so varied that any comparison made should be treated with caution. There are over 3,000 certificates that exist in over 700 qualifications ranging from levels 1 to 3. Level 1 qualifications include GCSEs (grades D–G), Business and Techonology Educational Council qualifications (BTECs), Diplomas and NVQs. Level 2 qualifications include GCSEs (grades A*–C), Oxford Cambridge and RSA (OCR) National Certificates and the Diploma (at level 2). Level 3 qualifications include AS/A levels, the International Baccalaureate, BTEC National Diplomas, the Diploma (at level 3) and National Vocational Qualifications (NVQs) (also at level 3).

Complex funding arrangements that span the 14–19 range of qualifications makes talk of a coherent set of qualifications difficult. Qualifications for 14–16 are currently funded by local education authorities or in some cases directly from central government. Funding arrangements for pre-16 vocational provision and post-16 education come under the auspices of the Learning and Skills Councils, although how long this particular arrangement is likely to remain is unclear. Three new bodies will play a leading role in shaping the 14–19 qualification system. The Qualifications and Curricular Development Agency (QCDA) and Joint Advisory Committee for Qualifications Approval (JACQA) are advisory bodies and the Office of the Qualifications and Examinations Regulator (Ofqual) will be a statutory body with regulatory powers. JACQA will be responsible for advising the Secretary of State on which 14–19 qualifications should be publicly funded.

The Diplomas

In Chapter 2 we outlined a range of policies from different governments that have attempted to create vocational qualifications that have parity of esteem with their academic counterparts. The Diplomas represent the current attempt by governments to continue this tradition. Designed by Diploma Development Partnerships and led by Sector Skills Councils, employers have had a significant say in the development of the Diplomas. With English and mathematics at their core, the Diplomas are intended to be a blend of general education and 'applied learning' (McNeil, 2008). Each diploma has been designed to meet the needs of a key employment sector and have been designed in partnership with universities and employers. The intention is to provide a qualification that brings together theoretical, practical work-related and work-based learning. The Diploma subjects that will be available to all learners from 2013 are:

- construction and the built environment;
- creative and media;
- engineering;
- information technology;
- society, health and development;
- manufacturing and product design;
- business, administration and finance;
- hospitality;
- hair and beauty studies;
- environmental land-based studies;
- travel and tourism;
- public services;
- sport and active leisure;
- humanities;
- retail business;
- science;
- languages.

The Diplomas have been designed so that pupils from the age of 14 can study a foundation (L1) or higher (L2) diploma at school in Years 10 and 11. This means that

Table 4.1   Diploma equivalency

The Diplomas will be offered at four levels:

Diploma level	Academic equivalent
Foundation level 1	5 GCSE passes at level 1
Higher level 2	7 GCSE passes at level 2 (A*–C)
Progression level 3	2 A levels
Advanced level 3	3.5 A levels

pupils have effectively to make a significant decision in Year 9 in terms of their future educational trajectories. That said the Diplomas have been designed so that pupils can study them along side the compulsory national curriculum. Each Diploma is made up of component parts that include:

- principal learning (relevant to the sector, the specific mandatory subject content that defines the diploma being taken);
- additional specialist learning (ASL) – learners can chose to study an extra option, e.g. learners might wish to take an A level in mathematics to complement their L3 Diploma in engineering;
- personal learning and thinking skills (PLTS) – this includes skills related to independent inquiry; creative thinking; team-working; self-management; reflective learning; effective participation;
- functional skills – in order to qualify for the Diploma functional skills tests in English, mathematics and ICT must be passed;
- generic learning (broad mandatory skills and knowledge necessary for learning that include PLTS and functional skills);
- a project (an internally assessed research project);
- work experience – each diploma carries with it a minimum of 10 days' work experience;
- extra-curricular activities – (related to the Diploma being taken).

Delivery of the Diplomas requires strong collaboration between institutions through the formation of local 'consortia'.

 M-level thinking: 14–19 competition and collaboration?

The 14–19 agenda, as spelt out in the government's 2005 White Paper, emphasises the need for collaboration between institutions if the Diploma project is to be a success. Consortia of different educational institutions have to work together to provide the entitlement for all learners across the country to study a Diploma by 2013. This is because, in most cases, no one institution can offer a Diploma

qualification at level 3 in isolation. What tensions can you identify between collaboration and a competitive marketised system of education in which schools compete for funding and 'bums on seats'?

Ensuring the right infrastructure is in place also requires partners to work together to develop area-wide strategies for issues such as timetabling, transport and development of the teaching force. The 14–19 partnerships are developing these local strategies in all areas (DCSF, 2007). By November 2008 12,000 young people had registered for the Diplomas (mostly at level 2) which was some way short of the expected 40,000 places the government hoped would be taken up.

Functional skills

All learners need level 2 achievement in functional skills (English, mathematics and ICT) as part of any learning pathway. This means, for example, that no GCSE can be awarded at grade C or above unless the functional skills have been passed. Functional skills are not new. Their predecessors were the key skills of communication, application of number and ICT. Functional skills are the latest attempt by government to raise standards of literacy, numeracy and ICT while making the curricula more relevant to employment and higher education.

 Discussion point

There are lots of reasons why the government has decided to replace key skills with functional skills. McNeil (2008) notes that that many school-leavers who have achieved GCSE English and mathematics at A*–C do not have the applied communication and numeracy skills they need at work, let alone the team-working, self-management and problem-solving skills employers argue are essential. Universities make similar complaints and this does not take into consideration the fact that just under half of all school-leavers in England leave with less than a level 2 qualification. Roach (2007) also notes that seven million adults are illiterate. This figure is made more worrying when considering that three-quarters of all long-term prison offenders have level 1 literacy skills or less. Bynner and Parsons (2006) have shown that people with poor levels of literacy and numeracy have a wide range of disadvantages, including poor health, lower standards of accommodation and higher rates of family breakdown. To what extent can the introduction of functional skills address the needs of universities, employers and society as a whole?

While functional skills have been embedded in the secondary curriculum, they are also available as free-standing qualifications for all learners aged 14 and over. Not only are they integral to the Diplomas (pupils will not pass the Diplomas unless they have passed the functional skills) but they are also an integral part of the extended project. Candidates will also not be able to gain GCSE A*–C in English, mathematics or ICT unless they have achieved a level 2 in the relevant functional skill.

The extended project

Although the extended project plays a significant role in the Diplomas it is also available as a stand-alone qualification (worth one AS qualification). It is 100 per cent internally assessed and, in addition to the submission of the written work, requires an oral presentation that is formally assessed. It requires a high degree of planning, research and autonomous working.

Personal learning and thinking skills

These skills are not only integral to the Diplomas but are also embedded throughout the 11–19 curriculum. The framework of PLTS skills comprises six groups of skills. McNeil (2008) summarises these groups of skills as:

- team-working, for example, working collaboratively with other people, taking responsibility and resolving issues;
- reflective learning, for example, setting goals for learning and work, monitoring performance and reviewing progress;
- creative thinking, for example, generating ideas, tackling problems and finding imaginative solutions;
- independent enquiry, for example, planning and carrying out investigations, taking informed decisions;
- self-management, for example, being organised, showing enterprise and responding to new challenges;
- effective participation, for example, playing a full part in school, college or the wider community.

Despite the government's desire for these skills to be one of a range of pillars of the qualifications framework, PLTS will not be formally discretely assessed.

The International Baccalaureate (IB)

The IB is an internationally recognised qualification for learners aged 16 to 19 and is based around detailed academic study of a wide range of subjects, including languages, the arts, science, mathematics, history and geography. Most learners who take the IB diploma programme go on to some form of higher education, and the qualification is recognised by universities in more than 100 countries. It takes a variety of forms that vary from country to country and institution to institution, but normally is composed of two years of study. The IB is mostly assessed through examinations that are marked externally. However, in nearly all subjects, some of the assessment (coursework) is carried out by teachers. From 2008 entry onwards, successfully completing the diploma officially counted towards Universities and Colleges Admissions Service (UCAS) tariff for getting into higher education. Wales has championed the IB with an enthusiasm that is largely lacking in other parts of the UK.

Although the IB varies from institution to institution it normally takes the form of a compulsory 'core' (consisting of the theory of knowledge, an extended essay focusing on an area of interest and involvement in some form of artistic or community-based endeavour). In addition to this core, learners will chose one subject from each of the following areas:

1. A first language (normally the student's mother tongue).
2. A second language.
3. Experimental sciences (biology, chemistry, physics, design technology).
4. Mathematics and computer science.
5. The arts (visual, music and theatre).
6. Individuals and society (for example, history, sociology, psychology and geography).

Towards the end of his premiership Tony Blair promised that by 2011 every local authority must have at least one educational institution that offers the IB. Only time will tell if this promise is fulfilled by successive governments.

Key Stage 4

At the time of the publication of the 2005 White Paper the curriculum was broadly divided into academic and vocational subjects. The former, at Key Stage 4 were assessed through the General Certificate of Secondary Education (GCSE). The latter were assessed through the General National Vocational Certificate (GNVQ) Part 1, eventually to become vocational GCSEs. However, Key Stage 4 qualifications take a variety of forms, all of which are defined at level 2 (intermediate level). Learners can follow nationally defined programmes of study for mathematics, English, citizenship, science and information technology. Physical education is compulsory and students study religious education from a locally agreed syllabus. New entitlement curriculum areas, including arts, design and technology, the humanities and modern foreign languages, are available to learners who wish to study these subjects.

The most common form of public assessment at Key Stage 4 is the General Certificate in Secondary Education. These are academic qualifications assessed through public examination after two years of study. In September 2002 a range of 'applied' GCSE courses were introduced across eight subject areas (applied art and design, applied business, engineering, health and social care, applied ICT, leisure and tourism, manufacturing, applied science). The VGCSE (the 'V' stood for 'vocational') replaced the GNVQ Part 1 in a range of vocational qualifications. It is assumed that the Diploma pathways will lead to the eventual demise of these qualifications, although that is far from certain.

 Discussion point

How ironic it is that weaker and perhaps more vulnerable learners, who might not get the required GCSEs to stay on in their sixth forms, are the ones that get ferried off to other institutions. In other words, many schools 'expel' students in Year 11 for not getting the required GCSEs to stay on; whereas those learners who 'perform' well in examinations retain the security of the schools that have been their base for the past five years. To what extent do you believe that children should be excluded from school sixth forms on the basis of qualifications?

A-level reform

Amid media furore over supposed falling standards, increased student stress and rising assessment burdens for teachers, A levels were once again reformed in 2008. AS/A-level studies are assessed in individual subjects in much the same way as their GCSE counterparts. Learners take two units at AS and two units at 'A2' in each of their subject areas, with most learners choosing to take three subjects. Students in their A2 year can also opt to take additional AS subjects if they and their teachers feel they can cope. So-called 'Stretch and Challenge' is addressed by having fewer structured and short-answered questions, more open-ended and essay-style questions and greater emphasis on 'synopticity' that is, the ways in which learners can show how different parts of the specification fit together (McNeil, 2008). An A* grade is awarded to candidates who achieve more than 90 per cent on the Examiner's Standardised Mark Scale (This can be viewed on www.edexcel.org.uk.) In most subjects coursework (so much a feature of Curriculum 2000) has been scrapped. Many subjects have replaced coursework with new-style questions where research methods have to be studied and where knowledge of them can be demonstrated.

Existing vocational Key Stage 5 qualifications

All level qualifications taken at Key Stage 4 can be taken at Key Stage 5. Advanced level 3 qualifications are in a process of change. In reality most learners take qualifications that follow on from their successes at GCSE levels. Many learners take the Advanced

Vocational Certificate in Education (AVCE). This is a level 3 vocational qualification assessed in a similar way to its level 2 counterpart. Learners sit public examinations but also submit a teacher-assessed portfolio. Single or double awards are offered (single award being equivalent to one A level). Business and Technology Education Council qualifications have grown in popularity, having first been offered in the FE sector and now growing in numbers in schools. They are assessed mainly at level 2 (BTEC First) and level 3 (BTEC National) (although level 1 and level 4 are also available).

Keeping abreast of the changes

One of the many tensions that is likely to continue as the 14–19 agenda gathers pace is the contradiction between, on the one hand, government rhetoric of collaboration and cooperation between institutions and, on the other hand, a system of funding based on market principles and competition between institutions. For a system that is largely funded on the basis of competition (for example, league tables) one of the challenges is for the provision of individual planned programmes for students where they may well have to have access to different providers in their chosen courses. As you continue your training as a teacher, it is your responsibility to make sure you are aware of how these curriculum changes affect your own subject area. Parents and students need access to sophisticated guidance and counselling systems in schools and colleges because of the plethora of different academic, vocational and work-based learning routes possible. Despite the wide range of careers advice available, parents and pupils are more likely to seek advice from you because of the unique relationship you have with them.

 Case study

Michael qualified as a psychology teacher last year and is working in one of London's academies. Compared to many teachers he is very lucky in that he has been given the opportunity to attend a variety of training days made available as a result of the breadth of 14–19 curriculum changes taking place. He enthusiastically describes the effects these training days are having on him: 'It's brilliant – there is so much going on if you look for it. The exam boards lay on loads of training days and I have also joined my subject association which offers training days, resources etc. I think the real benefit though is that where I work I am the only full-time psychology teacher and I don't get the opportunity to meet up with other teachers of my subject. At these training days it is great because you get all the formal stuff but equally useful is to make contacts with other teachers – we email each other all our lesson plans and resources and I find that so helpful'.

There is lots of guidance and advice for teachers who are trying to keep up to date with all these curriculum changes. Try to find out about your subject association. These organisations are great for meeting other teachers who teach your subject and are a great source of resources, news and advice. Examination boards will also usually offer free sessions updating developments within the subject specifications. Finally, keep an eye out for flyers about training events that often get sent to heads of departments who, unintentionally, often forget to pass these on to other members of the teaching team: do not blame them though – they, like you, are busy bees!

Similarity and difference: Scotland, Northern Ireland and Wales

Scotland

No distinct 14–19 phase exists in Scotland. The emphasis of the Scottish Executive is firmly placed on entitlement rather than requirement (Roach, 2007). Every school in Scotland is required to have established partnerships with at least one college for pupils, although there is no single model for how this takes place. Between 2004 and 2008, A Curriculum for Excellence (ACfE) introduced a single-phase curriculum from age 3 to 18. These developments provided a unified system of vocational and academic awards calibrated within a national credit and qualifications framework. The ACfE has also been designed to encourage interdisciplinary working and provide pupils opportunities to gain vocational learning post-14. Skills for Work is a programme which provides pupils with vocational learning opportunities. Intended as an integral part of the school curriculum Skills for Work leads to nationally recognised qualifications.

Northern Ireland

Northern Ireland shares a qualifications framework with England and Wales and therefore some of the features of recent reforms in England and Wales apply in Northern Ireland (for example, the introduction of functional skills and the extended project). Currently, 14–19 reforms are contextualised by the government's response to the Bain Report, *Schools for the Future: Funding, Strategy and Development* (Bain, 2006). The New Entitlement Framework for learners guarantees every student an entitlement to select from a minimum of 24 academic and vocational subjects. The framework is intended to promote opportunity for learning to all young people. Schools and colleges ensure that at least one-third of the subjects on offer are vocational. There is no element of compulsion to study. A Diploma route of qualifications is also under development but details of the reform process are currently unclear.

Wales

The National Assembly in Wales announced its own consultation with major 14–19 stakeholders, and its progress has been extensive and reflects many of the concerns of Westminster. Issues related to parity of esteem, increased entrepreneurship, creativity, and a focus on personal and social skills are familiar themes. However, Wales is ahead of its English cousins with the piloting of learning coaches, a seamless transition within the 14–19 age phase and the introduction of the Welsh Baccalaureate. Wales has led the way in UK with its IB, and their version of the qualification can be taken in a conventionally academic, vocational pathway or combinations of both. It is worth 120 UCAS points and there is an intermediate one-year qualification. The introduction of 14–19 learning pathways provides individually tailored opportunities for young people. This, coupled with wider choice of academic and vocational learning, is regarded by the Welsh Assembly as a key platform for raising expectations for learning beyond 16 and incentivising young people to learn (Roach, 2007).

Chapter links →

Themes and ideas explored in this chapter link to corresponding ideas in Chapters 2, 3 and 12.

Suggested further reading 📖

Hodgson, A. and Spours, K. (2008) *Education and Training 14–19: Curriculum, Qualifications and Organization*. London: Sage.

References

Abbot, I. and Huddleston, P. (2007) '14–19 curriculum reform', in V. Brooks, I. Abbot, and L. Bills (eds), *Preparing to Teach in Secondary Schools*. Maidenhead: McGraw-Hill.
Bain, G. (2006) *Schools for the Future: Funding, Strategy, Sharing*. Report of the Independent Strategic Review of Education.
Bynner, J. and Parsons, S. (2006) *New Light on Literacy*. London: NRDC.
Department for Education (DfE) (2004) *14–19 Qualifications and Curriculum Reform – Final Report of the Working Group on 14–19 Reform*. DfE Ref 0976/2004. London: DfE.
Department for Education and Skills (DfES) (2005) *14–19 Education and Skills*. White Paper DfES Ref. 02/05 176940. London: DfES.
Department for Children, Schools and Families (DCSF) (2007) *Expanding the 14–19 Diploma Programme*. London: DCSF.

Hodgson, A. and Spours, K. (2008) *Education and Training 14–19: Curriculum, Qualifications and Organization*. London: Sage.

Leitch, A. (2006) *Prosperity for All in the Global Economy – World Class Skills Final Report*. London: HM Treasury.

McNeil P. (2008) '14–19 reform – "pressures and priorities"', *Social Science Teacher – The Journal of the Association for the Teaching of Social Sciences*, 37(2): 24–8.

Roach, P. (2007) *A Better Future: 14–19 Education – an NASUWT Perspective*. London: NASUWT.

Wylie, T. (2006) Speech given at 2nd Annual 14–19 Diploma Conference, Hotel Russell, London, 20 September 2007.

SECTION 2
PROFESSIONAL SKILLS

CHAPTER 5

THE HABITS OF A GOOD TEACHER

Objectives

By the end of this chapter the reader will be able to:

1. define the term 'reflective practitioner';
2. see the importance of the idea of reflection for teacher training;
3. apply the idea of reflection to the day-to-day practice of a professional teacher;
4. apply the usefulness of diary- and journal-keeping to the process of teacher education and training and the recording of 'critical incidents';
5. understand the relationship between reflection and the teacher's professional identity.

Becoming a reflective practitioner

Initial teacher training qualifications are a journey in which those taking part are able to construct a professional identity and through which in-service trainees are able to further reinforce and shape their already existing identity.

It has long been recognized that for effective teaching to take place, teachers need to unite both theory and practice – they are two sides of the same coin. Practice uninformed by theory is never going to be critical and will be blinkered – it will be always kept in the dark. Whereas theory uninformed by practice will be pointless and merely abstract. Uniting theory and practice is essential for sound reflective thinking – being able to see the connections between what you do, how you feel about it, how you evaluate it and what research and theory also tells you. The unification of theory and practice is referred to as 'praxis': attempts to link them result in a far greater outcome than simply having theory and practice separate from each other.

Much of the existing teacher education literature draws upon the idea of reflection. The notion of reflection is seen in a variety of ways:

1. Reflection is a means to improve one's own practice through criticism and evaluation.
2. It is a means through which practitioners can 'de-bunk' their prior assumptions, leading to a greater insight.
3. Being reflective is seen as a major part of the critical and 'distanced' role to be adopted by all professionals.
4. Reflectivity is seen as a means through which to better construct one's own professional identity and to better know one's self.
5. Reflection is a means towards 'praxis': it can allow professionals the space to make connections between their practice and wider theoretical concerns.

Reflection is the act of 'meaning-making' – putting order and sense into the world around you. As a professional-in-the-making it involves thinking about the role you are occupying, your own actions and practice within this role, and how and why things happen as they do. It allows you to think about why some things do not happen. Reflection is seen as a vehicle through which to explore practice that has not as yet happened. It is a form of introspection with the goal of self-improvement.

The term 'reflective practitioner' coined by Schön (1983) makes use of two different notions of reflection and reflective practice:

1. Reflection-in-action.
2. Reflection-on-action.

While reflection in action is 'thinking on our feet', making choices as we do them 'in the moment', reflection-on-action occurs after the event. Reflection-on-action takes the memory of the experience or the event and allows us the time and space to think about it with the kind of hindsight that enables the drawing together of other linked experiences. Through reflection-on-action, after the action itself, we can make connections, apply theory and seek the advice and support of mentors, peers and other colleagues. Experienced practitioners are able to draw upon the sum total of their thoughts, reflections and engagement with theory. Through the combination of both types of reflection you are increasing your 'stock' of tools and resources at hand at any given moment.

Argyris and Schön (1974) suggested that thinking about the role of critical reflection in our practice means we need to also think about theory and what it is and how we might use it. They suggest that as professionals we adopt two different ways to theorise and to use ideas about our practice and the contexts that our practice occurs within:

- Theory 1 – 'theory in use'. In other words, these are the ideas (often assumptions) that we make about our actions, practice and performance as professionals. We draw upon these types of theories on a daily working basis as the basis on which we might make sense of our actions at any time, within the context of our professional role that we have adopted. They are the common-sense held ideas of the profession that we are socialised into.
- Theory 2 – 'espoused theory'. In this sense, theory acts as a means through which we can think about and communicate to others what we do and why and how we do it.

These are both described as being 'theories-of-action'. They are the sets of ideas that we draw upon in order to build our understanding of what we do. If 'theory in use' is how we make sense of it all in our own head, then espoused theories are the ways in which we wish to be seen to think, when we explain our actions to others.

Argyris and Schön argue that for maximum efficiency within an organisation, and for maximum effectiveness as an individual professional practitioner, both 'theories in use' and 'espoused theories' need to be as closely knit and as congruent as possible. The only way to make how we think and how we explain ourselves to others as congruent as possible is through open and critical self-reflection.

Usher et al. (1997) describes the consequences of Argyris and Schön's ideas – being a reflective practitioner and doing reflection-in-action – as 'artful doing'. We might wish to see classroom practitioners as carrying with them an invisible tool kit of approaches that they can dip into and use in the classroom depending upon the situation and their reading of it. Through their memories, experiences, reflections and planning, good teachers are able to 'artfully' craft responses to the immediate situation in hand.

 Case study

To illustrate the value of reflective practice, consider this example. Rebecca was an experienced teacher in an FE college, having worked at her post for a couple of years, with a further two years' teaching experience in a previous institution. Over time, Rebecca realised that one of her second year A-level classes was becoming increasingly more 'difficult' to teach: They were noisy, sometimes disruptive and often off task. This realisation seemed to catch up with her from nowhere, despite her years of practice. By her own later admission, she had stopped reflecting upon her practice with the demands of the job taking over her time. She felt a little caught out by this sudden realisation. Speaking to her

(Continued)

(Continued)

colleagues about her teaching of this group was really useful for Rebecca, since it allowed her a space within which to begin to reflect upon her teaching and in particular her work with this class. She also invited colleagues to come and observe her, to see if they could offer a fresh insight from an outsider's viewpoint. Interestingly (and sometimes it is this simple!) one of the colleagues suggested moving the classroom layout around. Changing where the tables and chairs were and, more importantly, removing the teacher's desk forced Rebecca to stand during her lessons. Within a couple of lessons Rebecca found that she was able to control the class much more easily. It took a simple piece of reflection and the reflections and observations of her peers to allow Rebecca to see something that she could not see before. After going on to apply this insight to many other classes, Rebecca became a much more confident teacher and even came to deliver training sessions within her team on new ideas for classroom layout.

Jarvis (1992) says that we only learn something – anything – in relation to our experience; that for us to 'learn', we need to link it to what we already know and compare and contrast it to ideas we already have about the world. This is what we are asking of you in this chapter – to try to link your experience to your actions, to what your peers have to say and to what the research literature suggests. This is important in order for your own professional identity to become established. In the same way that we would hope you are able to encourage your own learners to become reflective learners, we are asking the same of you. Moon (2004) says that reflective learning and experiential learning are mutually supportive. Activities which help you to reflect upon your experience in turn aid the experience as you live it the next time. Equally, experiential learning involves reflection both during and after the event.

Kolb's learning cycle

A popular and well-regarded model of the role of reflection and experience in learning is provided by David Kolb (1984). For Kolb, there are four processes to undertake when engaging in critical reflection – and each process follows the next, in sequence, as a cycle:

1. Concrete experience.
2. Reflective observation.
3. Abstract conceptualisation.
4. Active experimentation.

Put simply, you have an experience – you 'do something' within your own practice (concrete experience). You then make a judgement on this initial experience; you analyse it and reflect upon it, building meaning as you do so (reflective observation). In this stage you start to ask yourself questions about the meaning and significance of the experience. When thinking about how we might improve on the practice a next time (abstract conceptualisation) we think into the future using our experience as a template to action plan and imagine future practice as yet conducted. Finally, we try out the new practice (active experimentation), and then engage in the cycle all over again.

In this model learning comes through the self-articulation of thinking about future practice before we do it. This thinking about the future can only take place by putting it into context through reflection on past practice. The Kolb learning model can be applied to all learners (and therefore to your own learners by you as a teacher), and it is important that we recognise that teachers are also learners at the same time.

 ## Discussion point

We have found it useful to think of our practice in the classroom as akin to having a 'tool kit' – an invisible metaphorical bag of ideas – that we carry into every classroom with us. Over time, we need to update the contents, change the organisation of the bag and generally remind ourselves what we might have hidden away. We can do this through reflective practice in all its many guises. What tools do you think, at this stage, will be the most useful?

 ## M-level thinking: Critical theory

The theoretical background to reflective thinking comes from the social scientific perspective of 'critical theory' most often associated with the Frankfurt School of thinkers in Germany (and later America) from the 1930s onwards (Adorno, 1976; Horkheimer, 1972). This theory supported the philosophical ideal that individuals and groups of individuals were able to achieve their own enlightened potential through the development of their own agency – the exercise of their own free will and the resulting liberation from the tricks and illusions of ideologies clouding and colouring their judgements and perceptions. Thus, 'critical thinking' or 'critical

(Continued)

(Continued)

reflection' was a tool to be adopted to enable us to recognise that there is no privileged view and no objective truth. We all have insights to make about the situations and practices we find ourselves in and only by discovering, testing and being critical of all our assumptions can we begin to recognise social situations and encounters for what they are. Applied to professional practice, we draw from this view the notion that for professionals to act they must do so not in a self-serving way, but by being critical of their assumptions and questioning all that is taken for granted about the roles that they find themselves adopting.

What assumptions are you making abut teaching, learning and learners at this stage in your professional development? Where do you think these assumptions come from?

Carr and Kemmis (1986) describe praxis as a 'risky' form of, and foundation for, knowledge and self-knowledge. In trying to achieve praxis – to unite theory and practice together – it means we are obliged to find 'a wise and prudent practical judgment about how to act in this situation' (Carr and Kemmis, 1986: 190). What this means is that praxis requires us to be reflective and to try to change our actions in some way. It is 'risky' in the sense that we need guidelines to follow that enable us to understand why some actions might be more prudent and more ethical than others. As teachers and as professionals we need to understand that classroom practice and the wider aspects of our role and identity have moral dimensions and values attached: we need to be thinking and reflecting not just about what choice to make, but which is the right choice to make. We need to fit into both the professional standards as laid down by our professional bodies (GTTR, TDA, IfL, LLUK, and so on) and the ethics and ethos of the institution that we work within.

〜〜 M-level thinking: Values and education

There is a growing body of literature on values in education, dealing with the question, what are the professional values that teachers should hold? This notion of the professional following a set of values and belonging to a wider body of practitioners all doing the same, leads to some other important questions concerning identity and power within the teaching profession: who should set the values? How are they monitored over time?

The most important thing is that reflection has a purpose: an end result. It is not 'navel gazing' but a tool to be deployed to improve and change action. This is also true for the evidence and theories we use as professionals when we reflect upon our experiences: 'Theories are not bodies of knowledge that can be generated out of a vacuum and teaching is not some kind of robot-like mechanical performance that is devoid of any theoretical reflection' (Carr and Kemmis, 1986: 113).

Many teachers – and certainly many trainee teachers – find reflection difficult and equally find theory somehow distanced and separated from their experiences of their own practice (Griffin, 2003). While most trainees value and see the importance of their 'field experience' – their teaching practice as we tend to call it – the other side of the coin, theory is usually ignored and at best used in a clinical and cynical fashion for the writing of essays and assignments. We argue here that this misses the point of what being a professional is fundamentally about. Field experience is invaluable – being in the classroom as a practical exercise is clearly essential – but practice without reflection and without critical thinking is ultimately of surface value only.

Writing a journal

Many professionals find reflection easier if they have a written focus for their thoughts. This focus often takes the form of a journal or a diary that you use to record your observations, thoughts, feelings and action planning.

Reflective writing itself is made up of four elements:

1. Personal descriptive accounts of your experience.
2. Writing about how you later make sense of your experience – what you think it means.
3. Evaluative accounts of your practice – saying what worked and what did not and to what extent.
4. The use of research, theory and dialogue with others to inform all of the above.

It is important to recognise that in order for your writing to be reflective, it must be evaluative and not simply descriptive. It is also important that your evaluation and critical awareness of your practice is linked to theory and research. This takes us back to the notion of 'praxis' – your development as a professional should be a journey taking into account the unification and connection of all aspects of your learning.

Moon (2006) suggests that it is absolutely important for the learner to make the reflective writing their own and to engage with it in a routine that suits themselves. It should not be forced, but should become a regular, normal habit.

We would like to add a warning to reflective writing while on a teacher education programme: think about the audience for your writing. If you are on a teacher training programme make sure that there is always an ethical dimension to what you do and record, and how you document it. Ensure that you do not use names of colleagues, pupils, students and, maybe, even the name of the institution you are placed within.

Many professionals use their diary or journal for the recording of what we call 'critical incidents': these are insightful and practice-changing observations. They are moments in time when suddenly we feel hit by an observation which completely changes how we think and feel about an aspect of our practice. After a critical incident, and the subsequent reflective processes, we are not quite the same professional that we were.

Lesson evaluation

As a trainee, it is often difficult to know where to begin when thinking about lesson evaluation. It can often seem an overwhelming experience. A useful place to start in deciding on any lesson, would be to think about previous practice. In this way, all planning and all teaching becomes a continuous narrative of reflection and action planning. This is perhaps best expressed in the notion of Kolb's learning cycle, above.

A very simple set of questions to ask yourself would be:

Planning stage

- What did I learn from my previous reflections and evaluations of previous lessons?
- What do I wish to target in this forthcoming lesson?
- How will the learners meet the objectives that I set?
- How will the learners' be actively engaged for the duration of the lesson?
- What 'distance' will the learners travel from the start to the end of the lesson?
- What is the shape of the lesson like? Are there enough activities or too many? Is there enough variety?

Post-lesson evaluation stage

- Were the aims achieved?
- If not, why not? Were the aims unrealistic or were the activities or classroom situation not conducive to meet them?
- Were the learners engaged?
- Did learning (at the appropriate level) take place?
- What was successful?
- What 'distance' did the learners travel from the start to the end of the lesson?
- What was less successful? Why did it occur? What could be done instead to solve/avoid the problem?
- What will you focus upon for development and evaluation in the next lesson?

 Discussion point

Evaluating lessons is one of the hardest things a teacher can do – yet one of the most powerful ways to improve one's own practice. We found we became much 'better teachers' when we rigorously and systematically made some notes after each lesson about what worked and what did not, and what we would do better next time. Over time you are able to build up a really useful living document of ideas, solutions and suggestions that help you extend your range of approaches. As a learner, what methods work for you at the moment?

Evidence-based practice

In recent years the notion of practitioner-research or 'evidence-based practice' has become popular in education. The notion of practitioner-research is that it is desirable for those professionals involved in practice (usually teaching or health care) to be able to evaluate and assess the effectiveness of their performance and their provision with a view to making further improvements.

Those in favour of this approach see it as reversing the trend for teachers to feel alienated and outside academic and theoretical research on education and teaching. It is worth noting that with the introduction of the Teaching and Learning Masters degree this situation may well change. Many teachers feel that theoretical debates exist separately from, and disconnected to, their own classroom teaching. And yet, at the same time, teachers are often looking for a 'what works' pragmatic approach. By undertaking their own inquiries and investigations, teachers – through reflection – are able to see what works for them and change accordingly. This challenges notions of what is theory and what is research? It might help teachers to 'take back' knowledge and research from academics and place it back into the hands of practitioners.

Critics of this view raise three main concerns:

1. The complained about distance and separation between academics and teachers is what places academic research on a different level: academic debate and research is able to separate itself off from the subjective concerns of those who conduct the actual practice. An outsider viewpoint is able to see things differently.
2. Evidence-based practice is seen to be a way of saying to teachers – 'find what works', but does not usually provide any funding or resource development for the work to take place. It is therefore evidence and research on the cheap. Critics who raise this point often also argue that it justifies the reduction of government and research bodies' spending on education since it asks teachers to do their own research, creating their own evidence.
3. Despite the arguments above, finding what works is difficult! What does this mean, and how can we measure what works – especially if we are looking at our own classes? In a sense, it is a circular argument:

> I want what works!
> How do I know it works?
> I saw it working when I tried it.

There is a sense in which only looking at what we do that 'works' might limit our own practice since it might close us off to other, new, possibilities. Nonetheless, despite the debates above, rooting your practice in the evidence from your own reflections and critical self-evaluation is a key aspect to the professional identity of a teacher.

Doing your own action research

The term action research refers to practice which is reflective and transformative in nature. Action research derives from the writings of American psychologist Kurt Lewin (1948). For Lewin, action research was conceived as a strategy for collaborative participation of a workforce within an institution as a means to improving practice. Action research was originally seen as a means through which to involve communities in self-evaluation and collective endeavour. This original sense of action research – as a collaborative process – is more than simply the previous notion of evidence-based enquiry coming from an individual. It is often based upon the notion of group work towards a shared goal – colleagues working together to assess, improve and change their practice.

Many teachers find engaging in action research a really helpful and productive experience (see Chapters 19 and 20 for further ideas that you might adopt if you are interested in this approach). The idea is that you identify from your own reflective work an aspect of your practice that you wish to improve and you then go about an enquiry based upon this practice: you experiment, review the outcomes and find new and more profitable ways of working. Thus, your action is the very research you are doing and your research is the actions you are making in the classroom.

We have suggested here that a key aspect to your emerging professional identity is the unification of theory and practice and that reflective thinking (and writing) is the tool to achieve this. We have also used a metaphor that, hopefully, you will find useful – that of the tool kit of approaches. With each lesson the tool kit gets a bit bigger and heavier, building up over time to a whole scheme of approaches. From time to time, trainee or experienced practitioner alike, it is important to go back to your tool kit and clean it out, update it and refresh it. This is the habit of a good teacher. Reflective practice becomes a habit, but practice does not become simply habitual.

Chapter links →

Themes and ideas explored in this chapter link to corresponding ideas in Chapters 6, 7, 8, 9, 10, 13 and 14.

Suggested further reading 📖

Koshy, V. (2005) *Action Research for Improving Practice: A Practical Guide.* London: Sage.

Moore, A. (1984) *The Good Teacher: Dominant Discourses in Teaching and Teacher Education.* Oxford: Routledge.

Schön, D.A. (1983) *The Reflective Practitioner: How Professionals Think in Action.* New York: Basic Books.

References

Adorno, T. (ed.) (1976) *The Positivist Dispute in German Sociology.* London: Heinemann.
Argyris, C. and Schön, D. (1974) *Theory in Practice: Increasing Professional Effectiveness.* San Francisco, CA: Jossey-Bass.
Carr, W. and Kemmis, S. (1986) *Becoming Critical: Education, Knowledge and Action Research.* Lewes: Falmer.
Griffin, M.L. (2003) 'Using critical incidents to promote and assess reflective thinking in preservice teachers', *Reflective Practice*, 4(2): 207–20.
Horkheimer, M. (1972) *Critical Theory.* New York: Herder and Herder.
Jarvis, P (1992) *The Paradoxes of Learning.* San Francisco, CA: Jossey-Bass.
Kolb, D.A. (1984) *Experiential Learning Experience as a Source of Learning and Development.* Englewood Cliffs, NJ: Prentice Hall.
Lewin, K. (1948) 'Resolving social conflicts; selected papers on group dynamics', in G.W. Lewin (ed.). New York: Harper and Row.
Moon, J.A. (2004) *A Handbook of Reflective and Experiential Learning: Theory and Practice.* London: RoutledgeFalmer.
Moon, J. (2006) *Learning Journals: A Handbook for Academics, Students and Professional Development*, 2nd edn. London: Routledge.
Schön D.A. (1983) *The Reflective Practitioner: How Professionals Think in Action.* New York: Basic Books.
Usher, R., Bryant, I. and Johnston, R. (1997) *Adult Education and the Postmodern Challenge.* London: Routledge.

CHAPTER 6

STARTING TO THINK ABOUT TEACHING AND LEARNING: WHAT MAKES A GOOD LESSON?

Objectives
.
By the end of this chapter the reader will be able to:

1. understand the importance of learning as a measurement of 'good teaching';
2. see the relevance of the notion of 'distance travelled' as a means to judge the successfulness of a lesson;
3. apply competing notions of 'good teaching' to their own practice;
4. recognise tools through which to think and reflect upon the nature of good teaching and learning;
5. assess practical advice for reaching the highest standards possible with their own classroom teaching.

Focusing on the learning

What is a good lesson? A lesson where there is 'good learning'! This is perhaps the most trite thing we can say about teaching, and yet at the same time it is one of the most powerful. We use the phrase 'distance travelled' to refer to the process or journey made by the learner through the lesson, the scheme of work or their whole educational programme. This is the way to think about good lessons: what has the learner done? How have they progressed and developed? What 'distance' have they travelled from the start to the end of the lesson?

Questions for reflection

Ask yourself the following questions about each teaching group you meet:

1. Who are the learners?
2. What have their previous educational experiences been like?
3. What are their needs – as a group and as individuals?
4. How can I best motivate them?
5. How can I challenge and inspire them?
6. How can we, collectively, build the most productive learning atmosphere that we can?
7. How can I show these learners that I value their education?

Use these as the basis from which to think about how you support learners to learn and what messages this support gives them.

The 2000 Hay McBer Report identified a number of essential 'teaching skills' that all effective teaching needs to demonstrate:

- Teachers need to value their learners and to have high expectations of them.
- These high expectations need to be communicated to learners themselves.
- Good teaching is based on thorough planning.
- Lessons need to flow and learners need to be engaged.
- Teachers need to plan time within lessons effectively.
- Teaching needs to draw upon appropriate strategies for the learners in question.
- Learners need to have their learning and their behaviour managed by the teacher.
- Assessment needs to be regular, fair and supportive of learners and their future learning.
- Lessons, homework and assessments need to be challenging and rewarding.

 Discussion point

A long time ago, a colleague of ours referred to good teachers as 'sparkling' in the classroom. This idea has stuck with us ever since. Teaching is a performance, and it is one where the good teacher can capture and enthuse the young people

(Continued)

(Continued)

in front of them. It is a performance where, if judged and crafted correctly, the teacher can foster a joy for learning in the classroom. This cannot take place, however, without adequate assessment, support, clear structure and goals and learners having a sense of their own self-worth. Do you remember a teacher who has sparkled? Have you seen a teacher like this? How did they manage to demonstrate this rather elusive quality?

In simple terms, a good lesson is where learning takes place and all learners are engaged and involved all of the time, being stretched and challenged at an appropriate level. We might see such lessons as working in distinct stages:

Pre-lesson

- Learners need to enter the room in an appropriate fashion.
- Learners need to be ready to learn as soon as possible.
- Learners need to have available (provided by the teacher or brought by the learner) appropriate tools and equipment – including homework and class exercise books/folders/notes.

Starter

- Prior learning should be recapped.
- Learners should be captivated and engaged.
- All learners should be all-involved and all-active as quickly as possible.
- Homework could/should be used as a means to focus the learning at the start.
- The lesson needs to have clear aims and objectives that are understood by the learners.
- Learners need to see where this lesson 'fits in' with their previous learning.

Mid-lesson

- Learners need to be on task.
- Learners need to be active.
- Learning classrooms can be noisy and learners need to talk and interact with one another.
- Learners need to have their needs met in a differentiated fashion.
- The lesson should have pace and variety.
- Assessment of the learning should take place.

End

- The learning itself should be solidified by being recapped.
- Learners themselves need to see what they have learnt and how it 'fits in'.

- Assessment of the learning should take place.
- Learners need to leave 'wanting more' and being excited about the next lesson.

Where does this leave us? Hopefully, we have a strong image of a good lesson coming through here. It is an exciting and inspiring experience – valued by those who participate in it, and skilfully crafted, manipulated and orchestrated by the teacher.

〰 M-level thinking: Double-thinking

Leach and Moon (2008) note that research suggests that most teachers perform what they describe as a 'double think' when it comes to thinking about learning. On the one hand, many teachers are very sympathetic to the idea that learners need to construct the meaning of their own learning for themselves. Yet, on the other hand, most teachers plan lessons to take place in a step-by-step process of knowledge transmission with the teacher at the front and centre of everything that takes place. Leach and Moon suggest that this double-thinking about teaching and learning, this contradiction, is largely the result of government policies and research about teaching that assess teachers on the basis of common criteria across the whole of the UK. Individualised learning is a rhetoric since the pressure on 'national standards' and world class testing drives attention away from individual learning. How much do you think that we can support individualised learning in classrooms? How would this work?

Race identifies 'five factors underpinning successful learning':

1. Learners wanting to learn.
2. Learners seeing the need for their learning.
3. Learners learning by doing.
4. Learners learning through the feedback they receive.
5. Learning having the opportunity to 'make sense of things' as part of the learning process (Race, 2005: 26).

What this is saying, is that successful learning is underpinned by a sense of ownership in the learning process by the learners themselves. Learners can be 'trained' to remember things off by heart, but true learning only really takes place once learners feel a sense of value in what they are doing and their efforts are rewarded through their manipulation and mastery of the (intellectual) tools they are given. Learners will only develop such mastery if they understand where they are located in their learning at any one time – hence the absolute importance of assessment and feedback for the learners' learning to intensify.

Develop your own style!

In becoming the sort of classroom teacher that you wish to, reflect upon what your assumptions are about learning. How do you think the process of learning takes place? What implications does this have for how you set up your lessons and how you interact with your learners?

Over time, you will through experience come to develop your own teaching style. This will take into account factors such as:

1. How will you set standards at the start?
2. How will you establish discipline?
3. How will you maintain discipline once established?
4. How will you assess learners?
5. How will you interact and talk to learners?
6. How will you motivate and challenge all learners in your class?
7. What atmosphere would you like your lessons to have?
8. How will you arrange the seating in your class and to what affect?
9. How will you ensure that all learners understand the progress they are making?
10. How will you develop trust with your class?
11. How will you demonstrate to learners that you wish to support them and that you value their learning?
12. What role will learner choice and the learner voice play in your planning and lesson preparation?
13. What resources will you develop and how will you use them?

〰 M-level thinking: Discourses of teaching

A 'discourse' is a way of thinking and speaking about an aspect of social life. These discourses, these ways of thinking, are seen to be either controlled by those in power or they are seen as vast 'battlegrounds' upon which different groups with different interests fight and struggle with each other for power. Education is a site for the struggle for power, as especially seen in the way that discussions and debates about 'education, education, education' take place at times of elections.

Moore (2004) argues that the notion of 'good teaching' is itself a discourse: it is something that is not neutral, but the site of massive political struggle – between teachers, parents, politicians, unions and academics, all trying to get their ideas on good teaching heard and establishing their notions as the 'truth'. Moore suggests that discourses about good teaching have changed each decade since the New Right political agenda in the 1980s (see Chapters 3 and 4):

The 1980s – teacher as 'charismatic' and inspirational 'sorcerer'.
The 1990s – teacher as a 'professional educator' and a 'reflective practitioner'.
The late 1990s – teacher as skilled and trained craftsperson.
Post-2000 – the teacher as a 'pragmatist' seeking only that which is 'effective'.

As we can see, notions of what a professional teacher is change over time. Which of these discourses is the closest match to how you view teachers and teaching? Why?

Thinking about learners' skills

A very powerful idea, known to most teachers as 'Bloom's taxonomies' (Bloom and Krathwohl, 1956), is an excellent way to start to think about lessons and how to structure the learning that takes place within them. This idea is very useful in terms of thinking about lessons, lesson planning, scheme of work construction and developing learners' skills (see Chapter 13).

Bloom's argument was that learning can be divided into three distinctive sets of skills or processes:

- cognitive (thinking) skills;
- affective (relationship, emotional and interpersonal interaction) skills;
- psycho-motor (physical) skills.

Each of these skill-sets, or 'domains', can be understood as a hierarchy or a taxonomy ranging from basic skills to more complex ones. Learning, in this model, involves the learner moving through the range of skills from the low/simple skills up into the 'higher order' skills at the top of the taxonomies.

We can illustrate these three domains here, building from the 'lower-order' skills up to the 'higher-order' skills within each taxonomy:

- the cognitive domain – made up of knowledge, comprehension, application, analysis, synthesis and evaluation;
- the affective domain – made up of attention, response, value, value system and generalisation;
- the psycho-motor domain – made up of procedural task, partial performance, coordinated performance, conscious control and mastery (Bloom and Krathwohl, 1956).

Many teachers feel these domains and taxonomies offer a useful way to think about teaching and its interplay with learning: if we plan by focusing upon learners' skills and how they develop – within lessons and across schemes of work over many weeks and months – we are able to think clearly about their 'distance travelled'.

Observation schedules

Depending on the nature of your teacher training course and the sorts of institutions that you are being prepared to teach in, the frequency of observations throughout the year will vary. You are likely to be observed by staff from the institution in which you are training (for example, your university). But you will also be observed by members of staff (including your school-based mentor) in the school/college and so on where you carry out your placements. We have developed an observation schedule that we adopt when working with our own trainees. This might be useful for you when considering the sorts of observation targets you might like to agree with your tutors as you progress through your training. The model is based around six observations carried out through one academic year, with each observation taking place every half-term:

- *Observation 1 – 'the feel-good factor'*. For many trainees their first observation can be a nerve-wracking experience. We therefore treat this as a warm 'introduction' to being observed and a boost of confidence for the trainee, with gentle pointers, lots of praise and the opportunity for the trainee teacher to realise that there is nothing 'threatening' about the observation process.
- *Observation 2 – a focus on questioning skills*. Questioning (see Chapter 14) is a much underused teaching skill and yet one that trainees can easily master. By drawing on educational theories (for example, Bloom's taxonomy) trainee teachers can quickly establish themselves with new classes as both an authority and in authority by the careful targeted deployment of questions to named learners. At the end of Observation 1, a target is given to all trainees to make sure that in Observation 2, at some point in the lesson the trainee will 'fire' questions at a range of learners using Bloom's taxonomy.
- *Observation 3 – mark books and differentiation*. This challenging observation addresses many of the issues surrounding assessment records and differentiation that so many trainees have difficulties with. For example, many trainees find it hard to understand what sort of data is professionally useful to them. In Chapter 10 we examine the role of assessment and record-keeping and how this is a vital ingredient to raising achievement. At the end of Observation 2 trainee teachers are set a target that involves the use of their 'mark book'/assessment records, lesson plan and the deployment of the lesson to be observed.

   The trainee is required to highlight *four* learners from their assessment records (to be shown to the observer during the lesson) in the class to be observed. Each of the four must be chosen for different reasons (for example, gifted and talented (G&T) behaviour). The trainee is given free choice as to which learners are chosen but the assessment records *must* back up that evidence (for example, excellent homework grades, GCSE grades, low motivation levels, involvement in class, 'hands up'). These four learners must then be highlighted on the trainee's lesson plan, indicating clearly what their particular sets of issues are and how the trainee teacher will differentiate the lesson for them (without them knowing). For example a lesson that uses more complex group-based learning strategies (see Chapter 16) will automatically do this as will the deployment of a variety of questioning strategies (see Chapter 14). Finally, the observer will watch the lesson to see that what is embedded in both the mark book/assessment records and the lesson plan is actually carried out during the lesson without the four realising that this lesson has been differentiated for them.

- *Observation 4 – homework*. In Chapter 16 we examine the many strategies that excellent teachers deploy when incorporating homework into their teaching repertoires. There is a weight of literature surrounding the benefits to learning that homework creates when deployed skilfully by teachers. Sadly, however, there is also much written about how homework is poorly used (for example, as a 'finishing-off' activity) and poorly instructed (that is, last minute of lesson with bells ringing, and so on). At the end of Observation 3 trainees are therefore set the target of creating Observation 4 around a lesson that is contingent on the homework set in the previous lesson/week.

  This challenging target requires the trainee to have procedures up and running for the setting, collecting and monitoring of homework. Remember this is an observation two-thirds of the way through training, so by now trainees should be familiar with their learners and the institutional mechanisms they can draw on when work set is not carried out. It requires that the trainee can be assured that homework will be carried out by learners and that, if not, then they are using the institutional procedures to chase up non-compliance in learners. Finally, this target ensures that trainees understand how homework can complement and feed into the construction of dynamic lessons that raise achievement for all they are teaching.

- *Observation 5 – advanced group-based active learning strategies*. It is hoped that by this stage the trainee will not only be using group-based learning as part of their repertoire but using them in such a way that all members of that group are fully engaged in the learning process (rather than just one or two of the more motivated members). The target, set at the end of Observation 4, is to show that they can deploy more advanced strategies and is designed to allow the trainee to 'show off' how they can use group-based strategies in a way that guarantees that all members of the groups during the particular phase of the lesson are fully involved in that activity. In so doing it confirms the ability of the trainee to provide stimulating lessons that both differentiate and motivate all learners in their care. It also provides excellent evidence of differentiation and behaviour management strategies.

- *Observation 6 – putting it all together*. In this final observation the trainee is free to plan a lesson utilising their own creativity and without the constraints of previous targets. We assume that the trainee is ready to go into the classroom in the next academic year as a professional teacher. We therefore return to the 'feel-good' factor in Observation 1 and, acting as a critical friend, offer guidance on any issues where the teacher can 'sharpen' up their already excellent practice (for example, furniture layout, task-transition, use of ICT).

Because of the variety of training pathways that exist throughout the different sectors in the UK it would be unwise to recommend a particular model that can be 'superimposed' on the training. We do hope, however, that this might prove useful to you as a source of reflection and something that you can bounce off your own experience as you progress through your course.

Getting grade 1s for your observations

In Chapter 8 we discuss more fully issues to consider when being observed. Below is a checklist of questions that you can run through before any lesson observation (ideally before *every* lesson). It should help you get better grades but, more importantly, these are the sorts of questions that excellent teachers address, without thinking, every time they teach:

- Is the room appropriately laid out for the session (including health/safety)?
- Have I noted any learners with sight/hearing problems and room layout?
- Do my classes start on time?
- Does my lesson start with a clear outline of what will take place?
- Does my lesson connect clearly with the last lesson and are learners aware of this connection?
- Is reference made to any work set in the previous lesson?
- Is there a scheme of work (SOW)?
- Does the lesson fit into the planned SOW?
- Can learners understand how this lesson fits into the planned SOW?
- Does the lesson use a range of teaching approaches to assist learning for all?
- Do the learners fully understand my exposition/didactic delivery?
- Are learners left entirely on their own (in/out of classroom to work)?
- When learners are in paired/group work, am I circulating/helping all in class?
- Am I using a range of resources/stimuli in the session?
- Do I issue instructions clearly, with simplistic terminology and to all listening?
- Do I check with my learners that they fully understand all tasks set?
- Do I make sure that I do not stay in one position for too long when teaching?
- Am I flexible enough to be able to change strategies depending on the lesson?
- Do I take a register?
- Do I monitor any assessment outcomes in my mark book?
- Do I know their names?
- Do I use gender/ethnicity/ability as a seating strategy?
- Do I have a seating strategy?
- Do the learners have a version of the SOW that they understand?
- Is there a lesson plan?
- Is material prepared and customised for the particular session/class?
- Does the lesson plan show that this has been done?
- Is additional work set and how often is it set?
- Is work collected and marked on time?
- Does my lesson plan show this?
- How do I assess individual performance?

- Do I know the ability levels of my learners?
- How do I know the learners understand the work?
- How do I assess the progress of individual learners?
- Are my reports helpful in identifying strengths and weaknesses for learners?
- Do I have appropriate display material in the room?
- Do I give detailed feedback from the work set?
- Do I explain to learners how they can do better?
- Do I prepare learners for all elements of assessment (for example, practice tests/ examinations)?
- Do I set work at the appropriate levels of differentiation?
- Do I help those weak on parts of the work and stretch those who can do more?
- Do I refer learners frequently to other sources of information?
- Do I frequently relate the work they do to their formal assessment (for example, examinations)?
- Do I refer learners to workshops for additional support where necessary?
- Do I ask support staff for help (for example, ask them to look at resources in advance)?
- Do I involve support staff in the planning of my lessons?
- Are learners punctual for my lessons? If not, why not?
- Am I aware of the teacher–learner talk ratio? (Do I talk too much?)
- Do I ask questions to named learners?
- Do I make sure that learners do not get used to me being in one position all the time (for example, front of class)?
- If I (actually the learners) need silence – how long does it take me to get it?
- Are bags, mobile phones and so on off all table/desk tops?
- Do I stand at the door greeting learners as they come into the class?
- Is there an activity on the tables for learners to do as they enter class?

We cannot guarantee a grade 1 for your observation, even if you manage to deal with all of these questions. However, you will be an exceptional teacher if you can aim to have most of these issues addressed in every lesson you do. Over time, we can guarantee that learners will respect you and want to turn up to your lessons and learn – which is what the job of being a teacher is all about.

Getting your learners grade As

Being a trainee teacher who is asked to take over a class that is being entered for public examinations can be a really stressful experience. We hope that the following pieces of advice can help you ease that transition and make your learners grateful for the fact they have you as a teacher:

- If you are teaching a subject that will be publically examined (for example, GCSE mathematics; A-level history), introduce learners to the examination at the very start of the year. Get them 'used' to the terminology, skills, marks, format, and so on. You can incorporate this knowledge into your assessment strategies, for example, when questioning learners in class you can easily use the mark scheme as a source of reward (for example, 'Well done Shamima, all you needed to do was add the year to that excellent answer and you would have been given four full marks in the exam next summer').

- Use the examination board websites to locate mark schemes, past papers and examiner's reports. Study these and aim to give your learners all the past papers under timed conditions in your classes.
- Join your subject association and get to know other teachers who teach your areas. Gain from them resources, tips, schemes of works and so on, and a sense of which units should be taught and when.
- Set homework where learners have to study the examination website – and write their own examination paper.
- Set learners past papers to plan, as homework, and get them to bring these plans into your classes. In pairs (with limited time) they can go through these knowing that you will chose *one* to do under timed conditions.
- All subjects have their own explanations/theories, key words/concepts, key people, evidence and evaluation possibilities that examiners are looking for – what we refer to as the 'five magic ingredients'. Use these five ingredients to inform the setting of homework, classroom activities, and so on. Make learners aware of how these ingredients emerge in their subjects.
- Providing your colleagues allow you to, get learners to decorate the classroom – or part of it – with all the key words for your examination subject. Use this regularly as a memory exercise (as a starter/plenary) so that learners automatically fall into the habit of using these words.
- Make sure you have a 'time-line' in your class so that learners can identify key dates/eras/epochs for your subject.
- Work with learners on the start of each paragraph they write for your subject. Before learners hand in homework/class activities to you, get them to highlight the first three words of any paragraph they have written. Have alternative phrases/link words/signpost phrases to hand (On the ceiling? On handout?) – phrases like 'on the other hand', 'in addition to this' and so on. Get learners to identify a new phrase every week that they can incorporate – do this from week one!
- Set up groups of tables each with flip-chart paper and a past examination question. Allow each group 5 minutes to write one paragraph for this question and then move the groups on. Each group must now write a new paragraph to the question confronting them but they cannot repeat anything that has already been written. This competitive and noisy activity works brilliantly as a revision task – and you can then collate the class answers, type up and give back to them the following week.
- Call in their 'folders'/revision exercise books on a regular basis. This 'folder check' needs to be enforced with a 'stick and carrot' mentality by you, the teacher, but will really make a difference to the organisation of the learner. Do this regularly (once a term/half-term?) *and* they will be implicitly revising as they prepare this for you. Get them to put everything into plastic wallets (for example, a maximum

of two handouts for each wallet). Make sure they have included dividers that are labelled and offer a prize for the best folder.

- Get learners to create their own revision cards (get them to use the five magic ingredients referred to above) – offer prizes for the best looking cards – but make sure they have limited amounts of words on each card; the idea is that they can then use these to revise *easily* (for example, on a bus journey, walk home).
- Take learners to revision classes run by the examination boards; these are invaluable not only for the learners but for *you*, their teacher. It is great for the learners to hear the so-called 'experts' repeat the good advice you give them but its also invaluable for you to see what examiners are looking for in your subject area.
- So many learners run out of time during examinations. When getting learners to write under timed conditions always make sure they do this with a watch in front of them (even if the class has a clock). Reinforce that they *must* look at this every 5 minutes to get them into the habit of time management.

By introducing the language of the examinations early on, you will reduce the damaging levels of stress that so many learners face in the build-up to examinations. Ideally, they should look at a paper in the final public examination and mutter 'not that again'!

Distance travelled?

Teachers, like learners, also have a considerable distance to travel. Moving beyond the statement that good lessons are those with good learning is by no means simple. As we have seen in this chapter (and in Chapter 5) there are many complexities and contradictions in educational theory. This is where the role for the individual teacher comes in: by assessing their own evidence-based practice and devising strategies that 'work for them'. Be mindful of the theory and, equally, be mindful of what your learners are saying about their own learning. See what works and reflect upon why. To refer again to competing discourses and notions of 'what makes a good teacher' (Moore, 2004) – we are professionals, pragmatists, reflective, charismatic and above all craftspersons … probably all at the same time!

Chapter links →

Themes and ideas explored in this chapter link to corresponding ideas in Chapters 10, 11, 13, 14 and 17.

Suggested further reading

Hay McBer (2000) *Research into Teacher Effectiveness: A Model of Teacher Effectiveness*. London: DfEE.

References

Bloom, B. and Krathwohl, D. (1956) *Taxonomy of Educational Objectives*. New York: Longmans Green.

Hay McBer (2000) *Research into Teacher Effectiveness: A Model of Teacher Effectiveness*. London: DfEE.

Leach, J. and Moon, B. (2008) *The Power of Pedagogy*. London: Sage.

Moore, A. (2004) *The Good Teacher: Dominant Discourses in Teaching and Teacher Education*. London: Routledge.

Race, P. (2005) *Making Learning Happen: A Guide for Post-Compulsory Education*. London: Sage.

CHAPTER 7

MAKING A GOOD START: MENTORING, TEACHING PLACEMENT AND FIRST ENCOUNTERS WITH LEARNERS

Objectives

By the end of this chapter the reader will be able to:

1. understand the importance of the first placement visit;
2. identify the necessary observational tools needed to critically assess the nature of placement institutions;
3. write a plan of action for the first visit and be able to reflect upon the placement institution once the first visit is over;
4. put in place a set of actions to maximise the opportunity of the first encounter with learners;
5. develop an awareness of the mentoring role and how to maximise mentoring support.

Understanding your placement institution

Educational institutions – schools and colleges alike – can be confusing and alien places. It might help if we see educational institutions as examples of 'total institutions': they have complex structures with rules both formally set down (often in UK law) and informally shared by communities of individuals in a common-sense fashion. Their routines are formally timetabled and mapped in planning documents, and yet the 'feel' of the routines in these institutions varies – often from class to class or teacher to teacher. Entering into such total institutions is alien and unsettling (think how Year 7 learners feel moving up from primary schools!). Membership of these institutions changes your identity in some way, for both learner and teacher.

For the outsider, becoming comfortable within an educational institution is not a simple matter. You need to get to grips with:

1. the legal aspects which underpin the teacher role and the teacher–learner relationship, as now governed by the Every Child Matters legislation (see Chapter 19);
2. the timetable of the institution and the 'pace' and 'feel' this gives to the working day (for example, some schools have now adopted a two-weekly timetable);
3. the meeting schedule, cover rota and yearly calendars which add another level of planning, organisation and structure to the daily timetable;
4. the rules of the institution, many of which will be both unspoken and not written down in staff handbooks. (This is what we mean, when we refer to rules as being 'common-sense');
5. and, as a trainee teacher, you need to develop strategies designed to 'present your self' to learners, managers, mentors and other staff in appropriate ways.

We can use the term 'habitus' to describe how the pattern of the routines feel for those who work and learn inside these institutions. Habitus refers to how culture patterns our actions and gives us a scripted set of rules and frameworks appropriate to different situations and encounters. We learn what we can and cannot do and how to act. Over time, this even patterns how we think and respond to others, to encounters and to other roles. Working inside an institution both affects and regulates you. You need to learn what the pattern of these routines is, and how it affects and structures your working life. These are really important, but all too infrequently spoken, aspects of teacher education: you need to take time to assess what it means to work to the confines of a timetable and how this compartmentalises your day and your interactions with groups of people, colleagues and learners.

The first visit

In order to maximise the opportunity of the first ever visit to your placement institution, you might wish to consider the advice below. You can see this as a useful checklist to follow:

1. Before you visit.
   - Look at the institution's website and read what it says about itself – its mission statement and how it describes itself and its learners.

- Find out the variety of subjects that are taught that are closely related to your own. Find out what levels and what types of qualifications are offered.
- Dress smartly (and then find out what the institutional codes are for dress once you arrive there).

2. During your first visit.

Please be careful how you manage the process of finding out the following information. It is usually better to allow the institution to direct what you are initially told and how you find it out. Do not push within the first few minutes all the answers to the following questions but allow them to develop. Follow them up at the end of your visit if you need to. Try to find out:

- What is the name of the head teacher/principal/director?
- What is the name of the member of the senior management team (SMT) that is responsible for overseeing trainees for the duration of their placement?
- Does the institution have a copy of a flow chart illustrating the organisation and structure of the institution?
- What is the name of the head of the team you will be working in?
- Find out how many subjects are taught by the team you are going to be working with and how many classes they have.
- Roughly speaking, what are class sizes like for the classes you are most likely to be working with (they will almost certainly not be able to issue you with a complete timetable as yet, but would have a rough idea)?
- How many learners are in the institution as a whole?
- What specification and what examination board do they follow (if you are teaching examination classes)? Alternatively, are there schemes of work in place and, if so, who is responsible for their creation/coordination? (Once you know this you then have some serious follow-up work to do – see below.)
- Ask for a copy of both staff and learner handbooks/rules/guidelines.
- Ask for or organise for yourself a tour of the campus (if one is not provided). If one is provided, try and find time to have a quiet walk around on your own, taking into consideration the points raised in the next section of this chapter).
- What is the name of your mentor?
- What is the average working day like in terms of hours and structure? (These vary quite considerably.)
- Is there a meeting rota? How much are you expected to contribute/take part?
- Where will you be located? (Do not expect your own desk but do expect to have a semi-regular place to be and to work.)
- What are the procedures for reporting staff absence (just in case)? Who do you need to tell and how? What telephone number should you use?
- Do the team have textbooks or other resources to lend to you?

It may be difficult to find all this out in the first visit – it might take a couple of visits to do so. If that is the case, do not worry. Allow the school or college to guide and direct you, at least initially – most institutions have a well organised and planned structure in place for the induction of trainee teachers and it might simply be easier to allow the information to come to you piece by piece. Certainly do not make too many demands upon new colleagues – you must remember that you need to fit around and into the teams that have been set up before you and that will continue to operate long after your training is over. This is not to say you do not have a massive contribution to make while training – you do. But manage the 'self' you present to others so that you fit it.

 ## M-level thinking: Presentation of self

Sociologist Erving Goffman (1969) uses the term 'presentation of self' to refer to the various ways in which we 'act out roles' in society according to the situations we find ourselves in. He suggests that when we encounter others, we adopt techniques of 'impression management' – we carefully try and manipulate and control the ways we want others to see us. In many respects, being a teacher, and taking on this identity, is a process of understanding and then acting out a role. The role of teacher is shaped by where you work and it is also shaped by what the ethos of the institution is that you work within. Equally, as a new teacher entering a new institution or even just meeting a class for the first time, you will also want to 'manage your self': control the impression that you gives others the first time they meet you. What elements do you think you will use to build your professional identity?

 ## M-level thinking: Situated learning

Lave and Wenger (1991) use the term 'situated learning' to describe the learning that takes place within a community of practice. What this means is that this is a type of learning that is undertaken where it is also applied in practice. This learning is co-constructed by the meaning-making and negotiation of colleagues and members of the same communities. The knowledge is not imposed and not 'detached' from experience, but is fundamentally a part of the actions and practice of those taking part.

Try and see your own placement as an exercise in situated learning: you are learning to teach, while teaching and working alongside other teachers who are part of the same community as you. Good teaching is not possible in isolation – bearing this in mind, try to work with your colleagues and mentors, seeking support and advice at all times. Start placement and your career as you mean to do on. Given your situated learning, what do you think your support needs are at this point in time?

3. After your first visit.

    - If you keep a diary or journal (see Chapter 5), write down what your first impressions and thoughts are of the institution – the staff, the learners, the space and the atmosphere.
    - Use the website of the appropriate examination board to look up the specification(s) that you will be delivering (if they are able to tell you). Download and print off the specification plus other useful materials such as teacher's guides and past examination papers and specimen assessment materials if they exist.
    - It might be a worthwhile exercise to find the college's most recent Ofsted report and take a look at what it says about the subject team you will be working with. However, doing this comes with a warning – staff might have changed, the reports are often written in a very particular tone and style (see for yourself what we mean by this) and the inspection itself could be all of four years ago. A lot can happen to any institution in the meantime. Treat this as a guide only – nothing more.

Knowing what to look for? And knowing how to see it

It takes time to really feel settled into your placement institution. Everyone feels like this. It is important to remember two things:

1. Most teachers have themselves been through training and have had the same feelings of uncertainty at their own placement.
2. Really take the time to thoroughly induct yourself into the life and ethos of the institution you will be training in. Try to understand it as much as you can.

 Discussion point

When we speak of the factors that might shape the success of educational institutions, we often speak of 'in-school' and 'out-of-school' factors (see Chapter 12). The out-of-school factors that would shape the nature of your placement institution

(Continued)

(Continued)

have a lot to do with the class and cultural make-up of the local area. You might wish to search the pages of the local authority for statistics about the area – housing, social deprivation, employment. These will help you to understand the context within which the school or college operates. What is the context within which your placement, school or college operates?

When thinking about the school or college as a learning community, it is vital you understand its ethos – the educational spirit and atmosphere – and how the actions of teachers and learners alike set the tone of this atmosphere.

1. Observing the environment.

    - What is the building like?
    - How old is the building?
    - Does the reception seem welcoming? How does it, or does it not, give this impression?
    - How does the security of the school or college operate?
    - What posters, art work, displays in the front reception are there? What do these say about the teachers and learners?
    - What are classrooms like? How are they laid out? What is the furniture like? How modern is it?
    - What electronic resources do classrooms have? Are they being used?

2. Observing classes.

    Most initial teacher education programmes will ask you to record observations of experienced teachers. Do not underestimate the importance of this opportunity. It will be, sadly, one of the very few times in your career where you will have such access to a diverse variety of teaching styles and methods and so really make the most of it. Do not rush in to start your own teaching, but learn from others first.

    We provide a more complete set of observational questions in Chapter 8, but consider the broad ideas below. Be mindful of these, they might help you to understand placement institution better, and all the quicker:

    - How do learners enter the classroom?
    - Where do learners sit? How much direction or input does the teacher have/should have in this?
    - What does the teacher do before the lesson officially starts? How much interaction is there and what is it like?
    - Where does the teacher stand or sit? Why do you think this is? (And was it the right decision?)

- What do learners do at the start with their bags and equipment – if anything?
- How does the teacher initially capture their attention and start the lesson?
- Are learners motivated? How can you tell? How were they motivated?
- Are lessons noisy or quiet? Is the noise 'productive'? (Many teachers think that silent classrooms do not necessarily mean that learning is taking place!)
- How does the teacher draw the lesson to a conclusion?
- Is there a plenary – an end to the lesson that brings to class together? If this is the case, then how is it structured?
- How does homework get set (if at all/if at the end)?
- How do learners exit the room and under what directions and circumstances?
- What does the teacher do at the end of the lesson?

 Discussion point

Be careful! Contained within the many questions above are some deep-rooted and implicit assumptions we are making about teaching and lessons and about what is and is not a good lesson. Try not to be completely swayed by the path these questions might lead you down; try and unpick from the questions what our own assumptions are – they may well be very different from that of the teacher you are observing and indeed from yourself. Given this list, what do you think our view is on what makes a good lesson? Do you agree? Have you observed any excellent teaching you can use as the basis for reflection and professional learning?

These questions serve, hopefully, as a starting point for you to think carefully, precisely and in depth about the nature of classrooms and what does (and should not) happen within them. You may observe these informally in your first visit simply by walking around: being in corridors and in the playground/communal areas at appropriate times!

3. Observing what institutions privately and publicly say about themselves.

- Take a look at the prospectus – what image does it give you of the institution?
- What do you think the message is from the front of reception? Look at how visitors are welcomed and the displays and notices: what is being said?
- Is there a staff room or common room? Do teachers sit and work in teams or as a whole? Are there formal or informal structures to who sits where? What does this tell you about how teachers do their work?
- What information is on display in staff rooms and team rooms?
- Take a read of the staff guidelines/handbook – these might be stored on an intranet on the staff pages if they are not an actual physical document. What do you think are the key official institutional messages that staff need to know?

- Does the institution have a teaching and learning policy? If so, how does it describe the nature of good teaching? Do you agree?
- Does the institution 'stream' or 'set' classes? What rationale is given for this if it does happen?
- How is the 'learner voice' captured? What voice do learners have and how are their comments recorded and acted upon?

4. Observing routines and daily patterns.

- How is the timetable structured?
- What is an average working day like?
- Is there a cover rota? How much are staff expected to contribute (if at all)?
- How do staff communicate with each other? Is there a message board? Do people have pigeon-holes and in-trays? How much is email used?
- Does the institution have an email policy? (As a rule of thumb, most institutions prefer you to talk to people, rather than email them, if at all possible!)
- What do the day-to-day interactions between teachers and learners seem like?
- How are discipline and standards maintained?

That should keep you occupied! (It would be a full-time job to record all of these!) However, this does give you an insight into how complex educational institutions are, and the list above does hopefully serve as a helpful breakdown of all the aspects of organisational life that teachers and trainee teachers need to get to grips with.

Beware those toxic dragons!

Beware the nay-sayers! All institutions have colleagues who tend to talk the loudest and moan about their work – these are usually the people who feel under pressure in some aspects of the job. Unfortunately teaching is no different. Beware of these colleagues! Make your own mind up but, as a general rule, if teachers criticise the institution and criticise the learners they are probably in the wrong job! Do not be swayed. It is almost always impossible to make sweeping generalisations about a 'bad year' or a 'weak group'. Our job is to understand our learners and support them to move forward.

Double-loop learning

Argyris and Schön (1974) (see also Chapter 5) have coined the term 'double-loop learning' to refer to the process whereby a practitioner learns through reflecting upon experience but by also questioning the values and assumptions at the very heart of the practice and institution they are within. For example, a teacher could make mistakes – have a lesson not go well – and think about new solutions for the same lesson to improve it. This would be referred to as 'single-loop learning' – a kind of reflection cycle: experience, reflection, action, experience, and so on.

Double-loop learning occurs by adding a second reflective process to this cycle in conjunction with the first, which still continues: while practitioners reflect upon their actions (which still needs to occur), at the same time they also question the very foundation and taken-for-granted values that lie at the heart of what they do. Without doing this, all we are doing is working within a system that goes unchanged, never questioning if it is the structure imposing upon our practice that is at fault.

Making sense of what you see

It is difficult to build a comprehensive image of a learning community after a brief visit, but over time you will know what to look for, and the more practice you have in understanding institutions the better you get at it. This will be invaluable practice for when you start to attend job interviews, where you will need to assess in a short space of time if you think the institution is for you. Try speaking with another trainee about your institution – try and articulate out loud what its essential characteristics are.

As a means to summarise your reflecting – in a journal or a diary – try and think about:

- what its expectations of staff are;
- what its expectations of learners are;
- what its expectations of trainee teachers are – and how are these the same and different from 'staff' in general?

Alternatively, you could think about the 4 Rs:

- rules;
- routines;
- resources;
- record-keeping.

 Discussion point

Learn the institutional norms of your institution (you are obliged to follow them), but do not necessary always believe them immediately. Engage in double-loop learning: question and reflect upon both your own actions and practice, and the

(Continued)

(Continued)

institutional structures and frameworks that contextualise what you do. This sounds subversive, but it is not meant to be. Simply question everything – sometimes schools and colleges get things wrong. But be sensitive to how you might communicate this and what this might mean for where you start looking for jobs once qualified. What are the norms of your placement institution? How do you know? How were they communicated to you?

Dealing with your subject mentor on placement

The process in which teachers are 'mentored' in institutions varies significantly from country to county, and remember that not all schools and their mentors get 'paid' for the work they do with you. In both England and Wales the partner schools within school/ university teacher networks receive payment for placement responsibilities. In Scotland, initial teacher education (ITE) is overwhelmingly the responsibility of HE institutions (in contrast to the movement towards school-based provision in teacher education in both England and Wales). That said, there are movements in Scotland to draw school staff much more fully into the mentoring and assessment processes (Hulme and Menter, 2008). In Northern Ireland the partnership arrangements in initial teacher education are voluntary and there is no transfer of funds to schools for any training that takes place.

This all means that when you go into your institution and meet your mentor for the first time, they may well be offering their services to you because of their passion to work with emerging teachers. Depending on where you are training to be a teacher your mentor may or may not receive any other material benefits for giving up their time. Knowing this means that you need to treat them in exactly the same way that you would hope that they treat you – with sensitivity and respect.

Although mentoring varies from institution to institution your subject mentor will probably be responsible for:

- the timetable for your observations;
- the focus of these observations;
- joint planning of weekly targets for your professional development;
- a review of those targets;
- critical review of your planning, teaching, monitoring and assessment;
- reviewing your own lesson evaluations.

In addition to these more formal tasks your mentor will be a valuable source of knowledge, resources, advice and guidance (as well as the occasional shoulder to cry on). Help them to help you by doing the following:

- Make sure that you have passed on to them all the relevant documentation from your university/training institution.

- Give them the names and email addresses of significant contacts from your institution (for example, tutor, administration).
- The balance between being a 'needy' trainee and showing that you can work independently is a tough one to manage. Try to use your initiative as much as you can – but remember, too, that good trainees will not be afraid to ask questions. Seeking advice and comments from your colleagues is evidence of your own emerging professional values.
- Show them resources and lesson plans well in advance of the class you are about to teach (anything up to a week is normal). Not only does this show evidence of your high professional standards but it also allows you to make those vital adjustments that more experienced teachers will be able to spot as necessary.
- Always let your mentor know well in advance when your university tutor is coming in to visit.
- Ensure that your mentor has a good sense of the sorts of issues you are covering at your university or training institution – if possible, give them a copy of your lectures/timetables and so on, so that they can plan their training to complement what is taking place at the university.
- Be critical about your own lessons and show your mentors the areas of weakness that you feel you may have – remember, they were trainees once! All mentors appreciate a trainee that is critical of her/his own practice as this makes it easier for them to offer formative advice and guidance.
- Have a list of questions that you wish to ask your mentor in the weekly meetings – if possible, go through the standards/competencies and see which ones you might like to address, using them as the basis for your questions.
- Ensure that you have a fixed agreed time and date for the next meeting.
- Clarify any targets that have been set and make sure that these are reviewed in the following meeting.

The relationship that you have with your mentor is, in most cases, the most important you will experience during your training. That said, in some, very rare cases, that relationship will not necessarily be as productive as you might expect it to be. If that is the case then your ability to show sensitivity and wisdom will be crucial to your success in that institution. Remember that your university-based tutor is the person to talk to first if you experience any issues related to your placement that are of concern to you.

First encounters with learners

How you create that all-important first impression for many learners will set the scene for how they respond to you during your teaching practice. That is not to say that you cannot change first impressions – but rather to recognise that there are lots of things you can do in your first session(s) to improve the learning experience – for your learners and you as a trainee teacher. What follows are some tips and suggestions on how you can create an impression of an experienced and confident teacher – right at the start of your teaching practice:

- Get a list of the names in the class you are teaching well in advance. Become familiar with how to pronounce their names.
- Stand at the door as learners come into the class – greet them confidently and politely (as you get to know learners in coming lessons – try to complement the occasional learner, for example, 'great hair cut', 'nice bag').
- Get into the classroom you where will be teaching several days beforehand and when there is nobody in the class (for example, at the end of the day). Move around the class getting the 'feel' of the room. Experiment with saying a few sentences to get used to the sound of your own voice in the room. Move tables/desks around and see what you feel comfortable with.
- Make sure the classroom is neatly laid out (for example, no bits of rubbish on floors, tables and chairs neatly laid out).
- Have the title of the lesson, objectives and key words written or projected onto the board at the start – this looks professional and allows you to confidently refer to key concepts throughout lesson.
- If possible get into the class before the lesson and lay it out exactly as you wish.
- Have a task waiting for them on their tables as they arrive (for example, a simple sorting activity).
- Photocopy all handouts on coloured paper (this aids differentiation and adds a 'wow' factor).
- Have all paperwork, worksheets, exercise textbooks and spare pencils/pens arranged and to hand. Being unorganised gives the wrong impression to learners.
- Spot the name on a learner's folder/exercise book when they put these on the table and then confidently ask that learner to close the door (he/she will be amazed that you already seemingly know their name). The use of names in these very first lessons establishes respect and an authority very early on in your teaching.
- Try not to refer to your class as 'Year 9' or some similar generic term, particularly if your comments are really only directed to a handful of individuals. Those learners who behave will quietly resent the fact that they are associated with those that do not and *none* of us really like to be referred to en masse. If you have to, then find a more respectful way of addressing them (for example, 'ladies and gentlemen' which will produce initial smiles but also quiet respect).
- When greeting them at the door, try to listen to what their friends have called them if you have missed the book on the desk.
- Prepare colourful cards with learners' names on them. Place the cards at each desk and ask learners to find their cards. Before the lesson, create a seating plan where you are going to place the cards and draw yourself a classroom layout detailing where each learner is sitting.
- Ask each learner to stand up giving their name and one thing that they like and one thing that they dislike. Every learner must have a different like and dislike. Learners must try to remember the information. The learners then write their likes and dislikes on cards. These cards are then mixed up and handed out and the recipient has to identify the owner.
- Create a subject handbook, for example, an A5 booklet detailing the programme of study, modules to be covered, useful terms. On the inside cover leave a template for

learners to create a list of their expectations (for example, behaviour). Introduce this as the class's first activity.

- Stand at the front of the class and wait for silence without issuing any instructions – this is hard but just wait – stand calmly and make sure your body posture conveys that calmness and wait for the chatter to stop (in a matter of seconds you will here learners saying 'shhhh'). Do not say anything until you have that silence and then greet the class nicely. Introduce yourself.
- Write your name on the board and also give the learners an explanation about why and for how long you will be teaching them.
- Have a seating plan in your hand and do not let them know you are checking their names and places if you are unable to greet them at the door.
- Check with colleagues before the lesson who works well and who does not and sit them together (you can project the seating plan on the smart board/whiteboard). Put the learners who tend to be distracted by the learners who work well.
- During the lesson choose three learners and ask them to carry out a task, for example, 'Susanne could you hand out the worksheets, Mohammed could you give out these text books'. This will help establish your confidence and authority with the class and aid you in remembering their names.
- When first in and around the school, try to meet as many of the learners as you can and ask their name, before you take over a class. (I know this is hard, but it does work for some.)
- Print out pictures of learners and add them to a seating plan.
- Have a set of class rules already drawn up. Ask the class what they would add to it and then write up the rules again with any amendments included, and give them out the next lesson. Refer to this and specifically refer to the rules they have created.
- When setting tests get them to add two or three things about themselves. Use this as a conversation point next time you see them in corridor/playground.
- Buy (or get the school to buy) those plastic collapsible trolleys so that you can easily carry the array of materials/resources you need from class to class.
- Make sure you try out (when nobody is around) blinds, videos, computer, and so on, so that you do not get caught out with your audience.
- Have a box where you keep pens, paper, scissors, and so on. Let learners know where this is and direct them to it rather than you searching for these items when you are teaching.
- Call parents when a particular learner has done well. All too often parents are called for negative reasons. You will gain respect from learners if you are seen to do both.
- Avoid sarcasm on all fronts – young people are both sensitive to this and excellent at it – choose words carefully and be professional in your instructions, praise, criticisms and warnings on all fronts.
- Have calm music playing as they come into your class.
- Get learners into the routine of placing bags under desk, pens and exercise books out, and so on – and insist that this takes place immediately at the start of your lessons.
- Make sure you deliver your lessons with enthusiasm. Learners like teachers who are enthusiastic about their subject and an enthusiastic teacher will invoke enthusiasm in their learners.

- If you use any form of threat/promise then be seen to follow this through – for example, if you say 'see me at end of lesson' do this – and, if you forget, follow up by tracking down learners in the playground/dinner halls.
- Make sure you do your research on your new class before you take them over, for example, check what topics they have studied, areas in textbooks – so you avoid embarrassing repetition.
- Know what the institutional rules are (for example, when are children allowed to go to the toilet, detention policies). This minimises learners 'trying it on' with you.
- Ensure that you have full details of SEN learners and learners who may have physical needs, to help in planning, seating, and so on.
- For the first lesson, plan something that is fun and engaging with colourful resources and interactive elements. Let them know that you are a teacher who cares about them and is passionate about both the subject and teaching.
- As the learners are standing behind their desks and the bell goes, let the best behaved/hardest working learners go first, praising them as they leave.
- Find out about well-known troublemakers in the class; however, it is important not to prejudge a class or individual. Some learners with a bad reputation are not always given opportunities to prove otherwise.

Try and see each new class and your new placement institution in general as a new opportunity: an opportunity to make your mark and define who you are within your new teacher's identity and role. If you can set the rules, be clear what you expect and understand what you see around you, then you will make a good foundation for the rest of your teaching.

Chapter links →

Themes and ideas explored in this chapter link to corresponding ideas in Chapters 11 and 14.

Suggested further reading 📖

Lave, J. and Wenger, E. (1991) *Situated Learning: Legitimate Peripheral Participation.* Cambridge: Cambridge University Press.

References

Argyris, C. and Schön, D. (1974) *Theory in Practice: Increasing Professional Effectiveness.* San Francisco, CA: Jossey-Bass.

Goffman, E. (1969) *The Presentation of Self in Everyday Life.* Harmondsworth: Penguin.

Hulme, M. and Menter, I. (2008) 'Learning to teach in post-devolution UK', in *Teaching and Learning Research Briefing no. 49*, Teaching and Learning Research Programme. London: TDLP.

Lave, J. and Wenger, E. (1991) *Situated Learning: Legitimate Peripheral Participation.* Cambridge: Cambridge University Press.

CHAPTER 8

HOW TO 'SURVIVE' TEACHING PRACTICE

Objectives

By the end of this chapter the reader will be able to:

1. understand the importance of teaching practice for their own professional development;
2. reflect on the most useful ways to prepare for the observation of their own teaching;
3. successfully observe the practice of more experienced colleagues;
4. understand the role of 'standards' in the assessment of teaching;
5. apply the relevant professional standards from the sector in which they are training to their own practice and development.

Is it really a case of 'survival'?

'Surviving' teaching practice seems to be such a strong theme dominating the titles of books on teaching that we are amazed that so many people want to go into the profession in the first place. The cliché 'don't smile till Christmas' compounds existing fears many trainee teachers have about classroom behaviour management. Referring to the initial period of teaching as one of 'survival', Shindler et al. (2004) argue that this time can involve feelings of inadequacy, stress, confusion and disillusionment. Hatch (1999) refers to the induction into the teaching profession as 'sink-or-swim socialisation'. Thankfully not all accounts of this magical profession are painted in this negative light. Researching the views of beginning teachers on their induction into teaching, Carter (2000) has suggested that the processes of becoming a teacher involve varying degrees of personal and professional growth. To this we must add that the very fact we are writing this book reflects our passion and enthusiasm for teaching and working with young people. That said there are a number of things that this chapter suggests you can do to ease the stress and confusion that Schindler et al. refer to.

How to observe experienced teachers

Before you start the bulk of your own teaching, it is desirable that you have the opportunity to observe the teaching of more experienced colleagues. This is a privileged and an essential opportunity for your own reflection and development. Never again in your career will you have the time available to you now to do this, so make the most of this experience. Do not rush in, eager to 'teach' but try and observe in as systematic a way as possible. What follows are some guidelines that will help you to make the most of the observation of others' classes.

Observation protocols

Here are some simple guidelines to follow when observing other colleagues' classes:

1. Confirm the observation with the colleague in advance.
2. Make sure you are clear about start times and where the colleague wishes you to sit in the room.
3. Don't write too many notes – write some, it will help your reflection afterwards, but if you write too many (and too obviously) it will have the potential to distract the teacher and maybe the learners too.
4. Arrange in advance if the teacher does or does not want you to join in – it may be inappropriate or might be welcomed as an offer of help. Especially during group work you could be 'an extra pair of hands', but only if your input is wanted.
5. If you keep notes, do not write anything negative – your colleague might wish to see them afterwards!
6. After the lesson, do not just walk out and leave your colleague. Try and at least speak to them if they have a few minutes – ask questions and show you were interested, but do not grill them ... they have just taught a lesson and been generous enough to allow you to observe!

There are many ways that you can structure your observations of experienced colleagues.

- The immersion method. In this type of observation you simply 'soak up the atmosphere' of the social situation you are entering. Do not write anything down, simply sit back and watch and reflect in action. Do not do this too often, but sometimes it is useful to make space for thinking.
- Systematic observation. In this method you develop a list of aspects of teaching to look out for (see Chapter 7) and you make notes against the categories as you see them displayed.
- The socio-gram method. Draw a picture of the layout of the classroom you are in showing the teacher, the learners and where they are seated. Once you have your map, try and observe where the teacher moves, who he/she speaks to and what type of interaction is taking place (it is, specifically, this map or web of interaction that is actually referred to as a 'socio-gram'). Are any learners ignored? Are any supported more than or differently from others? It is an excellent method to focus on the relational and interactive nature of teaching.
- Teacher talk. Make a list of what the teacher says – verbal instructions, questions, replies, and so on. Do this only if you have agreed this with a colleague in advance! It could feel quite exposed to someone unaware that you are going to try it. Try and see from your list if there are any patterns in language and communication. For example, does the questioning technique follow an order (high to low order?) or are some learners rewarded for different things than others, and why might this be the case?
- Timed event recording. Start with a blank sheet of paper. Make a decision to neutrally describe what occurs at a regular timed interval – say every 4 or 5 minutes. Ignore everything in between and just record each event at the designated time. During the course of the observation you will create a narrative of the lesson which unfolds before you.

 Discussion point: Is 'neutral' observation possible?

The nature of observation is such that how you observe inevitably shapes the outcome you get, that is, your method of observation dictates the data and sensory experience you receive. Your very presence in the room – not being a 'usual' part of the routine of the lesson – will affect that lesson and your observation of it. To what extent do you believe that learners and teachers will act differently if they know they are being observed?

Other things to try!

1. Shadow a student or a class for the day! Get their timetable and go to every lesson they do! See what the experience of being in a school or college is like from the learner's perspective – you will be amazed how disjointed lessons

(Continued)

(Continued)

are and how much learners are expected to do. No wonder they get tired! Have some sense of how they experience lessons and learning.

2. Observe as many different and varied subjects as you can – you will find a genuine difference between some subject specialist pedagogies and also some genuine similarities between all learning. Equally, you might find some learners responding and acting very differently between different teachers and different subjects.
3. Shadow an experienced teacher for the day – see how they change their teaching for the class and the needs of the learners.
4. Join a lesson and 'act like a learner' – actually doing the exercises they do and completing all the work they are set: really try and develop an understanding from their side of the teaching–learning interplay.

Preparing for lesson observations of your own teaching

Being observed during your teaching practice can be a stressful experience, particularly if it is associated with some sort of grading or assessment process – either by your colleagues in your school or by your university tutors. There are lots of things you can do to make the process less stressful and make it one of the most rewarding experiences during your training (see Chapter 6). The temptation will be to 'go for the safe option', that is, not to take risks but deliver a lesson that has little or no dynamism to it. Avoid 'pedestrian' lessons at all costs during observations. Your tutor (and you) will value the observation far more if you are seen to be experimenting and moving beyond your comfort zone. Doing this and having a 'critical friend' watching you teach will accelerate the speed at which you become an excellent practitioner.

Before your observation discuss with your observer what it is that they will focus on (for example, starters and ends to lessons). Ask them to specifically focus on areas you might be worried about (for example, questioning strategies, classroom layout). Remember that if this is a first observation the chances are your tutor will ask you what particular lesson you would like observed, so choose one where you feel your subject knowledge is strongest. Try to choose observation times that are either first periods of the day and/or after break/lunch times. This allows valuable time for you to get into the classroom before the lesson and set up the way you would ideally like the room to be. Speak to colleagues and find out (ask nicely!) if it is ok to rearrange tables, chairs and so on (just make sure you move them all back – even better, ask learners to help you).

If targets have been set from a previous observation, show these targets, well in advance, to your colleagues and mentor to guarantee that you can find ways to meet them. Make sure that you also show copies of your lesson plan, resources, and so on to another trusted colleague before your observation takes place. This will allow you to develop the lesson and make sure there are no glaring mistakes (for example, forgetting to refer to homework, differentiation). Remember to go through any official standards/competencies that are associated with your particular qualification and check that everything you have planned 'ticks' the relevant boxes. If the observer is from your university remember to let key staff from your school (for example, reception, subject mentors, professional tutors) know of their visit in advance. Greet them with an offer of a cup of tea/coffee. Not only does this set the mood for the observation but also your tutor will be grateful (this might be her/his third observation of the day with little/no time for lunch/coffee).

On the big day make sure there is a place for your observer to sit and that you have given them all the documentation they need (for example, lesson plan, scheme of work, copies of resources and your assessment records). Check blinds and technological equipment before the lesson (this avoids opportunities for learners to laugh because you do not know how to turn on the projector). Remember that the observer's visit is designed to move you on from one stage of teaching to the next. Inevitably this means that they will be constructively criticising you as a 'critical friend'. Prepare yourself for this and do not be overly defensive about the strategies you deploy or the criticisms that they may generate. The moment the lesson finishes start to think about elements of the lesson that you were pleased about – but (and far more importantly) think about how the lesson could be done again with improvements. Your tutor will be expecting you to be able to critically deconstruct the lesson and your own teaching. Remember – even if a lesson goes badly it is possible to get a better grade if you can show an awareness of why the lesson went the way that it did.

Being clear about the goal of the lesson – the learning!

Elsewhere in this book (see Chapter 5) we have made the point that the goal of teaching is learning. This is central when you prepare for observations of your own teaching right from the planning stage onwards.

Ask yourself the following questions:

1. Where will learners start the lesson from? What is their prior knowledge? How does it fit into the point of the lesson today? How will prior learning be assessed?
2. Where will learners need to get/be by the end of the lesson? What is the end point they need to reach in terms of their development?
3. What processes do they need to go through in order to reach the learning goals by the end of the lesson?
4. What activities will most easily maximise the skills development/knowledge transmission needed for the lesson goals to be achieved?

What this means, is that successful lesson planning is often a process of 'planning backwards' from the end point of the lesson (see Chapter 13 for a fuller discussion). If you can be absolutely clear about the end result you can then be clear on how your learners are going to get there and write resources accordingly.

A model of lesson planning

Lesson planning often takes the following shape:

- Stage 1 = identify the aspect of the curriculum (usually from the scheme of work) that you wish to base your lesson upon.
- Stage 2 = assess and reflect upon the prior learning of the learners: what do they already know and what can they apply to this new lesson topic? How will you track this with them and make clear the connections in their learning?
- Stage 3 = identify the aims and then the objectives of the lesson: what is the point of the learning within the time period set for the class?
- Stage 4 = plan (often backwards) the student activities, taking into account the differentiated needs of the learners (see Chapter 17) and any key/functional/cross-curricular skills that need to be addressed.
- Stage 5 = create the resources needed to achieve the aims and objectives.

Do not forget the hidden stage – stage 6. After the lesson, ensure that you reflect on and evaluate the teaching and the learning and the interplay between the two. You could ask for the learners themselves to evaluate their own learning as a means to establish if both you and they feel the aims and objectives of the lesson have been met.

If applicable, you might wish to try and adopt the ideas of Bloom and Krathwohl (1956) (Chapter 13), and the notion of skill 'domains' within your lesson planning.

Bloom and Krathwohl suggest that different learning takes account of the development of different sets of skills. They identify three domains or areas of skill-sets in all:

- cognitive (thinking) skills;
- affective (relationship, emotional and interpersonal interaction) skills;
- psycho-motor (physical) skills.

Many teachers find the language of these domains useful when they are considering writing the aims and objectives of the lesson. This is a key issue that your observer will be looking out for! To clarify these:

Aim = the overall point of the lesson, reached by the very end.
Objectives = smaller goals throughout the lesson enabling the overall aim to eventually be achieved.

It is considered essential that you make the aims and objectives of the lesson clear to learners at the start to 'locate' them and their learning; so they can see the point of the lesson and be as clear as possible. This will help their ownership of the learning process.

Stating the aims and objectives

It is considered good practice to make sure that learners understand the aims of the lesson so they can own the process of their own learning (see Chapter 14 for a fuller discussion). There are, as with everything in teaching, a number of ways that you can do this:

- You could verbally state your aims.
- Learners could have a process of recording the aims of each lesson.
- Learners could assess their own learning at the end of the lesson based upon the aims.
- You could do a starter, and then make clear your aims afterwards – especially if your starter assesses prior learning. If you do this, make sure you can show your learners (and your observer) how everything 'fits together'.
- You could have your aims and objectives written down on the board or on a Microsoft PowerPoint slide.
- You are best advised to ask your learners to tell you what the language of your aims and objectives mean! Get them to decode and deconstruct the aims so you can see they are as clear as possible.
- At the end of the lesson, ask them to remind you and themselves what the aims were.
- Learners could evaluate their learning or evaluate the activities/content of the lesson against the announced aims.

You can announce that you are 'not going to announce the aims' and ask the learners at the end to be able to tell you what they were! In this sense, the aim is actually for the learners to see and understand the context of their own learning. Be careful how you do this – especially if you are being observed! But it does show you that there are no absolutely rigid rules, just guidelines for you to adapt and manipulate.

The most important thing when being observed, is that you make the process of your thinking and planning about the lesson as transparent as possible to the observer – through your lesson plan, accompanying documentation and your actions and instructions to learners while in the class. You might find, depending upon the lesson and your subject specialism, that you adopt one of the three domains more than the others, or that different tasks require different skill domains at different times. It is also the case that in many lessons the domains will overlap. For example, a lesson where learners are developing their understanding of a new concept would draw from the 'cognitive domain', but if they worked in groups to share their understanding then they would need skills from the 'affective' domain to work profitably and would in turn be learning how to work with each other while doing so.

The language of the domains might help you to write your aims and objectives. Consider Table 8.1. As you can see, you can describe aims and objectives as being

Table 8.1 The language of the domains

For the cognitive domain we might use language such as:	For the affective domain we might use language such as:	For the psycho-motor domain we might use language such as:
Low to high:	Low to high:	Low to high:
Define Outline Recap Repeat	Listen Pay attention to	Following Copying Sequencing
Recount Explain Illustrate	React Answer Respond	Breaking down activity or skill into components
Transfer Apply	Being responsible Being respectful Taking into consideration	Combining components of a skill Merging skills and activities together
Break down Pulling apart	Acting Illustrating understanding through behaviour	Showing mastery through applied effort
Putting together Review Assess	Application of understanding/behaviour	Embedding elements seamlessly into performance

about the learners' 'understanding' or their 'comprehension'. You could plan for learners to develop 'evaluation' or 'mastery'. Do not forget the importance of the affective domain – in your teaching and your lesson planning. If learners are working together, you need to provide opportunities for them to develop the skills of cooperation: essential for learning and also for their lives after school and college.

If you can plan for these in your lessons while on placement – and especially for those where you are being observed and assessed – you will really be setting yourself up with a solid foundation for a very enjoyable career. The tendency when being observed is to think that the focus is on your teaching; but your teaching is only ever a vehicle for their learning. If you plan for this and think about lessons like this from the very start, it will help you to maximise your training experience while on placement.

Achieving the standards: secondary

Although the experience of training to become a teacher varies, depending on which of the four countries in the UK you train, there is a trend for convergence (for example, there is a move towards integrated professional development frameworks based on standards or their equivalent). Hulme and Menter (2008), in their review of arrangements for teacher education across the UK, draw attention to the existence of a 'competence framework' in all four countries. These include: 'Professional Standards' (England and Wales); 'Benchmarks' or 'elements of Standard' (Scotland) and 'Competence Statements' (Northern Ireland). In all four countries these standards broadly address:

- professional values, attributes and practice;
- professional knowledge and understanding;
- professional skills and abilities.

While it is not possible to draw up a 'wish list' that is wholly consistent for all four countries, the following is a list sources of evidence that we feel will help you when compiling your standards/competence files.

- lesson plans;
- lesson evaluations;
- schemes of work of lessons planned and taught by you;
- minutes of any meetings you attend;
- letters/emails to other staff/parents/external bodies;
- resources you have produced or used;
- any paperwork associated with trips you attend with learners;
- documentation of any additional courses attended during your training;
- observation notes (by you or any other member of staff);
- documentation confirming visits by you to other educational institutions;
- any awards/merits that you have created for your learners;
- copies of marked work showing comments you have made;
- communications with tutors, Heads of Year (HOY), Heads of Department (HOD) and so on about your learners;
- documentation that ties you to any extra-curricular school activities;
- subject knowledge 'audits';
- evidence of subject knowledge updating, for example, conference attendance;
- entries from your professional journal;
- pages from your mark book, assessment records, pupil-tracking, and so on;
- testimonies from other professional colleagues about the work you do;
- photographs of displays of work by learners for you;
- photographs of classroom layouts used by you when teaching.

It is not always easy to get your hands on all of these sorts of evidence. What follows is a list of tasks you can do during your training that will help you generate some of the evidence you require:

- Offer to take minutes in a departmental meeting.
- Using 'Microsoft Moviemaker' to create a 10-minute film about why learners should study your subject.
- Develop a spreadsheet/database that 'tracks' where the functional skills (mathematics, ICT and numeracy) appear in your subject.
- Attach yourself to a form tutor and gain experience of the pastoral side of teaching.
- Shadow a member of the senior management team (SMT) of your school/college.
- Shadow a member of the special educational needs team.
- Produce an ICT revision pack for your subject.
- Shadow a pupil who receives some sort of additional support.
- Visit your local pupil referral unit and carry out observations.

- Spend half a day in the area of the school where learners are referred to for bad behaviour – talk to the learners and find out their perspectives on why they are there.
- Shadow a 'gifted and talented' pupil for the day.
- Carry out observations in an institution above and below the key stages that you are being trained to teach in.
- Team teach a citizenship/personal, social and health education (PSHE) lesson.
- Differentiate a resource you have produced for an English as an additional language (EAL) student.
- Offer to lay on an exhibition with your learners on a subject related area that can be displayed in the foyer of your school/college.

These tasks will not cover all of the standards/competencies you require but they will create evidence for the areas that trainees often find difficulties in accumulating. We believe that doing these tasks will make you a better teacher, but please make sure that when you carry out the tasks, you have secured the permission of your tutors, mentors and the professionals in the institutions you visit.

Achieving the standards – post-compulsory

Unlike the secondary initial teacher education routes, the PGCE, Certificate in Education (Cert. Ed.) for the post-compulsory education and training sector (PCET), Diploma and Post Graduate Diploma do not lead to qualified teacher status (QTS). The secondary PGCE leads to QTS at the end of the training year with the award of the qualification after tests, whereas the PCET version – qualified teacher learning and skills (QTLS) – is awarded by the Institute for Learning (IfL) after a period of employment and 'professional formation' which could last up to five years.

The LLUK standards

The document *Equipping our Teachers for the Future: Reforming Initial Teacher Training for the Learning and Skills Sector* (DfES, 2004) laid out the reform of teacher education in the PCET sector and the establishment of new professional standards for teacher education starting September 2007, as coordinated by Lifelong Learning UK (LLUK).

Lifelong Learning UK define the 'teacher role' as opposed to the 'associate teaching role' (or 'instructor role') as comprising the following elements:

1. Initial assessment.
2. Preparation and planning.
3. Delivery.
4. Assessment.
5. Evaluation.
6. Revision based on evaluation (LLUK, 2007a: 11).

Teachers are seen to have responsibility for the management, assessment and coordination of the six areas of professional responsibility as outlined above. The professional standards against which all initial teacher education for the PCET sector is assessed are to be found in the LLUK document (2007b) *New Overarching Professional Standards for Teachers, Tutors and Trainers in the Lifelong Learning Sector*. The standards are categorised into six areas of professional practice – referred to as 'domains':

Domain A   Professional values and practice.
Domain B   Learning and teaching.
Domain C   Specialist learning and teaching.
Domain D   Planning for learning.
Domain E   Assessment for learning.
Domain F   Access and progression.

Code of professional practice

The IfL has its own code of professional practice for teachers and trainers working in the lifelong learning sector (see Chapter 3 for a discussion of these terms and the nature of this provision). There are seven 'professional behaviours' but the first four concern us here:

1. Professional Integrity.
2. Respect.
3. Reasonable care.
4. Professional practice (IfL, 2007).

This code of practice for professionals within the lifelong learning sector is seen as an attempt to re-professionalise the FE workforce in the light of parallel developments in the professional regulation of other teachers at both primary and secondary level. At the same time, it is an attempt to articulate the recognition that the make-up of the FE workplace is different from that of teachers employed in the secondary sector – teachers and instructors (different levels of role in the eyes of the IfL) do not necessary need to be graduates, depending upon what they teach/instruct, and many have vast vocational and professional experience to draw upon. This reflects the sectors large employability and vocational basis beyond the curriculum designed for 14–19-year-olds.

The IfL code of practice and the wider legal obligation to join the IfL and to undertake 30 hours' continuing professional development (CPD) is seen as a measure to give a professional voice to the FE workforce while, at the same time, 'raising standards' and centralising professional activity within the remit of a national body.

Changing professional landscapes?

As we have seen in this chapter, the world of education is open to increasing review and assessment (see Chapter 1 for a fuller discussion). The notion of teachers as 'professionals' is of high importance in terms of how initial teacher education is assessed and the resulting 'competences' or 'standards' that apply to both secondary and post-compulsory training. Despite the differences in language and legal obligation, both sets of standards are united by the recognition that professional teaching (and therefore adequate initial teacher education) is measured by how one supports learners to learn, and how one plans, tracks and coordinates this learning. In this sense, the landscape is not that different.

Chapter links →

Themes and ideas explored in this chapter link to corresponding ideas in Chapters 19 and 20.

Suggested further reading

Hulme, M. and Menter, I. (2008) 'Learning to teach in post-devolution UK', in *Teaching and Learning Research Briefing no. 49*. Teaching and Learning Research Programme. London: TDLP.

Lifelong Learning UK (2007) *Guidance for Awarding Institutions on Teacher Roles and Initial Teaching Qualifications (Version 3)*. August. London: LLUK.

Lifelong Learning UK (2007) *New Overarching Professional Standards for Teachers, Tutors and Trainers in the Lifelong Learning Sector*. London: LLUK.

References

Bloom, B. and Krathwohl, D. (1956) *Taxonomy of Educational Objectives*. New York: Longmans Green.

Carter, M. (2000) 'Beginning teachers and workplace learning: an exploration of the process of becoming a teacher', paper presented at the 13th Annual International Congress for School Effectiveness and Improvement (ICSEI 2000), New South Wales Department of Education and Training.

Department for Education and Skills (DfES) (2004) *Equipping our Teachers for the Future: Reforming Initial Teacher Training for the Learning and Skills Sector*. London: DfES.

Hatch, J.A. (1999) 'What preservice teachers can learn from studies of teachers' work', *Teaching and Teacher Education*, 15: 229–42.

Hulme, M. and Menter, I. (2008) 'Learning to teach in post-devolution UK', in *Teaching and Learning Research Brief no. 49*. Teaching and Learning Research Programme. London: TDLP.

Institute for Learning (IfL) (2007) *Statement of Intent: Code of Professional Practice*. July, www.ifl.ac.uk/professional-standards/code-of-professional-practice

Lifelong Learning UK (LLUK) (2007a) *Guidance for Awarding Institutions on Teacher Roles and Initial Teaching Qualifications (Version 3)*. August. London: LLUK.

Lifelong Learning UK (LLUK) (2007b) *New Overarching Professional Standards for Teachers, Tutors and Trainers in the Lifelong Learning Sector*. London: LLUK.

Shindler J., Jones, A., Taylor, C. and Cadenas, H. (2004) *Don't Smile till Christmas: Examining the Immersion of New Teachers into Existing Urban School Climates*. Los Angeles, CA: Charter College of Education.

SECTION 3

THEORY

CHAPTER 9

EDUCATIONAL THEORY: USEFUL TOOLS AT YOUR DISPOSAL

Objectives

By the end of this chapter the reader will be able to:

1. question what is meant by 'intelligence';
2. comprehend theories related to teaching and learning;
3. understand how theories can enhance your classroom practice;
4. understand how theories can assist in evaluating planning, teaching and assessment.

There is nothing so theoretical as good practice

Kurt Lewin (1890–1947), seminal theorist on action research and experiential learning, was famously quoted as saying 'there is nothing so practical as good theory' (Lewin, 1951: 169). The consistent theme in Lewin's work was his interest in the integration of theory and practice. Our philosophy for this book is to endorse this by adding that there is nothing so theoretical as good practice.

During teaching practice it is so easy to forget the importance of educational theories. Lesson planning, schemes of work, rushing to the photocopier and worrying about that Year 9 class all seem far more relevant and immediate than what appears to be the abstract ideas of university professors far removed from today's classroom. And yet educational theories have the ability to not only transform teaching practice but also to enable you to reconsider the very nature of education itself. Educational theories can be emancipatory (that is, they can help you transform the lives of those you teach), descriptive (that is, they can tell you things about teaching that you might not necessarily have known or thought about) and normative (that is, they can imply that 'this is the way things should be done' and we would argue that you should always view critically what others say about teaching and learning).

Theories are just that – theories! Educational theories are the products of the particular historical and social context in which they are generated. In many cases they are informed by political agendas, scientific, technological and popularist thinking. It is worth remembering that the 'male-stream' psychological theories that informed much educational thinking in the nineteenth century encouraged the idea that because women had smaller brains, certain types of activity (for example, political debate and scientific endeavour) were unsuitable for women and deemed not 'feminine'. In other words theories can be so powerful (however daft they may appear in hindsight) as to influence professional thinking at the time. It is worth bearing all of this in mind when considering the theories in this chapter. However, it is also worth remembering that many theories offer tantalising glimpses of the kind of teacher you might want to become – so, respect and honour the theories in this chapter and glean from them as many ideas as you can about the sort of teacher you want to be and the sort of institution you want to teach in.

Intelligence

The idea that intelligence is something that you can measure, test and quantify has its origins in nineteenth-century theories related to education and psychology that have dominated much twentieth-century (and some twenty-first-century) thinking about not only intelligence but the construction of education systems, setting, streaming, the design of curricula and the array of different types of schools that exist throughout much of the UK. It underpins much of the sorting and sifting of learners into different forms of schooling and choice of subjects based on 'ability'. In this sense it has added to the patterns of inequality of educational achievement according to class, gender and ethnicity (see Chapter 12). So called 'IQ' (intelligence quotient) tests and other similar standardised forms of examination were first constructed in France by Alfred Binet (1857–1911) to assess children's educability in schools. Psychologists and educationalists developed these ideas to argue that there were different 'types' of children that could be identified by these tests. Critics argue that such tests are culturally biased working in favour of 'white' middle-class children and discriminating against those who have English as their second language.

Ongoing research on 'multiple intelligences' is famously encapsulated by the work of American psychologist Howard Gardner. Rather than having an intelligence defined by somebody's 'IQ', he argues that humans are better thought of as having nine or more intelligences – the most significant being:

- Linguistic – the ability to learn, explore, play and develop language or languages.
- Logical/mathematical – the ability to excel in mathematical problem-solving or lateral thinking.
- Musical – the ability to recall music (be it pitch, rhythm or timbre) on first hearing and/or the ability to 'naturally' pick up a musical instrument and play melodies without instruction. The ability to listen to, and discern differences in, a variety of musical styles.
- Spatial – the ability to map read, recall and describe places by picturing them in your mind and perhaps the ability to conceptualise thoughts in diagrammatical form. The ability to re-create visual experience.
- Bodily kinaesthetic – as exemplified by athletes, dancers and other physical performers, this refers to the ability to control and orchestrate bodily motions along with the ability to handle objects skilfully (for example, jugglers and footballers).
- Naturalist – the most recent of Gardner's intelligences this refers to the ability to recognise and categorise natural objects.
- Interpersonal – the ability to read other people's moods, feelings and motivations and other mental states.
- Intrapersonal – the ability to access one's own moods, feelings and motivations and draw on them to guide behaviour.
- Existential – the ability to raise fundamental questions about existence, life, death and finitude.

Gardner argues that both interpersonal and intrapersonal intelligences (above) are what other writers often refer to as 'emotional intelligence'. The concept of emotional intelligence has been most famously written about by American psychologist Daniel Goleman (1995). Goleman's theories focus on the development of the limbic brain, which regulates emotional responses. According to Goleman, this part of the brain examines everything we do and relates it to the emotions of past experiences. He argues that educators need to consider the emotional brain, which controls 'personal intelligences', or a learner's interpersonal and intrapersonal skills. Goleman claims that it is essential that teachers change the way they teach to include the following five dimensions of emotional intelligence:

- Self-awareness – the ability to recognise and understand moods, emotions and drives and their effects on others.
- Self-regulation – the ability to control and/or redirect disruptive impulses and moods along with the propensity to suspend judgement (to think before acting).
- Motivation – a passion to work for reasons that go beyond money or status, pursuing goals with energy and persistence.
- Empathy – the ability to understand and respond to the emotional make-up of other people.
- Social skill – proficiency in managing relationships, building networks, finding common ground and building rapport.

Lozanov and Evalina (1988) offer some suggestions in light of the above that many teachers might indeed find hard to put into practice because of the idea that such practice challenges conventional 'discourses' about teaching. Their research into highly successful 'accelerated learning' techniques for language learning argues that the learning process should have three phases:

- introductory music with deep breathing to achieve an optimal learning state;
- an active/vibrant piece of music where the information to be learned is read in time to expressive music;
- a passive/calming piece of music where learners hear new information against a background of music.

 Case study

Vikki is in her first year of working in a further education college in Birmingham and describes what happened when she started to use music in the class: 'I remembered hearing about the effects of music on learners and I thought I would give it a go. All I did was to make sure there was gentle music playing before classes started. I had this one group first period and their punctuality was terrible. But over the coming weeks a few of the latecomers actually started to walk into my class 10, 15 minutes early! It took me ages to make the connection between the sometimes classical, sometimes jazz music I played and their early arrival. I eventually chatted to them about it and they said that the calm environment this created was in complete contrast to the mayhem some of them faced at home – they really liked it – even though the music was not the sort of music they would normally listen to.'

McNeil (1999) argues that this type of research based around the emotions is hugely underestimated in terms of its potential impact in the classroom and asks teachers to focus on two questions when formulating lesson plans:

- How can or do teachers plan to use the learners' emotions in a positive way to enhance learning?
- What kinds of collaborative opportunities do learners have where their emotions can assist in their learning?

While 'linguistic' and 'logical/mathematical' intelligences (the first two of Gardner's intelligences) inform much of what has traditionally been understood as 'intelligence', multiple intelligence theories make two significant claims that teachers in the classroom can bear in mind. First, that all human beings possess all these intelligences. Secondly, we all possess different 'profiles' of these intelligences regardless of our genetic or environmental background. A third claim made by other commentators (for example, Sale, 1998) is that as teachers we tend to teach to the particular 'profile' we possess. If this last claim is true, then automatically we are *not* teaching to the needs of the majority of learners in our classroom. The implications for teachers are obvious if we are to take such thinking seriously. Our lesson strategies need to reflect the profiles of the learners in our class, rather than the profile of the teacher giving the lesson.

Three learning paradigms

Three schools of learning theory are really helpful when looking at teaching and learning styles, namely, behaviourism, social constructivism and humanism. All three paradigms pose different types of relationships between the teacher and learner, and all three raise questions about the sort of teacher you want to become and what sort of institution you would like to teach in. Broadly speaking, behaviourist approaches (see Skinner, 1957; Thorndike, 1911; Watson, 1913) to learning allow for a focus on teacher and learner behaviour. Like Pavlov's (1927) dogs, the focus of such approaches within the classroom considers 'rewards' for learners (for example, certificates, praise and the speed in which marked work is returned to learners). However, such rewards can also be 'negative' and consist of detentions, extra homework, and so on. Behaviourist views emphasise a process of knowledge transmission and the expert role allocated to the teacher rather than the learning activities of learners. Value is placed on the behaviour, performances and outcomes of learners and teacher trainees.

In contrast to behaviourist approaches, social constructivist schools of psychology contribute to learning theory by focusing on the thinking processes when learning takes place. The constructivist approach is more concerned with processes of learning and the role of the learner in particular and assumes that there is no such thing as 'fact' in that all facts, scientific or otherwise, are socially constructed in the first place. Knowledge is therefore assumed to be constructed by learners themselves and learning is seen as an active process of construction and knowledge accumulation. The teacher is no longer assumed to be the deliverer of knowledge but the facilitator of active learning. Learners 'restructure' what they see and hear, think and rethink ideas until 'personal meanings' are formed. This particular pedagogic approach assumes that 'mistakes' are 'OK' providing learners 'talk', solve problems, make decisions and form opinions. The teacher is no longer assumed to be the deliverer of knowledge but rather a 'facilitator' of the learners' active learning. Value is therefore placed on the variety of active learning that learners take up along with the facilitator role that the teacher occupies.

Humanistic approaches (for example, Froebel, 1900; Montessori, 1909; Rogers, 1969) to education focus on the importance of meeting the emotional and developmental needs of learners. The role that emotions play in the classroom is stressed under this approach with greater emphasis on personal development rather than purely intellectual. Much importance is placed on the holistic development of the individual including their emotional growth. This approach views learners as being afforded the opportunity to pursue their own interests within a non-threatening environment. Carl Rogers (1969) typifies this particular philosophy arguing that learning will occur by the educator acting as a facilitator by establishing an atmosphere in which learners feel comfortable to consider new ideas and do not feel threatened. Rogers argues that:

- Human beings have a natural eagerness to learn.
- Facilitative teachers are less protective of their constructs and beliefs than other teachers.
- They listen to their learners, especially to their feelings.
- They pay as much attention to their relationship with learners as to the content of the course.
- They can accept constructive feedback (both positive and negative) and use it add further insight into themselves and their behaviour.
- Learners should be encouraged to take responsibility for their own learning.
- Learners should provide much of the input for the learning which occurs through their insights and experiences.
- They should be encouraged to consider that the most valuable form of evaluation is self-evaluation.
- Learning needs to focus on factors that contribute to solving significant problems or achieving significant results.

We do not argue that one particular paradigm is better than another. In fact, really good teachers tend to have elements of all three paradigms embedded within their practice. However, we do argue that, sadly, the day-to-day reality of teaching in many schools, colleges and work-based environments gives little priority to the humanistic paradigm, despite the best of intentions. Considering that Britain as a whole has one of the lowest post-16 participation rates in education in Europe, it might well be worth reconsidering humanistic approaches to education in our secondary schools.

 Discussion point

Shut your eyes and think back to your own experiences of being a pupil in a primary school. Try to recall the layout of the classroom and the sorts of activities you did. Remember the plants, animals, reading carpets, bright colours and wonderful array of items you could touch and play with? Remember how small the school was in comparison to what followed? Contrast this warmer, personalised and friendly institution with what, all too often, is the uninspiring, cold environment that makes up many secondary classrooms. Which would you prefer to study in? With this in mind – discuss to what extent and why you believe that humanitarian approaches to education more closely embed British primary schools than those of the secondary and tertiary sectors.

Theories of learning

When reviewing literature of any sort, taking a broad historical perspective not only helps in an understanding of the context of much of the educational theory that has been generated in recent decades but also serves to remind teachers that theories come and go in much the same way that styles of music emerge, vanish or are 'reinvented'.

Bloom's taxonomy and the twenty-first century classroom

Benjamin Bloom (1956) and his 'taxonomy' of learning offers teachers a framework for considering different types of learning as well as understanding many of the skills required in public examinations today. Originally designed as a classification of goals within any education system, his taxonomy focused around three domains: the cognitive (including knowledge, intellectual abilities and skills); the affective (including interests, attitudes, emotions and values) and the psycho-motor (ranging from simple reflex movements to more advanced articulation and kinaesthetic activities, for example, dancing/sport and so on). Drawing on the work of Bloom (1956), Anderson and Krathwohl (2001) have created a classification of educational objectives focused around thinking skills. Table 9.1 contains these skills. Experiment by using this table when planning your next lesson. Use the column on the right to create imaginative activities. Aim to incorporate each of the thinking skills in every lesson.

Table 9.1   Thinking skills activity matrix

Thinking skills	Examples of instruction words for your activities	Activity
Remembering	Who? When? What? Recall; list; define; name; describe	
Understanding	Why? Summarise; contrast; interpret; discuss; translate	
Applying	Solve; classify; discover; predict; apply, demonstrate	
Analysing	Compare and contrast; connect; analyse; order; explain; separate	
Evaluating	Rank; summarise; evaluate; conclude; assess; decide	
Creating	Compose; design; integrate; modify; combine	

 Discussion point

Take a look at the examination specifications for your subject area (for example, GCSE/GCE/Diploma). Study carefully the examination skills that your subject demands of its learners when sitting the examination. Discuss with your colleagues on your course the commonality of these skills across all subject areas. See how closely the skills that the examiners are looking for today reflect the ideas of Bloom from over half a century ago.

Discussion point

The skill of questioning is a really hard one for trainee teachers to develop quickly and we explore this more fully in Chapter 14. Once mastered it not only raises achievement but acts as a powerful form of classroom management (learners will pay attention if they feel you might ask them a question at any time during the lesson). One of the many ways that trainee teachers can practice this skill is by using Anderson and Krathwohl's (2001) thinking skills. Try this exercise with one of your colleagues on your teacher training course. In pairs each decide upon a favourite topic or hobby you know something about (for example, cooking, photography). Starting at the top of the taxonomy take it in turns to formulate and ask a question that reflects each level of the hierarchy. Do not stop until you have worked your way to the bottom of the taxonomy. Once you have done this repeat the exercise but this time focusing on your own subject discipline – experiment by applying these thinking skills the next time you ask questions in the classroom.

The activity supported by Table 9.2 draws together the work of Gardner (1993) and Anderson and Krathwohl's (2001). Use this template to generate as many teaching ideas as possible and in doing so you will find that you automatically differentiate your lessons for all your learners.

Table 9.2   Activity matrix comparing learning skills and learning styles

	Linguistic	Logical-mathematical	Spatial	Bodily-Kinaesthetic	Musical	Interpersonal	Intrapersonal
Remembering	In pairs match the ...						
Understanding		Identify trends in ...					
Applying			Draw a diagram that ...				Write a short story about ...
Analysing				In this corner of the room I want you to ...			
Evaluating					Compose a song with lyrics that ...		
Creating						Take part in a mini-election in which your party must ...	

Sociocultural theory

Lev Vygotsky (1978) argued that learning is a social and cultural process in which all learning is shaped by the social context (for example, the family, the religion and the classroom). Vygotsky's work centred around the idea that there was a crucial role for culture and language in the development of cognitive abilities. It is through social interactions that we acquire language and, with language comes knowledge of the culture in which we live. His focus on language emphasised how children's discussion should be an essential element in the teacher's repertoire. Two concepts Vygotsky puts forward for teachers to consider are:

- Zone of proximal development (ZPD) – this refers to the zone between what learners' level of development is (their actual level) and the level of development they could reach with suitable teaching (their potential level).
- Scaffolding – the framework that a teacher puts in place to assist the 'learner' to learn.

By recognising a child's ZPD teachers can understand that while two children may be at the same level of learning in a subject, one may be able to achieve far more than the other. This is particularly useful when, for example, we consider children who may only recently have arrived in the country and, in the short term, may be performing below average compared to class mates but, in the longer term, show huge potential.

Cognitive growth

Jerome Bruner's (1960) work develops Vygotsky's interests in the environmental, social, cultural and experiential factors that effect learning. Education is, for Bruner, a function of the particular culture in which it operates. Cognitive growth develops in three stages of representation according to Bruner:

1. Enactive representation – takes place in the early stages of a child's development as they learn through personal action. Learning to crawl, sit up and walk are processes in which the child is learning about the world they inhabit.
2. Iconic representation – children start to understand the world through the use of images, for example, through pictures and diagrams.
3. Symbolic representation – as children move into adolescence they start to engage more with symbols when understanding the world around them, for example, through mathematical symbols. This particular stage of representation emphasises the ability to work at an abstract level of thinking.

The implications of Bruner's theories for teaching rest on the ability of the teacher to match the activity, resources and tools (for example, computers) to the mode of the child. Learner development takes place as children become more skilled in swapping from one mode to the next. In this way, according to Bruner, there is no academic subject that is out of reach of any child – rather the emphasis is on the teacher to make sure that the mode of teaching (whatever the subject) matches that of the child's cognitive developmental stage. Such thinking challenges much of the philosophy behind the British secondary curriculum which rests on the assumption that certain subjects cannot be taught to younger pupils (for example, psychology, physics).

Learning styles

Much has changed in recent years about the way we conceptualise 'learning'. During the 1960s and 1970s learning was viewed as (and compared with) a set of 'computing processes' whereby learners were conceived as 'intelligent systems'. Thankfully, with academic attention being drawn more to the 'emotional' side of teaching and learning, much literature exists about 'models of learning' that provide useful 'prompts' for how one might wish to structure lessons. Many of these 'models' come from work that examines how the brain processes information and how this is related to learning styles.

Frank McNeil (1999) has written extensively about brain research and learning and, quoting research by Goldschmeid and Jackson (1994) he argues that the young brain develops at an astonishing rate in response to streams of information via the senses of touch, smell, taste, hearing, sight and bodily movement. He argues that this illustrates how the young mind can sustain concentration when the learning environment and tasks in hand are very carefully structured with these senses in mind. Developing the theme that a variety of 'stimuli' are required in a successful learning environment, Adey et al. (1999) refer to research into 'right brain/left brain' learning styles. Such research attributes the right-hand side of the brain with non-verbal, holistic, concrete, spatial, creative, intuitive and aesthetic forms of conceptualisation. Left-brain learning styles, it has been claimed, tend to focus around verbal, analytical, abstract, temporal and digital modes of conceptualisation. Though more recently contested, this research does provide a useful checklist for teachers when planning a variety of activities for learners.

In Chapter 5 you were introduced to the work of Kolb (1984). Drawing on his work Dennison and Kirk (1990) refer to a 'Do, Review, Learn, Apply' learning cycle in which an activity is undertaken (Do) by learners who exercise choice in planning their approach. This is followed by a process of reflection and evaluation (Review). Learners monitor their progress and review their learning and planning in terms of goals, strategies, feelings, outcomes and context. As a result a meaning or hypothesis is formed (Learn). New insights and understandings are noted and factors that have influenced progress are identified with new strategies devised for further enquiry. This then allows for the planning of future action (Apply) in light of any new understanding achieved. Honey and Mumford (1986), inspired by the stages of this 'learning circle', suggest that certain learners have 'profiles' that contain a variety of 'styles of learning'. Identifying four such styles they suggest that:

- Activists involve themselves in new experiences and tackle problems by brainstorming.
- Reflectors like to stand back to ponder experiences and observe from many different perspectives.
- Theorists like to analyse and synthesise while focusing on assumptions, principles, theories and models.
- Pragmatists like to try out ideas to see if they work in practice, often taking the first chance to experiment and apply.

Both models suggest that when structuring a lesson, a teacher can call upon some of the concepts above to incorporate the more reflective and evaluative traits that examiners are looking for, particularly in the higher-grade boundaries.

Much has been made in recent years about the success of girls within formal education at the expense of their male counterparts. However, the variety of research that has been carried out throws up often confusing data. For example Botrill and Lock (1993) argue that 13-year-old boys learned significantly better from text-only worksheets than from text-plus-pictures worksheets but for girls of the same age there was no difference. Adey et al. (1999) argue that, while much research has been carried out looking at sex differences and learning styles, nothing conclusive has been found. Nevertheless, our own interpretation of such data certainly now stops me from seating males together in any one group that I teach.

Bandler and Grinder's (1981) work on neurolinguistics programming (NLP) increasingly permeates the language of teaching. Their complex sets of beliefs, skills and behaviours revolve around the notions of 'neuro' referring to what they argue to be a nervous system where experience is received through the five senses, 'linguistic' representing innate verbal and non-verbal language capabilities and 'programming' referring to the ways in which people can be 'trained' to think, speak and act in new ways. The implications for teachers are that learners' internal mental processes (for example, problem-solving, memory and language) consist of representation systems that focus around the:

- visual (that is, what we see);
- auditory (that is, what we hear);
- kinaesthetic (that is, what we feel, touch and how we move);
- olfactory (that is, what we smell);
- gustatory (that is, what we taste).

Bandler and Grinder (1981) argue that our internal sensory representations are constantly being formed and activated. It is therefore the job of the teacher to stimulate each and every one of these systems for successful teaching to take place. In practice, schools and teachers that refer to visual, auditory, kinaesthic ('VAK') tend to use the first three of these systems when creating resources or planning lessons. As a rule of thumb we would argue that good teaching needs to always incorporate 'VAK' elements into every lesson.

M-level thinking: Neuroscience versus learning styles

Many educational programmes claiming to be 'brain-based' have been produced without the involvement of neuroscientific expertise and are rarely evaluated in their effectiveness. To some extent the rapid development of neuroscience and its application to educational theorising is problematic for teaching. There is much in mainstream educational theory that neuroscience challenges from the 'Braingym' and 'Accelerated learning' industries that have flourished in recent years, to the very notion of preferred learning styles. Recent work by Andrew Pollard and the Teaching and Learning Research Programme (TLRP) introduces the theoretical and methodological issues arising within this emerging interdisciplinary field of enquiry. To what extent do you believe that neuroscientific ideas challenge conventional educational theories?

Pedagogy – what's pedagogy?

Pedagogy refers to a science of teaching embodying both curriculum and methodology. Throughout most of Britain the term 'pedagogy' by and large is absent from teacher vocabulary – a fact that would surprise the majority of European teachers who, in most cases, are inculcated with 'educational science' throughout most of their teacher education. European research has also shown that learners with more elaborated conceptions of learning perform better in public examinations at age 16, with lower attainment at that age correlated with perceived pressure from adults and higher attainment positively related to independence, competence and a meaning-orientated approach to learning.

Malcolm Knowles (1980) makes a clear philosophical distinction between the use of the term 'pedagogy' and 'andragogy' when referring to the characteristics and values of teachers and learners. Pedagogy (referring to the teaching of children) implies a dependency on the teacher by the learner. The teacher is cast as a figure of authority who assumes that readiness to learn is uniform by age and curriculum. Knowles argues that this is in stark contrast to andragogy (referring to the teaching of adults). This distinction casts the learner in a far more self-directed and autonomous role. The teacher is viewed as a guide and facilitator in which the readiness to learn is not uniform by age and curriculum but rather develops from tasks and problems put in place by the teacher. While his views on pedagogy have been subject to significant criticisms – we would argue that a combination of his interpretations of both pedagogy and andragogy can be combined when teaching across all age ranges. We also think it is helpful to consider the many roles that a teacher occupies, that is, that of instructor, guide, facilitator and consultant. It is perhaps worth considering that learners might tend to become more dependent on an 'instructor', perhaps more interested in a 'guide', more involved with a 'facilitator' and arguably more self-directed with a 'consultant'.

Critical pedagogy

Two names that are often under-represented within teacher training/education courses in the UK are Henry Giroux and Paulo Freire. Both are associated with critical pedagogy, an area of education that is accorded greater attention and status in much of mainland Europe. Emerging from the ideas associated with the civil rights movements, the Frankfurt School of thinkers in Germany, and the growth of feminism in the 1960s and early 1970s, critical pedagogy encourages a critical stance on knowledge, power and authority at all levels of education. In contrast to many behaviourist notions of teaching, it moves power from the teacher (as instructor and authority figure) to one where power is shared by both learners and teacher. What is taught, when, and how are decisions to be shared by learners and teachers in a classroom viewed as a microcosm of an idealised egalitarian view of society. While critical pedagogy might appear for some not to be relevant to many British classrooms it is, in fact, an approach to teaching and learning that resonates with much current educational policy thinking, for example, pupil/student voice, personalised learning, student-centred teaching, negotiated curriculums and assessment for learning (see Chapter 10).

Towards 'blended learning'?

Whereas we might refer to the teaching methods and activities above as encouraging 'traditional learning' (group work, role play, scaffold support, question-and-answer), learning that takes place through the use of digital technologies is often referred to as 'e-learning'. E-learning might involve the use of the Internet as a research tool or the interactive smart board as a way to encourage learners to manipulate images and text. Today, we even speak of 'e-learning 2.0' to describe the way in which Web 2.0 innovations have and can change learning. By this we mean how instant messaging, social networking, podcasts and so on have changed the ways we can interact with knowledge and how teachers and learners can interact with one another. A fuller discussion of this can be found in Chapter 18.

As a distinctive theory of leaning, many propose that we should seek to 'blend' the traditional and the new – the non-digital and the digital – together. This is seen to maximise the ways we can interact with learners and to motivate learners. It is also seen as a source of differentiation if we can offer different learners a variety of approaches that they can choose from. In this sense, all teaching and learning is 'blended' since most of us choose from the range of theories on offer above and merge many ideas together.

E-learning is seen to offer both synchronous and asynchronous learning opportunities, whereas traditional learning is often seen to be limited to synchronous learning only. What this means is that learning can be at the same time as all other learners – synchronous – or can occur at varying times, whenever the learner chooses to do so – asynchronous. E-learning is often seen to be an 'any time, any place' form of learning and therefore flexible enough to meet the needs of learners.

E-learning often fits into a broader cognitive or constructivist approach since it is seen to offer, if done well, (inter)active engagement, learner choice and flexibility. (This discussion is taken up further in Chapter 18.)

 M-level thinking: Pedagogy before technology!

Beetham and Sharpe (2007) soberly remind us of the importance of 'Pedagogy before technology': in other words, we need to use and blend old and new approaches together for the right reason – namely, that they maximise and aid learning, not simply that they are the most 'modern' and fashionable thing to do. We need to be appropriate and careful in our choices, ensuring that we think of the learning first and the means to obtain it second. Why do you think that some teachers fall into the trap of using technology uncritically? When do you think it is appropriate to use technology in the classroom and when do you think it is not?

Maslow's hierarchy of needs

Maslow's (1987) hierarchy of needs (physiological, safety, love and belonging, self-esteem and self-actualisation) is a motivational theory in psychology that provides a useful evaluation framework for teachers when reviewing and planning the efficacy of their lessons. His theory argues that while people aim to meet basic needs, they seek to meet successively higher needs in the form of a hierarchy. The implication for teachers is that successful learning can only take place if all of Maslow's 'needs' can be fulfilled by the learner. In Chapter 19 we examine the implications for teachers with the arrival in 2008 of the Every Child Matters agenda. It is sufficient here to comment on the fact that, in relation to this agenda, all good teachers (particularly those working in the 14–19 sector) need to take on board to what extent they are aware that their learners fulfil each of Maslow's 'needs'. As tutors and teachers it really helps to cast an eye over Maslow's framework and to ask yourself the question: 'How, as a teacher, can I contribute to each of those needs in my learners'?

A study of the theories and concepts on offer in this chapter will, we hope, sensitise the reader to what she/he may well have forgotten about, never learnt in the first place, or – most importantly – need to be brought to the surface in today's increasingly mixed-ability classroom where the pressures of competition between institutions, performance-related pay and educational funding make demands that previous generations of teachers have not had to face – however well they may have been trained.

Chapter links →

Themes and ideas explored in this chapter link to corresponding ideas in Chapters 12, 14, 17 and 18.

Suggested further reading 📖

Adey, P., Fairbrother, R., William, D., Johnson, B. and Jones, C. (1999) *Learning Styles and Strategies – a Review of Research*. London: King's College.

Howard-Jones, P. (2008) *Neuroscience and Education: Issues and Opportunities*. London: Teaching and Learning Research Programme.

Useful websites

The Creative Learning Centre – www.creativelearningcentre.com/default.asp

Learning Theories knowledgebase – www.learning-theories.com

References

Adey, P., Fairbrother, R., William, D., Johnson, B. and Jones, C. (1999) *Learning Styles and Strategies – a Review of Research*. London: King's College.

Anderson, L.W. and Krathwohl, D. (eds) (2001) *A Taxonomy for Learning, Teaching and Assessing: A Revision of Bloom's Taxonomy of Educational Objectives*. New York: Longman.

Assessment Reform Group (1999) *Assessment for Learning – Beyond the Black Box*. Cambridge: University of Cambridge School of Education.

Bandler, R. and Grinder, J. (1981) *Reframing: Neuro-Linguistic Programming and the Transformation of Meaning*. New York: Real People Press.

Beetham, H. and Sharpe, R. (2007) *Rethinking Pedagogy for a Digital Age: Designing and Delivering e-Learning*. London: Routledge.

Bloom, B. (1956) (ed.) *Taxonomy of Educational Objectives. Handbook 1: Cognitive Domain*. New York: David McKay.

Botrill, J. and Lock, R. (1993) 'Do students learn more from pictures or from text – a pilot study', *School Science Review*, 74: 72–81.

Bruner, J. (1960) *The Process of Education*. Cambridge, MA: Harvard University Press.

Dennison, B. and Kirk, R. (1990) *Do, Review, Learn, Apply: A Simple Guide to Experiential Learning*. Oxford: Blackwell.

Froebel, F. (1900) *Pedagogics of the Kindergarten: The Origins of Nursery Education: The Froebelian Experiment*, History of British Educational Thought.

Gardner, H. (1993) *Frames of Mind: The Theory of Multiple Intelligences*. New York: Basic Books.

Goldschmeid, E. and Jackson, S. (1994) *People under Three*. London: Routledge.

Goleman, D. (1995) *Emotional Intelligence*. New York: Bantham.

Horkheimer, M. (1972) *Critical Theory*. New York: Herder and Herder.

Honey, P. and Mumford, A. (1986) *A Manual of Learning Style*. Maidenhead: Peter Honey.

Knowles, M.S. (1980) *The Modern Practice of Adult Education: Andragogy versus Pedagogy*. Cambridge: Prentice Hall.

Kolb, D.A. (1984) *Experiential Learning: Experience as the Source of Learning and Development*. Englewood Cliffs, NJ: Prentice Hall.

Lewin, K. (1951) *Field Theory in Social Science: Selected Theoretical Papers*. D. Cartwright (ed.). New York: Harper and Row.

Lozanov, G. and Evalina, G. (1988) *The Foreign Language Teacher's Suggestopedic Manual*. New York: Gordon and Breach.

Maslow, A. (1987) *Motivation and Personality*, 3rd edn. New York: Harper and Row.

Montessori, M. (1909) *The Montessori Method – Scientific Pedagogy as Applied to Child Education in 'The Children's Houses'*. New York: Frederick A. Stokes Company.

McNeil, F. (1999) *SIN Research Matters: Brain Research and Learning – an Introduction*. No. 10. London: School Improvement Network.

Pavlov, I.P. (1927) *Conditioned Reflexes,* translated by G.V. Anrep. London: Oxford University Press.

Rogers, C. (1969) *Freedom to Learn*. New York: Macmillan/Merrill.

Skinner, B.F. (1957) *Verbal Behavior*. Englewood Cliffs, NJ: Prentice Hall.

Sale, G. (1998) 'Matrix theory and practice', an Inset given on the application of Gardner's theories in the classroom, 24 August 1998, the Academy Conference and Training Suite.

Thorndyke, E.L. (1911) *Animal Intelligence*. London: Macmillan.

Vygotsky, L.S. (1978) *Mind and Society: The Development of Higher Mental Processes*. Cambridge, MA: Harvard University Press.

Watson, J.B. (1913) 'Psychology as the behaviourist views it', *Psychological Review,* 20: 158–77.

CHAPTER 10

UNDERSTANDING THE ROLE OF ASSESSMENT IN LEARNING

Objectives

By the end of this chapter the reader will be able to:

1. understand what we mean by 'assessment';
2. apply different assessment methods and models to their own practice;
3. apply the 'language of assessment';
4. understand how assessment fits into teaching and lesson planning;
5. see the importance of feedback and assessment as a tool to further motivate learners and to increase learning.

What is assessment?

Assessment means to find out, to judge, to analyse, to ascertain – to find out where your learners are with their learning; to measure and maybe test what they can do and cannot as yet do, and the level to which they are working. Assessment and 'testing' are not necessarily the same thing, and assessment does not have to be formal nor written down. Assessment does not even have to be planned for – you might end up assessing a learner after something surprising has happened! But this chapter deals for the most part with assessment that is accounted for in some way through the lesson planning process.

When we speak of assessment, we usually think of four broad categories into which the assessment tool and practice can fit into:

1. Initial assessment (often called diagnostic assessment). This refers to assessment tasks that occur at the start of a programme or even before enrolment to measure the starting level and needs of the learner, and to sometimes check the appropriateness of the course. Sometimes this type of assessment leads to setting and streaming (see Chapter 2) in classes and sometimes in the setting of predictive grades of achievement.
2. Formative assessment. This type of assessment takes place during the programme of study. It is ongoing, not final. It is used to check progress and to support further development.
3. Summative assessment. This type of assessment usually occurs at the end of the programme of study and is a final measurement of the outcome of the programme being studied. Having said this, it can also provide a 'snapshot' of the progress of the learner at any given point during the course.
4. Ipsative assessment. This usually refers to a process of learner self-assessment; the learner identifies their own position within their learning and assesses their own needs. This assessment method is often about the 'distance travelled' as identified by the learner themselves. It can happen entirely separately from the role or input of a teacher, as well as be supported 'from the side' by a teacher.

Consider the examples in Table 10.1.

Table 10.1   Types of assessment by approach

Diagnostic assessment opportunities	Formative assessment opportunities	Summative assessment opportunities	Ipsative assessment opportunities
• Computer-aided skills tests at enrolment into a new institution • 'Cognitive' diagnostic tests to set benchmark grades • Predictive grades set through previous educational standards	• Regular marked homework • Peer assessment in a lesson • Teachers using question and answer in the class *Note* It is worth noting that feedback to the learner is an essential part of any formative assessment method	• Mid-term tests (to provide a 'snapshot') • Final GCSE exams • Final A-level examinations • Final externally verified and moderated coursework components or portfolio submission • A final performance of a piece in arts curriculum, documented in some way by the institution or visited by an external marker/ assessor	• Learners setting targets as part of action planning • Learners marking their own work and setting targets to improve

It is possible that all these types of assessment can be either formal or informal: Given this, we end up with the positions in Table 10.2. For example, summative assessment is always formal, and ipsative assessment tends to be informal most of the time, but doesn't exclusively have to be.

Table 10.2   Comparisons and contrasts between assessment approaches

	Diagnostic assessment opportunities	Formative assessment opportunities	Summative assessment opportunities	Ipsative assessment opportunities
Formal	Yes (most often)	Yes	Always	Yes
Informal	Yes	Yes	Never	Most usual

Formative and ipsative assessment fits into notions of the 'learning cycle' (as discussed in Chapter 5). According to Kolb (1984), learning is best thought of as a cycle where the learner moves through four distinctive stages:

1. Concrete experience.
2. Reflective observation.
3. Abstract conceptualisation.
4. Active experimentation.

The assessment itself would be the concrete experience – say a test or a piece of homework. The learner then receives feedback from a teacher or peer or self-assesses their own work (we are now at the reflective observation stage), and then sets targets, taking us to the abstract conceptualisation stage. Putting the targets into practice becomes 'active experimentation' and then we are back at the start of the cycle. In this sense, the role of assessment is to move learners forward. The exception to this is summative assessment which is designed to provide a summary (and as such is often used for a measurement of and against national standards).

Formative and ipsative assessments are methods of assessment for learning (to take place), not assessment of learning after it has happened. This phrase 'assessment for learning' is essential in understanding recent national strategies on assessment practices, as discussed later in this chapter.

To our types of assessment models above, we can also add a fifth category, not often thought of:

5. Assessment of prior learning. In many vocational and employability programmes (often work-based provision), assessment of prior learning can be used as a mechanism by which some learners can be 'fast-tracked' through modules and early qualifications.

It is worth noting that assessment of prior learning (APL) is not necessarily the same thing as assessment of prior experiential learning (APEL): APL usually refers to prior learning that has been awarded a qualification or part of a wider qualification – it is 'accredited' by an awarding body allowed to do so; APEL is not formally accredited – there is no previous award – and yet the learner is able to find a way (usually through employment records, testimonials or the building of a portfolio) to demonstrate how their prior experiences are able to compensate for qualifications not officially gained.

Why do we assess?

We need to ask ourselves the questions: why would we assess? What is its purpose?

1. We can assess learners as a means to enrol them onto appropriate courses and programmes of study.
2. Assessment can be a tool to help establish ('diagnose') the needs of a learner.
3. We can assess learners as a measurement of the effectiveness of our own teaching.
4. Assessment can help learners to see where they are with their learning.
5. Assessment provides data that institutions can use to monitor both staff and learners alike.
6. Assessment can provide data that external bodies (LEAs, Ofsted) can use to monitor the provision within institutions.
7. If conducted correctly and sensitively, assessment can motivate learners.
8. Assessment can be used to provide feedback to learners.
9. Assessment can be used to provide feedback to parents.
10. Assessment can be used to establish the 'location' of learners within national qualifications and standards.

As you can see, assessment is a fundamental part of teaching; it ranges from practices within our classrooms (both formal and informal), right up to wider social and even global levels of nationally and internationally recognised qualifications.

 Discussion point

Assessment of learning is vital for the teacher to understand if the aims and objectives of the lesson have been met – and to help 'locate' the skills and needs of the learners for future lesson planning. Some colleagues use the following convention to help them with their lesson planning – they write under objectives:

- By the end of this lesson, all learners will be able to …
- By the end of this lesson, most learners will be able to …
- By the end of this lesson, some learners will be able to …

These are good differentiated learning objectives, but it is only through the assessment of learning that you can understand if these intentions have been fulfilled, or not. Why do you think we place so much emphasis upon learning rather than teaching? What implications might this have for planning?

Norm-referencing and criterion-referencing assessment models

The final outcomes of assessment tasks (the 'results') are often tested against and divided into those that are norm-referenced and those that are criterion-referenced:

- Norm-referencing – marks are allocated on a 'quota' against a notional normal distribution of all learners taking the assessment task. For example, so many learners will get A, so many a B grade, and so on. The learning cohort is banded together and measured against each other – hence the term 'norm'.
- Criterion-referencing – learners are judged against statements of skill or competence – hence the term 'criteria'. Learners are measured against outcomes rather than against each other.

While norm-referencing helps to identity the top and bottom learners who might need very particular aspects of support and challenge to further their learning, this system tells you nothing of the quality of the outcome. For example, the top 20 per cent of learners one year could have 80 per cent of the test result, whereas the next year the top 20 per cent could only have 60 per cent on the same test. And yet, under norm-referencing, each group would receive the same grade as an outcome!

The spirit of the criterion-referenced assessment model is to see testing as a means to reward for skills and work completed, rather than see testing as a competition of learners against each other. At the present time, the UK direction is heading towards criterion-referenced assessment practices for formal summative examinations.

 Discussion point

Many vocational qualifications are based upon the principles of criterion assessment. When faced with this type of assessment, it is absolutely vital that teachers are able to make transparent to learners the criteria under which they are being assessed and to make the criteria themselves understandable. Early lessons in the scheme of work would deal with these criteria for each module or unit – learners might be asked to rewrite them in their own words or explain what they mean verbally. You could make the criteria posters and display them in the teaching room as a constant reminder. Can you see yourself doing this? Are there other means by which you could make assessment criteria clear to learners, and if so, what are they?

Case study: 'Assessment as pantomime'

A number of colleagues of ours when we taught in schools and colleges found it difficult to ensure that all learners completed homework to deadline. If the informal assessment task is not completed, then learner and teacher alike are missing an important part of the picture. On reflection, our colleagues realised that when learners followed a performing arts curriculum their assessment was often partly associated with being physically present to do a performance or to work as a member of a group. This very 'public' assessment (the 'performance') created a challenge that most of the young people lived up to. We thought about how we could re-create these conditions in our own classes – how to make assessment and homework a public 'pantomime' as a means to ensure it gets done? A number of colleagues experimented with learner presentations, Viva questions and answers and public quizzes, with considerable success. When the assessment tool became a performance and was staged so that it was not possible to hide in the background, the learners completed all the work on time. This was only possible with sensitive handling and appropriate teacher support, but illustrates that public and performance assessment methods work and motivate learners as long as the challenge is not too great.

Predictions and benchmarks

There is a considerable movement within both schools and colleges to the setting of predictive grades following a diagnostic process. Often this process takes into consideration objectively measured and awarded qualifications and 'national levels' achieved in previous education, and in doing so can occur separately from the individual leaner having any involvement in the process.

Learners are set a 'predicted' or 'aspirational' grade and then their learning is measured against this outcome. The language of this is slippery, but the following three types of prediction apply:

- Predicted grade – what a teacher thinks a learner will get from a test.
- Aspirational grade – what a learner is working towards as a tool for motivation and challenge.
- Minimum target grade – (norm-referenced against other UK cohorts) this is the lowest expected of a learner, based upon a sample of previous learners with the same pattern of previous educational performance.

A criticism of some of these measurements is that, alone, they say little about what we refer to as the 'added value' of the institution. What we mean by this is the distance that learning goes through as it changes and improves. For example, learners might obtain a grade D in an examination, and this may be a massive achievement and demonstrative of a huge improvement in relation to what their past assessment might have indicated. For example, ESOL learners or newly migrated learners might need to work considerably harder to achieve similar results as other learners and their starting points need to be taken into consideration. The Office for Standards in Education takes 'value added' scores into consideration as part of the process whereby institutions have their practice and provision inspected. This illustrates an important point about the role of assessment – all assessment is only meaningful in relation to the groups of learners producing the learning outcomes being assessed. Assessment does not exist in a vacuum, somehow separate from other aspects of teaching and learning.

Speaking the language of assessment

When looking at the issue of assessment, a number of specialist terms and ideas are often used, as summarised and defined below:

- assessment tool – the physical resource that the assessment is produced on (that is, the examination paper);
- assessment practice/method – the technique or tool you are using in general terms (that is, writing an essay);
- assessment object – the work produced by the learner under the scrutiny of the assessment;
- assessment task – the precise tool and instructions the learner works to;
- assessment procedure – the steps and stages that setting-up, administrating and marking the assessment involves;
- outcome – the work to be assessed, produced by the learner at the end of the set task;
- feedback – what the assessor or teacher/tutor makes clear to the learner about their learning and how this takes place (could be written and/or verbal);
- high risk – assessment that has stakes that are deemed important and may be a once-only chance to perform;
- low risk – an assessment not deemed to have important stakes or seen to have little significant consequences or with many more chances to repeat the same practice.

A risky business?

The relationship of assessment to 'risk' is an important but sometimes neglected issue. Low-risk assessments might result in some learners not bothering and thus underperforming; while high-risk assessments might worry learners and cause stress and anxiety – also resulting in an underperformance. Having said this, on some occasions, high-risk assessment (with adequate preparation/support) can be highly motivating – many learners like to rise to a challenge.

M-level thinking: The 'burden of assessment'?

Many political criticisms of recent educational legislation and curriculum change – most notably in the wake of the developments known as 'Curriculum 2000' (see Chapter 2) – have attacked the UK education system for a 'burden of assessment'. The view is that too frequent examinations and tests with 'high stakes' lead to demotivated learners and such assessment actually stops the very learning taking place that it is supposed to be measuring. How might we, as classroom teachers, avoid the burden of assessment while at the same time be rigorous in our support of learners?

Principles of assessment

We can identify the following eight principles that all assessment needs to adhere to. All assessment needs to be:

1. Valid – it assesses what it is supposed to, and what you think it does.
2. Reliable – can the assessment and its judgement be repeated by another marker under the same conditions with the same result?
3. Adequate/sufficient – enough to get the data needed to tell you what you wish to know.
4. Fair – be possible given the teaching and support on offer.
5. Appropriate – linked to the skills needed for the actual programme of study.
6. Current – the learning behind the assessment outcome is not out of date.
7. Authentic – we need to know that the work being assessed is the product of the learner submitting it.
8. Transparent – those being assessed need to understand what they are being asked to do and why.

Where does assessment 'fit-in'?

Assessment is a fundamental part of the interplay between teaching and learning:

- You will be asked, during your training on lesson plans, how you assess the learning that takes place in the teaching session.
- You will only know if you (and your learners) have achieved the aims and objectives of the lesson if you assess learning against them (see Chapter 13).
- Schemes of work frequently ask teachers to record assessment methods and show how they develop and feed back into the teaching over a period of time (see Chapter 13).

- Teachers are recommended to start lessons with an assessment of prior learning from previous lessons – showing how the current lesson fits into a series.
- Teaching resources and activities can themselves also be assessment tools at the same time.
- Teachers often end lessons asking learners themselves to assess their own learning.
- Some teachers end lessons asking learners to assess the teaching – as a means to establish if the routines and schemes of work need to be updated for the ever-changing needs of the group.

'Subjective assessment'?

National tests, criterion-referenced assessment practices, summative assessment and final examinations are all seen to be relatively 'objective' forms of assessment: in other words, the standard is measurable and in some way moderated between teams of assessors. Given this, it is 'reliable'.

There is, however, a role that highly open and subjective assessment can play in the stimulation and motivation of learners. Open-ended tasks can be set for formative and ipsative assessment of learners where no norm-referencing would be possible since the outcome would be unique to the learner. For many learners, this freer/open type of assessment would be risky without support and an adequate rationale provided by the teacher, but under these conditions, might stretch and challenge learners.

Target setting

Many teaching colleagues adopt the SMART technique for action planning with their learners. This method provides learners with action points arising out of the assessment method used:

S = specific
M = measureable
A = attainable
R = realistic
T = time-framed.

No matter precisely how you provide feedback to learners and help them to target-set, it is recognised that formative assessment has missed the point if some sort of action planning or target-setting is not available. This is the core message of the 'assessment for learning' movement, as outlined below.

Techniques of assessment

There is a wide and complex range of methods and activities you can use to assess the learning of your learners. Some subject-specific pedagogies lend themselves to particular sorts of assessment methods more than others, but the rich variety of those on offer does mean that you are able, as a teacher, to adopt unusual and varied routines and really challenge, stretch and motivate learners. Of course, you need to prepare your learners for the nature of the summative assessment and replicate its rules and conditions. But along the way, have fun! Use a variety of appropriate formative assessment techniques to inspire and stimulate.

You could choose from these in Table 10.3, presented here as a guide, not an exhaustive list.

Table 10.3   The variety of assessment methods and tools

- Examination
- 'Mock examinations'
- 'Seen' examination papers pre-released before the examination date
- Essays
- Short answer questions
- Stimulus response questions
- Being observed
- Witness statements and testimonials of skills demonstrated
- Posters
- Practicals
- Performance
- Wiki chat
- Blog contributions
- Multiple choice questions
- Learner presentation
- Case study evaluations
- Report writing
- Making a project
- Keeping a diary or journal
- Discussing in groups and keeping minutes of the learning taking place
- Question and answer 'vivas'
- Interviews
- Building a portfolio
- Role-playing
- Learner produced 'movies'
- Exhibitions
- Learner produced podcasts (see Chapter 18)

Assessment for learning

Broadly speaking, all the goals of assessment come down to four key factors:

1. Assessment for national standards (gaining and giving qualifications).
2. Assessment for selection (into institutions, programmes, sets within institutions).
3. Assessment for the diagnosis of need (as a means to provide adequate and appropriate support).

And finally,

4. Assessment for learning.

The first three broad categories above (national standards, selection, diagnosis) are assessment of learning, rather than assessment for learning. This phrase, assessment for learning, has its origins in the research *Inside the Black Box* by Black and Wiliam (1998). In this research report, they pose some essential principles for assessment to help raise the quality and effectiveness of learning, rather than simply being used as a tool to measure final outcomes.

Inside the black box

1. Feedback should offer practical and concrete solutions for improvement.
2. Feedback should be precise and not vague.
3. Learners should not be compared together.
4. Learners should regularly self-assess to understand where they are with their learning.
5. Learners should have the opportunity to express their own understandings of their learning and their progression.
6. Feedback must make it clear how the same piece of work could be improved if it was to be completed a second time.

Based upon Black and Wiliam (1998).

The conclusion of Black and Wiliam is that regular formative assessment is a very powerful 'effect factor' in raising standards, and yet assessment practices themselves are often little understood by teachers and one of the least focused upon areas of teaching. And yet it can have one of the greatest impacts.

Feedback or feedforward?

Following the *Black Box* report of Black and Wiliam, it is claimed that learning and motivation for learning can be increased through the adoption of a 'medal and mission' approach to assessment and feedback.

1. Medal – show what is positive about the work (the 'reward').
2. Mission – set targets for future learning (the 'next steps').

In this sense, the assessment leads to 'feedforward' not feedback, since it is future-looking. Feedback is positive – helping learners to see where to improve.

 Discussion point

Although the 'medal and mission' approach is presently linked to notions of learner ownership of their own learning, previously this approach has been more closely associated with behaviourist techniques of reward and reinforcement (see Chapter 9). How do you think the use of rewards might motivate learners? Do you agree with this approach?

This approach has led some colleagues and institutions to experiment with not giving work grades, or at least, with the 'withholding' of grades until after the learners have self-evaluated and reflected, so as not to distract them from the process.

The Assessment Reform Group (2002) has suggested some key principles to follow when using assessment and testing to motivate learning, as we illustrate below:

Teachers should try to:

1. Allow for, and accommodate, as much learner choice as possible.
2. Encourage learners to take responsibility.
3. Always illustrate the purpose of the learning – show how it fits in.
4. Connect learning to previous and future learning.
5. Frame feedback in such a way that learners are clear what to do next and why.
6. Support all learners to work collaboratively.

Teachers should either avoid completely or at least do less of:

1. Focusing on testing learning rather than on learning itself.
2. 'Drilling' learners to get 'right answers' without actually understanding why such answers are 'right'.
3. Allowing learners to think that their success is based upon the grades they receive from assessment tasks.
4. Allowing too much competition between learners through assessed and tested tasks.

Traffic lights

Many teachers of younger learners are adopting a 'traffic light' approach to learner self-assessment and feedback: learners grade work or lessons according to red for difficult, amber for moderately OK, and green for easy. This is a relatively unconfrontational and unimposing way to develop the learner voice into your teaching.

The 14–19 agenda and assessment reform

In tandem with the policy Every Child Matters (see Chapter 19), the February 2005 White Paper *14–19 Education and Skills* (HMSO, 2005) identifies 'rigorous assessment in which all can have confidence' as a key aspect of 14–19 reform. The reform of assessment for this age range focuses upon the following:

- creation of a new national 'bank' of optional Key Stage 3 tests;
- reduction of coursework at GCSE;

- reduce summative assessment in each A-level qualification from six to four assessments;
- investment in national continuing professional development programmes aimed at in-service qualified teachers to improve and develop their assessment skills;
- a commitment to value e-assessment opportunities as a valid form of assessment.

Under the tenets of the Every Child Matters legislation, the need for teacher record-keeping of assessment and the transparency of this information to both the learner and his/her parents is essential. In addition we are seeing the construction of a national assessment database that will follow learners around from institution to institution and track their progress. This means that, unlike ever before, assessment is now a powerful political issue as well as a powerful pedagogic issue.

Record-keeping and organising your mark book

With the sophistication of computer programmes and computer-based assessment tracking, 'why oh why' we hear you ask, should you keep an old fashioned 'mark book'. As you pick up more and more hours throughout the year as well as attending parents' evenings, departmental meetings and so on, you will quickly realise that it is not always possible to be able to jump onto a computer and give people the information you, or they, require. Remember, too, that when you become a qualified teacher, you will, within a matter of weeks, have your first parents' evening with perhaps 200 or more learners whose parents expect you to give them quality feedback about their offspring. Your mark book is also invaluable for those priceless 30-second corridor conversations with other members of staff about learner X as you hurry between classes.

The categories in Table 10.4 are suggestions for the sorts of data you might want to keep in light of the ideas discussed in this chapter.

Try to think of ways to ease the recording burden. Try to invent some sort of coding or short-hand system, for example, in the homework sections you could colour code homework with red (not done); orange (unfinished); pink (work not in book); blue (book/work not seen). For the 'hands up' column you could enter a dot every time a particular learner puts his/her hand up in your class. By creating these categories you will 'open your eyes' to all sorts of assessment related issues that you might otherwise have missed and more importantly develop a deep seated and invaluable knowledge base about your learners.

Think assessment, think motivation, think feedback!

When we first think about assessment, we might be tempted to think rather narrowly about testing or simply 'marking' work. As this chapter has shown you, assessment is

Table 10.4   Possible data for record-keeping in teacher mark books

Useful data to keep in your mark book

Name/gender/ethnicity	Address/contact number	Year/house/tutor
Uniform/PE Kit etc.	Attendance – lateness	Detentions/referrals
Credits/merits/ prizes etc.	HOD/HOY report/referral	Homework (mark/targets etc.)
SEN/EAL/G&T	Reading age/spelling age	KS2/3 CAT/SAT scores
Target/assessment levels	Traffic lights/understanding	Mood/personality
Medical history/records	Learning support unit	Learning mentor
Contact – outside agencies	Concerns	Aspirational grade
End of topic tests	End of year results	Current level of achievement
Behaviour	Key/functional skills	Parental contact numbers etc.
Who/how well at questions	'Hands up' column	Targets set
Form/tutor group	Learning style	Cause for concern
Dyslexia/dyspraxia (needs)	Contributions in lessons	Date of birth
UCAS statement (versions)	Candidate number for examinations	Learners designated an LSA
Name/email of LSA	A 'forget list' (e.g. pen, tie)	Effort/motivation
Seen guardian/parents eve	This week's star learner	Siblings in school
Loss of merit/suspension	Personal reminders/follow up	Staff/departmental meetings
Examination/test dates	Coursework (dates/grades)	Lunch-time activities
After-school activities	Exercise book/folder check	Study support attendance
Diploma pathway	Work experience	Hobbies
Languages spoken	Level/rate of improvement	P/time job

vital for learning and can also raise motivation – which in turn is also vital for learning. The core message here is that assessment without adequate feedback at best leaves learners in the dark about their learning and, at worst, is so unmotivating it puts learners off learning. Get the feedback right however, and you will develop amazing relationships with your learners which will in turn result in some inspirational classroom sessions.

Chapter links →

Themes and ideas explored in this chapter link to corresponding ideas in Chapters 13, 14 and 17.

Suggested further reading

Black, P. and Wiliam, D. (1998) *Inside the Black Box: Raising Standards through Classroom Assessment.* London: NferNelson.

References

Assessment Reform Group (1999) *Assessment for Learning: Beyond the Black Box*. Cambridge: University of Cambridge School of Education.

Black, P. and Wiliam, D. (1998) *Inside the Black Box: Raising Standards through Classroom Assessment*. London: NferNelson.

Her Majesty's Stationery Office (HMSO) (2005) *14–19 Education and Skills*. London: HMSO.

Kolb, D.A. (1984) *Experiential Learning Experience as a Source of Learning and Development*. Englewood Cliffs, NJ: Prentice Hall.

CHAPTER 11

BEHAVIOUR AND CLASSROOM MANAGEMENT IN SCHOOLS AND COLLEGES

Objectives

By the end of this chapter the reader will able to:

1. understand the importance of the distinction between classroom management and behaviour management;
2. understand the significance of good communication skills in classroom management;
3. recognise the role of classroom layout in the management of behaviour;
4. appreciate how Behaviour for Learning (B4L) informs many successful classroom management strategies;
5. emphasise the role that relationships play in the management of classroom behaviour.

Behaviour management or classroom management?

For many practitioners 'behaviour management' is a pejorative term, that is, it treats active learners as passive objects using behavioural strategies. We favour the term 'classroom management' since it speaks more of the creation of a learning atmosphere and ethos. A factor that worries many trainee teachers at the start of their training period in schools is whether or not they can manage behaviour. We would, from the outset, argue that most challenging behaviour for trainee teachers can be eradicated by good classroom management, that is, planning, enthusiastic and knowledgeable teaching, and lessons that stretch the intellectual abilities of all learners in your classes. Get that right and there will be little reason for students to text, chatter or put on their make-up in any of your classes.

Summary: what's in a name?

'Behaviour management' – refers to the ability of the classroom teacher and the wider institution to manage, control, and set the behavioural outcomes of the learners. This is usually through behaviourist techniques (see Chapter 9), and usually due to reward, sanctions and environment manipulation.

'Classroom management' – sees the management of learner's behaviour as part of the wider project of the management of the learning process overall. In this view behaviour management is a by-product of the creation of a learning atmosphere in your classroom and wider institution.

This chapter does not deal with the sorts of extreme behaviour (for example, violence, bullying, drug taking) associated with 'social, emotional and behavioural difficulties' (SEBD). These examples of special educational needs as described in the Code of Practice (DfES, 2001) can and should be explored on your particular training course. In this chapter we deal with two of the most common categories of problematic behaviour that trainee teachers have to deal with:

- non-disruptive behaviour, for example, combing hair, staring out of the window, mobile phone texting under the desk, doodling on textbooks;
- low-level disruptive behaviour, for example, off-task chatter, late arrival to your class, throwing of items across the classroom.

We would argue that both forms of behaviour are, in most cases, useful indicators for you in terms of assessing to what extent you have planned and delivered the lesson to meet the learning needs of all learners in the class. In other words, our starting point for this chapter is that if poor behaviour exists it is probably caused by your teaching rather than the learners in your classes.

There are two ways to think about the relationship between classroom management and behavioural management. First, we can see them as separate but overlapping aspects of teaching (Figure 11.1).

The second approach – favoured by our work in this book – is to see behaviour management as a subset of a more general classroom management approach (Figure 11.2).

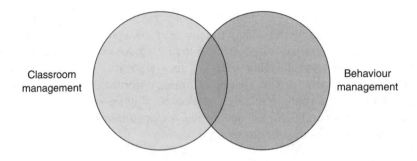

Figure 11.1   The interconnection between classroom and behaviour management: view 1

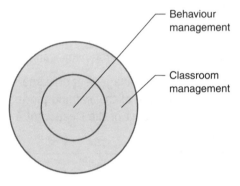

Figure 11.2   The interconnection between classroom and behaviour management: view 2

In this second approach, the management of good teaching and learning takes priority, along with a key emphasis upon the establishment of an effective learning atmosphere and positive relationships. This emphasis on relationships and ethos is sometimes also referred to as a 'Behaviour for Learning' approach.

Behaviour for Learning

What is 'Behaviour for Learning'?

An emphasis on positive relationships between teachers and learners and among students themselves lies at the heart of Behaviour for Learning approaches. According to these approaches, three sets of relationships underpin all learning behaviour:

1. Relationship with self: students who do not feel confident as learners and believe they are unable to succeed are more likely to engage in challenging behaviour.
2. Relationship with others: behaviour by students is not only triggered by factors internal to the learner but by interactions with other learners, teachers, and a range of professionals working in the school/college.
3. Relationship with the curriculum: behaviour and what is being taught are intertwined. Positive behaviour is contingent on the belief by learners that what is being taught is important and accessible to them.

Underpinning the 'Behaviour for Learning' approach is a commitment by the teacher to establish positive relationships and a learning climate that enthuses and supports all learners. Child (2004) argues that unacceptable behaviour is likely to be minimised when the teacher:

- personalises learning for each student identifying the most appropriate learning style;
- challenges and supports learners by planning activities with content that is intellectually stimulating, interesting and pitched at the correct level;
- monitors, recognises and rewards progress based on a range of well-developed assessment strategies.

Building good relationships

Classrooms should be warm, inviting spaces that learners wish to come into. Remember that your classroom can offer both the boundaries and the sanctuary that many students lack in their private lives. This places significant importance on the ways in which you forge relationships with your learners, both inside and outside the classroom.

One essential component in your communication skills will be the skilful way that you deploy praise. When used by successful teachers, it can be a powerful method of behaviour management signalling to the class the high expectations and outcomes that you have of them. Child (2004) argues that praise should be:

- personal – that is, targeted at the named person or group for whom that praise is deserved;
- specific – that is, targeted at the specific task/achievement/attainment, for example, 'well done Shamima for finishing question 5 so quickly'.
- genuine – that is, it must be sparingly used and only for those actions that you are genuinely pleased with – regular/over use will devalue its effectiveness as a behavioural management strategy.

Marland (1993) stresses how important it is for learners to see the more sociable, friendly you outside the classroom and how it is OK for this to contrast with the more 'formal' you in the classroom. At first glace this might appear inconsistent but Marland's point is that you will gain significant respect from your learners if you can successfully juggle these two elements to your professional identity and that, in doing so, your ability to manage classroom behaviour will improve significantly.

This requires significant 'backbreaking work' in your first few weeks in any new placement (especially when some of your colleagues are relaxing in the staff room at break or lunch time). In the long run, however, you will gain respect and your classroom management skills will improve significantly. We would advise you in your first few weeks in school/college placements to:

- See break/lunch times as opportunities to talk to learners in corridors, playgrounds, canteens, and so on. Stop and exchange a word or two in the corridor with any learners you teach – show them that the 'formal' you in the classroom can be offset by a more informal you that is friendly and interested in them (for example, their music, their sport, etc.).
- When walking from one part of the school/college to another, occasionally take the longer route to get a sense of who is where so that you maximise opportunities for these informal sorts of conversations. Not only will this convey confidence to learners you engage with but you will also pick up invaluable information about which peer groups your students hang around with – vital information for you as an emerging professional.
- Take any opportunity you have to do trips/excursions with your learners. While these can almost certainly be exhausting, they are also a fantastic opportunity for you to bond with learners and for them to see this all-important other side to your professional persona.
- Remember that the class that you might be taking over next term/year might also be the group of learners hanging around in a part of the building you do not normally frequent. The friendly sets of exchanges that you have with students now in those remote parts of the institution will pay dividends when you take over that same class later in the year.
- If, on one of these forays around the building you witness behaviour that is unacceptable (for example, fighting, smoking on site) do not walk away from this but, rather, (preferably with a smile) engage those learners involved – deal with the matter firmly and immediately send a student to get help. Walking away or turning a blind eye will ultimately harm your credibility with your learners.
- Never hold grudges. That means, for example, that if you have to authoritatively reprimand a student during one of your lessons and you see that student a couple of hours later in the corridor, greet them warmly. Let them see that your reprimand is to do with their learning and not their personalities.

Good communication and its role in classroom management

In many respects good teaching is about good communication and this is also true for good behavioural management.

- Avoid instructions where you change the instruction halfway through.
- Ensure that you 'count down' to when tasks start and end so learners know where they are at any one time.
- Encourage learners to express your instructions in their own language to check they have really understood.
- Do not give out materials unless you want them used immediately.
- Keep instructions brief.
- Do not make rhetoric questions.
- Back-up verbal instructions with written instructions so learners can remind themselves if needed.
- As the class gets louder you might want to try getting more quiet, forcing your learners to listen to you.
- Do not allow yourself to get distracted by questions or other derailing behaviour in the middle of an instruction or explanation.
- Always insist on being the only voice speaking if addressing the whole class – simply pausing often works.

Keeping these simple communication rules in mind will help you to avoid some aspects of undesired and off-task behaviours before they even begin.

Classroom layout

 Discussion point

Remember the colourful, vibrant and exciting spaces that primary classrooms are? Now contrast this to many secondary school classrooms and ask which sort of environment would you rather walk into. How would you like your ideal classroom to look?

The professional layout of the room should convey the very same professional values that you communicate to your learners. As such it is a vital tool in the repertoire of classroom management strategies. Learners should feel that when they walk into your room from break or another lesson, they are walking into a professional environment created by you to inspire them to learn (and therefore not to misbehave). This means that you should ensure that in every lesson:

- Any wall/ceiling displays and so on always look presentable (for example, carry some extra Blu-Tack with you to make sure no posters are hanging lopsidedly).
- If there are any plants in the room they are watered and healthy looking (nominate students to water the plants). If no such plants exist, buy some!
- Check where the teacher's desk is. All too often these are located at the front of the class and take up valuable classroom space (often encouraging the teacher to stand – or sit – at the front of the class instead of moving around). If you do not need the desk, move it! Slide it to the side of a wall/under smart board etc and see how much extra space you have created. This in turn frees up more space for you to experiment with new seating arrangements.
- Scan the room before any lesson starts and get rid of any bottles, crisp packets or rubbish on the floors – treat the room as if it were your sitting room and you were awaiting 'guests'.
- Note any broken cupboard doors, non-functioning blinds and so on, and notify the appropriate technicians.
- Note where resources are (books, pens, and so on) and make sure these are displayed neatly and professionally (items can be colour coded, labelled, and bookends can be bought etc.).
- Any resources prepared or used by you (for example, worksheets) look professional (no excuse not to with the ease of desktop publishing) – if possible, photocopy all resources on different coloured paper.
- Make sure that chairs/tables are not scattered around haphazardly but are ordered and are in a layout 'fit for purpose' (that is, if today's lesson revolves around paired work, then make sure tables are arranged accordingly). Ensure learners leave the room in the some state they found it in.
- Whiteboards, flip charts and so on should not have any writing left over from a previous lesson. Wipe boards clean and discard old flip-chart paper.
- Periodically get rid of any broken furniture, empty boxes, old books and so on.
- Try to ensure that you have a music player. Experiment with different types of music that you can have playing gently in the background as learners enter your classes. At first learners might find this strange but will appreciate the calming effect this can create on entry to your class.
- If you have both smart board/whiteboard and flip chart, use them! Have the flip chart at the opposite side of the room to where the board is so that you can move across the class and refocus learners on a different activity – this will provide added dynamism and energy as well as keep learners on their toes (and stop them from texting).
- Change display boards frequently and display learners' work – let them feel that you are proud of their accomplishments, for example, Best Homework of the Week.
- Make displays relevant and use them. Have subject key words displayed around the room and refer to them during your lessons (starter activities can be as simple as memorising 10 key words on your displays in 30 seconds).
- Display artefacts, posters and so on that relate either to your own subject or, indeed, to your own life. These sorts of personal touches will mark your classroom out as a special place of learning and caring, and will help you gain the respect of your students.

We fully realise that in many cases you will not be lucky enough to have a 'base room' in which your classroom teaching takes place all the time. However, if you are in this fortunate position, the care, imagination and fun that you instil in the way you decorate and arrange your classroom will (if not necessarily voiced) be appreciated by your learners. Whether you have a base room or not, there should be a 'wow' factor every time learners come into your class (however small that 'wow' is). But always remember to ask permission first before you move anything in someone else's classroom.

Seating arrangements

We present here five ways that you can organise your classroom to maximise management and minimise learners being able to distract each other and hide from view while being off task. The seating arrangements are based upon the following principles:

1. The teacher needs to be able to make eye contact with all learners.
2. The teacher should be able to move freely around the room – allowing the ability to move closer to all learners as needed.
3. Seating is 'fit for purpose', that is, it matches the activities that the teacher has planned for the lesson.

1 Horseshoe teaching shape

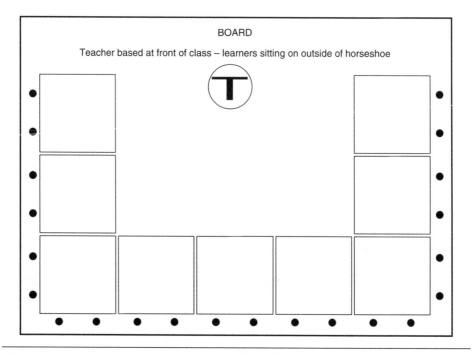

Figure 11.3   Arrangement 1: horseshoe teaching shape

Description

Arrange the desks and chairs as a large U shape facing the front of the classroom (Figure 11.3). Position yourself front and middle. All learners can see you, and they can see each other.

How does it help?

- This allows the teacher to remain as the central focus in the classroom, yet at the same time does also allow discussion between peers since most learners can see each other.
- The teacher can move around the group very easily, getting closer to learners for either support or behavioural management reasons.
- Learners can easily work in pairs.
- Some learners can move chairs to the inner side of the U shape with relatively little disruption thereby creating smaller 'groups' as needed.

Things to think about

1. You could create a seating plan ensuring that learners sit where you wish them to.
2. Prevent learners who habitually communicate off task from sitting opposite each other on the U shape – this might create even more disruption due to calling out.
3. It might be a good idea to position learners to talk to each other on the same rows – it is harder for them to make eye contact then.
4. Make sure you are moving into the shape as much as possible. Never simply stand or sit in one place.
5. If you are speaking to learners, simply kneeling down opposite them often creates the right message in terms of lowering yourself to their height.

2 Group work formations – diamonds

Description

Arrange the tables in diagonal formations of four learners but with the seating placed so that all learners can see the board and the teacher (Figure 11.4).

How does it help?

- This enables all learners to see the board as and when required but also facilitates group-based discussion.
- The teacher can move around the class easily circulating from group to group.
- This seating arrangement enables more advanced group-based strategies where learners are required to move from one table to another.

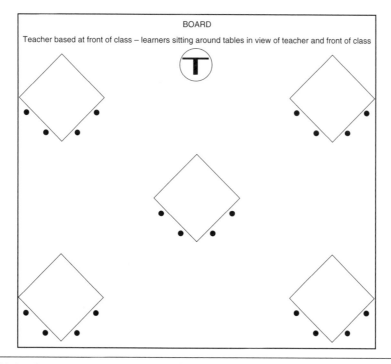

Figure 11.4   Arrangement 2: group work formation – diamonds

Things to think about

1. Carefully consider how each group is 'made up', for example, mixed ability, mixed gender.
2. If you are not actually using the teacher's desk, then move it. Slide it to the side so that you can free up much needed space.
3. Leave sufficient space between the tables and chairs to enable easy movement for both teacher and learners (particularly important if using 'ambassador' or 'jigsaw' strategies (see Chapter 16).

3 Group work formation – squares

Description

Arrange the tables in formations of four learners but with the tables flush against the wall. Space needs to be made between each grouping so that the teacher can move between each group. If required additional tables can be placed in centre of classroom (Figure 11.5).

How does it help?

- By pushing the tables against the walls this seating arrangement creates a surprisingly large amount of space often not realised in many classrooms.

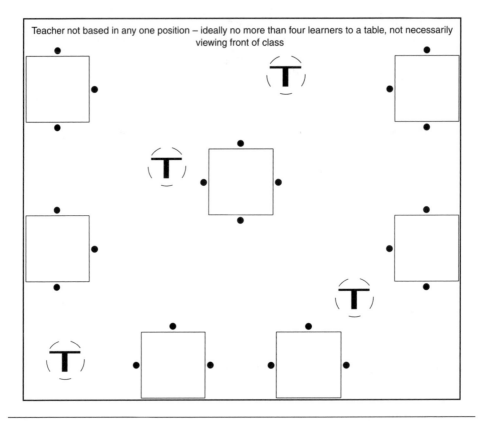

Figure 11.5   Arrangement 3: group work formation – squares

- Not only can the teacher move around the class easily, circulating from group to group but she/he can place themselves between groups. This is ideal when managing more advanced group-based strategies.
- The gaps between the tables are also invaluable when using questioning strategies, allowing the teacher to move easily from one part of the classroom to the next and 'firing' questions at groups or individuals.

Things to think about

1. Carefully consider how each group is 'made up' that is, mixed ability, mixed gender and so on.
2. This seating strategy is best used when minimum board work is required (you can always ask learners to shift their positions as and when the board is required).
3. Make sure that you ask permission from colleagues before you move the tables and, of course, put the classroom back into its original state at the end of the lesson (as you gain confidence you can ask learners to help you do this).

4 Circle seating with breakout tables for group work

Description

Arrange the chairs only at the front of the space in a large circle. At the same time, in the same room, have some tables arranged for group work, thereby creating two distinctive spaces within one classroom (Figure 11.6).

How does it help?

- This allows the teacher to remain a part of the group for opening dialogue and discussion where everyone sits together.
- The start of the lesson can take place in the circle, as could the plenary.
- Learners can move to the tables to do tasks, returning to the circle at the front for feedback, discussion and so on.

Things to think about

1. The discussion circle at the front should give the start to the lesson a calm feel.
2. This routine works well if learners need to listen to each other and receive feedback.
3. You might need to carefully manage the transition between the spaces to avoid disruption.

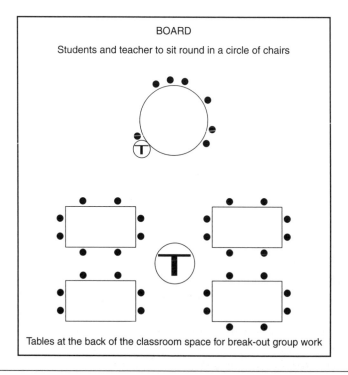

Figure 11.6   Arrangement 4: circle seating with break-out tables for group work

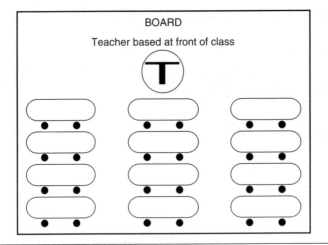

Figure 11.7   Arrangement 5: students sitting in pairs

5 Students sitting in pairs

Description

Tables and chairs are arranged in pairs (Figure 11.7). Remember to make sure that you can walk in between pairs (all too often 'pairs' in many classrooms are substituted for 'rows' restricting the ability for the teacher to move in between learners).

How does it help?

- This seating strategy is excellent for targeted paired work if that is the main strategy you are adopting in your lesson.
- This strategy can be really useful when taking over new classes where behaviour management is an issue. Make sure that the paired arrangements are really paired, that is, that sufficient space is made between tables to restrict inter-table 'banter'.

Things to think about

1. This strategy assumes that the teacher will be 'based' at the front of the class, however we argue in this book that you should be fully mobile. Make sure that you can get to anywhere in the classroom easily and do not let the seating 'dictate' your body position.
2. Think carefully about how the pairs are made up (ability, gender and so on) and which pairs are located where (for example, if behaviour is an issue with student 'x' then make sure student 'x' is seating near the front).

Body posture and voice control

Many trainee teachers are unaware of how important body posture and voice are in managing classroom behaviour. This is understandable particularly when you are experiencing classroom observations by other members of staff or your university mentor. One of the most useful things that you can do during your training is to audio-record (or, even, better, film) one of your lessons. This will very quickly highlight the myriad of mannerisms that we often deploy unbeknown to us as teachers (for example, 'shhhh's; 'do you know what I mean'; 'ermm'). As an exercise, record/film one of your lessons. When reviewing the recording carefully analyse it for the following:

* Your speed of talking.
* The time you allow learners to respond to your questions.
* The frequency that you speak (think of this as a ratio between the amount of time you speak in any lesson compared with the time you allow learners to speak).
* Study carefully your voice for volume, pitch and tone.
* In relation to both pitch and tone, study carefully the way you emphasise and inflect certain words/phrases (this is particularly important when issuing instructions).
* If you are watching a film of your teaching, pay attention to where you stand during the lesson and how often you move around the class.
* Examine your body posture to eliminate non-desirable body positions (for example, arms folded, hands on hips).
* Focus on your facial expressions. These can be a powerful behaviour management tool (for example, encouraging looks for confidence building during a question and answer session, stern looks to certain learners not on task).
* Mannerisms (for example, the flicking of hair, overuse of fingers on lips).

You can also use the above checklist as an observation schedule for one of your formal or informal observations by your colleagues in the school/college placement.

The 'dos' ✓

We cannot stress enough that tips alone will not be sufficient to ensure that you have superbly behaved learners. What will ensure this will be lessons that are planned by you containing dynamic and well-paced activities in which all students feel that they have clearly defined yet challenging tasks. We hope the following tips prove useful as you master the art of planning engaging lessons:

* Make sure that learners have something to do when they arrive in your classroom (for example, sorting activity on desks as they arrive, quiz, true/false).
* Learn students' names as quickly as you can. Not only will this speed up the respect learners have for you, but it will also rapidly accelerate the efficiency of classroom management.

- Start lessons on time and make sure that the first activity is important to the aims of the lesson (registers and copying down aims are what most learners are used to and bored with – so make sure they feel they must rush to your lesson for something worthwhile and new).
- From your very first lesson with a new class, get learners used to you moving among them and moving them around (for example, dynamic group work). Do not wait until week 3. This will eradicate the 'I don't want to sit with her' syndrome that many teachers face. If moving students quickly becomes an established part of your 'repertoire' they will respond quickly and efficiently to your requests for them to move in any group-based learning activity.
- If certain students are problematic working together, move them.
- If you teach mixed gender classes get boys to sit with girls. Remember that statistically girls outperform boys in mainstream education, so use this factor to raise male aspiration and expectation of the workload you wish them to engage with.
- Keep instructions short and simple, and never more than one instruction at a time.
- Issue instructions with a timed target, for example, 'you have 5 minutes to read the text in silence highlighting key words'.
- Issue instructions positively, for example, 'I would like you to …' rather than 'Don't …'.
- Never issue instructions over the talking of *any* student/s.
- Once you have issued your instructions to the class, wait and watch! Let the class see that you are 'policing the task' for the first minute or so. Only after this pause should you then move around and help learners. If you do not do this there is a danger that your instructions will not be followed by some groups and students will quickly go off task.
- Never remain in one position for longer than 2 minutes – learners should feel that you could be *anywhere* at any given moment in the class. Not only will this prevent that mobile phone from being brought out, but it will give you an invaluable opportunity to monitor any off-task behaviour.
- Ensure that the arrangement of tables/seating allows both your mobility and the separation of learners likely to distract each other (see Figures 11.3–11.7). You should be able to move around easily to all parts of the classroom at any moment in time. If you cannot, then rethink the table/seating strategy, changing it for the next time you have this class.
- Use questioning strategies (see Chapter 6) as a means to engage learners and keep learners attention on the task at hand. Questions should be directed at named students and used at various stages of the lesson to keep the attention of all pupils.
- If running a video/DVD/film clip, stop the clip after 15 seconds and fire a couple of questions at individual members of the class – this will raise attention levels on the film and highlight whatever elements you wish your learners to tease out from the film.
- If you have in-class support then liaise with them before the lesson. Many teaching assistants are underused and often would love to be more involved in teaching. Find out what they would like to do in your class. This will raise their status with learners and provide you with an additional and invaluable classroom management resource.

- Never have your back to the class. Give the impression that you are scanning the class at all times. When talking to groups move your body around to a position where you can see the whole class and never focus on one group/pair/individual for too long.
- When asking a student to talk/answer a question, move to the opposite part of the classroom to where the particular student is. This will accomplish two things: first, the student will have to throw their voice to you thereby allowing the whole class to hear their contribution; secondly, your physical presence in a different part of the classroom will pre-empt any off-task behaviour while that student is talking.
- Do not get learners to multi-task, for example, never give out instructions while giving handouts/books – only give instructions when learners are paying attention to the task you have given them.
- Make sure you are aware of the codes of conduct and rules that your school/college employ (for example, school uniform policy, music earphones).
- Make sure you are aware of the sanctions policy adopted by your institution and that you follow it (for example, informing tutors, advance warning of detentions).
- Phone home! Do this for both positive behaviour as well as negative. Learners are used to some teachers phoning for discipline reasons but you will mark yourself out as special for ringing home to say how well a student has done (make sure you have permission from tutors to do this). If learners are late or behave badly, get a 'reputation' for telephoning home – once this reputation is fixed you will actually need to do this less and less.
- Praise learners but do not over-praise as this will ultimately devalue its usage.
- Be consistent, that is, if you tell latecomers that you will see them at the end of the class make sure you do – and, if they leave, track them down in break/lunch time. This will send out a powerful message that you are relentless and will always carry through whatever you say.
- Use a behaviour board (this can be a section of your whiteboard) on which you write the names of learners whose behaviour is not acceptable. This has the advantage of dealing with that student in a calm, controlled manner without disrupting the lesson. It also acts as a record-keeping mechanism.
- 'Sell' the importance of any activity (this requires a little performance on your part) with urgency and enthusiasm (for example, link the activity they are doing to the GCSE or A-level examination they will sit at the end of the year).
- Whatever activity you are asking learners to engage with, remind them of the remaining time left (for example, 'Ladies and gentlemen you have three minutes left').
- If you are deploying group activities, praise the group that is ahead and let the class know where they are, for example, 'This group is on task 2 already – well done'. This gentle form of competitiveness will 'up' the level of expectation for the whole class and devolve behaviour management down to the group.
- Wait for silence once you have asked for it. The wait might take a minute or two but almost immediately you will be rewarded with the sound of one or two learners saying 'shhhh'. Without actually having had to do anything you will have got the class to be silent for you.
- If by any chance you do need to simulate anger or annoyance at classroom behaviour, lower your voice – do *not* raise it and never shout. The lowering of the voice

creates the impression of greater authority, calmness and control on you part to your learners. Shouting loses its effectiveness quickly and over time increases the level of classroom noise.

- Avoid ticking off the whole class, for example, 'Year 10 you will *all* remain in detention' – this inevitably will lose you respect from those learners who are behaving. Identify those learners who are misbehaving and deal with them at the end of the lesson, in break and so on.

- Tactically 'ignore' learners who are vying for your attention for the wrong reasons at the wrong time, for example, when you are issuing instructions for the next task a pupil complains that her neighbour has stolen her pencil. You can always return to that student once the task has been initiated.

- If hands go up as you are issuing instructions, do not stop your instructions to answer these questions. Acknowledge the student with a nod or hand gesture, finish the instructions and then either take questions from the class or, once learners are on task, go to the particular pupil and find out what the issue is.

- Always start a new day/week as a fresh page, that is, do not carry over grudges or give the impression to learners that what they did before colours how you see them now.

The don'ts ✕

- Do not turn a blind eye to behaviour in your class that you do not desire. Learners will quickly pick up on this and realise your low expectations in terms of acceptable behaviour.

- Do not forget or ignore any punitive action you have promised, that is, if you say that you wish three learners to stay behind at end of the lesson, make sure that they do – and if they leave then follow this up by finding them in break time and/or emailing/putting a note in the appropriate tutor's pigeon-hole.

- Do not chastise the whole class for the poor behaviour of a minority of learners. You will quickly lose the respect of the majority who work well for you.

- Do not refer upwards (for example, heads of year, tutors) for behaviour that you should be able to initially deal with (for example, lateness, lack of homework). Only if the behaviour persists should you then use the referral processes in your school/college. If you too easily use these, learners will perceive you as a soft touch in the classroom and respect you less.

- Do not be intimidated by stronger characters and let the class see that you only tell off weaker individuals. Consistency again is the key element to your practice here and learners need to see you treating everybody fairly.

- Do not use over-the-top punishments for lower-level behaviour issues and, if possible, give learners the opportunity to make amends before any punishment is given. For example, homework not done can be threatened with a larger piece of work – but allow the student to get the original work to you by an agreed date. Only if work is then not handed to you should you follow this threat through.

- Never use sarcasm in the classroom – ever! Teenagers are likely to be far better at this than you and will certainly not respect any teacher that deploys this form of communication.

'Don't smile till Christmas'?

This cliché is often the type of advice given to trainee teachers by some 'experienced hands' (remember our 'toxic dragons' that we looked at in Chapter 5). With so many young people in Britain voting with their feet and leaving education at the age of 16, we would argue that this philosophy has no place in any classroom today. However, you do need to make a distinction between 'being friendly with' and being a 'friend to' your learners. The former is something we would encourage and the latter something we would argue ultimately will impede your success as a classroom practitioner.

'Behaviour for Learning' informs many of the ideas we offer you in this chapter. The trick is to keep a degree of professional distance from learners while at the same time encouraging them not to feel intimated by you. This combination is particularly hard for trainee teachers who often feel the understandable need to be 'liked' by their learners. However, it is a combination that, if managed correctly, will endear learners to you and give them the confidence to approach you if they need to talk about personal circumstances that might impede their learning (see Chapter 19 on Every Child Matters). It is also an essential combination if high-quality learning is to take place, that is, learners feel confident enough to ask you questions and engage in that all-important on-task discussion without the fear of 'being wrong'.

Chapter links →

Themes and ideas explored in this chapter link to corresponding ideas in Chapters 12, 14 and 17.

Suggested further reading

Rogers, B. (1990) *You Know the Fair Rule*. London: Pitman.

References

Child, A.J. (2004) 'Managing Behaviour for Learning', in V. Ellis (ed.), *Learning and Teaching in Secondary Schools*. London: Learning Matters.
Marland, M. (1993) *The Craft of the Classroom*. London: Heinemann.
Department for Education and Skills (DfES) (2001) DfES 581/2007, The Special Educational Needs Code of Practice.

CHAPTER 12

EDUCATIONAL ACHIEVEMENT AND UNDERACHIEVEMENT

Objectives

By the end of this chapter the reader will able to:

1. identify patterns and trends in educational achievement related to class, gender and ethnicity;
2. understand the significance of the concepts of 'inclusion' and 'exclusion';
3. comprehend why 'inclusion' and special educational needs (SEN) are inseparable concepts;
4. distinguish between in-school and out-of-school explanations for educational underachievement;
5. understand the impact of poverty on educational attainment.

What are the patterns and trends?

It is easy to assume that because Britain is considered to be a multicultural society there must be a relatively meritocratic education system, that is, one that offers equal chances to all within it. On closer examination another picture arises where huge differences exist in educational performance in terms of class, gender and ethnicity.

Despite all the different government policies since the 1944 Education Act (see Chapter 2), students from working-class backgrounds, on average, achieve less within formal education than their middle-class counterparts. Evidence of this can be seen in examination results, lower reading scores in primary schools, higher leaving rates from school at the age of 16, and the fact that wherever streaming, setting or tiering takes place, working-class children can be seen to be disproportionately in the lower bands. Significant evidence shows that in times gone by women performed worse than their male counterparts in many areas of education whereas now many educationalists talk of a 'crisis in masculinity' when referring to the underachievement of boys in British schools. Equally, evidence of the performance of ethnic minority students in Britain is often complex and ambiguous. Comparisons over time are difficult because different classifications of minority ethnic groups have been used, for example, 'Asian' and 'Afro-Caribbean' are both misleading terms masking the multitude of countries and cultural differences these terms embrace. Such terms often obscure differences in the performance of different national cultures (for example, Chinese and Indian pupils often score above national averages in key stage tests).

In this chapter we examine some of the patterns, trends and explanations that lie behind differences in educational achievement. We hope that by drawing a variety of lenses onto the causes of why some learners do badly in British schools you will become sensitised to these explanations informing and transforming your professional practice.

Education and class

Historically, explanations for working-class underachievement vary. Some writers argue that certain 'structures' within British society produce inequality within it. Basil Bernstein (1990), for example, argues that the structure of the language that middle-class children use is the same as the language that teachers expect for examination success. Bernstein's argument focuses around the use of 'restricted' and 'elaborated' codes. The first is what, he argues, working-class children use and this consists of shortened phrases or 'slang' terms that communicate ideas well in certain circumstances (for example, 'innit') but not in those of formal education. Middle-class children use both 'restricted' and 'elaborated' codes. Elaborated codes are the words that are used by teachers and found in textbooks. He argues that middle-class learners automatically use these words and therefore perform well in the school system. The existence of homogenous working and middle classes with distinct speech patterns is open to question but his work draws attention to the assumptions behind the curriculum, resources and language that teachers use to assess and reward students.

Some biological structural explanations focus around the issue of 'intelligence'. Cyril Burt's influential (and now discredited) work on inherited intelligence informed many justifications for the tripartite system (see Chapter 2) in which more middle-class children attended grammar schools than their working-class counterparts. Many researchers argue, however, that as these tests are largely constructed and standardised upon middle-class professionals, they are culturally biased in favour of this group. Many Western IQ tests will be wholly unsuitable for non-Western cultures. For example, being asked to identify the odd-one-out in 'flute', 'shot', 'tumbler' and 'acrobat' requires the culturally related knowledge that the first three items are glasses for drinking different types of alcohol. Gillborn and Youdell (2001) argue that the term 'intelligence' has been replaced by the term 'ability' and yet still carries with it implicit assumptions that are culturally biased against children of working-class and Black/African-Caribbean heritage.

Boudon (1974) argues that it is harder for working-class children to aim for university and high-status jobs while at the same time easier for middle-class children. When middle class, the expectation from many friends, teachers and families is that you must enter a high-status profession (whether you want to or not). Boudon argues the opposite can be the case for working-class children particularly if there is no tradition in the family for anyone to attend university. Other, more 'interpretive' explanations focus much more on the processes within the classroom and the individual interaction between students and teachers, and students themselves. For example, Keddie (1973) has argued that teachers do not make judgements about students based on their performance but rather on their imagination as to what an 'ideal' student is. Teachers teach in a different way depending on what stream, set or tier students are placed in. This is a clear example of labelling and a self-fulfilling prophecy if the student then goes on to believe that they are bright or stupid, depending on the level they have been placed at by the teacher. Feinstein (2003) has argued that the main factor influencing educational attainment is the degree of parental interest and support. According to this view, a lack of parental encouragement along with lower levels of general knowledge, vocabulary and access to books is typical of many working-class families. However, it is important to realise that measuring parental interest is highly problematic; for example, a lack of attendance at parents' evenings may actually reflect the need to work nights to support the family rather than a lack of interest in the child's education.

∿ M-level thinking: The impact of cultural ∿ capital on educational achievement

Bourdieu (1993) argues that the cultural capital of the middle classes gives middle-class children an advantage over their working-class peers. By 'cultural capital' he refers to the tastes, knowledge and ideas associated with a particular class. Teachers and middle-class learners, he argues, share similar cultural capital and, as a result, teachers reward these learners with greater educational success than their working-class counterparts. Ball et al. (1994) argue that middle-class parents are in a better position to exploit the marketised education systems that give the illusion of 'choice' to all parents. They argue that such parents are in a better position to research schools, attend and perform well in interviews, and appeal if turned down. They can afford to pay for the public transport necessary to send their children to more distant schools, or buy houses in the catchment areas of the schools of their choice. Finally, they can also afford, if necessary, to pay for private tuition in the build-up to public examinations. To what extent do you believe cultural capital is a significant factor in educational achievement?

While many writers in the past have focused how on how class has played a major role in determining the educational success of learners, few sociologists today hold this view, preferring to combine gender, ethnicity and class when evaluating the educational success of students. Reay et al. (2004) provide a sophisticated account of the overlapping effects of social class, ethnicity and gender in the process of choosing which university to attend. By the beginning of the twenty-first century, university education is increasingly shifting from one formed by an elite group to a mass education system for all. Their study draws on qualitative and quantitative data to show how the welcome expansion of higher education has also deepened social stratification, generating new and different inequalities. While gender inequalities have reduced, those of social class remain and are now reinforced by racial inequalities in access. Students are seen to confront vastly different degrees of choice that are powerfully shaped by their social class and race. Courses such as media studies, business studies and IT tend to attract a lot of students from working-class and ethnic minority backgrounds. As these courses become more popular, they become devalued and employers offer jobs to candidates with higher-status degrees, more often taken by white, middle-class students. So, while more students have the opportunity to take degrees, the chances of getting a job on graduation remains dependant on class and social position.

Education and gender

A report by the male-dominated employer's organisation the Confederation of British Industry (CBI) in the late 1990s argued that if Britain were to remain economically competitive with other countries, its top 100 companies should be run by female managers. The report argued that not only did women make better team leaders and were more able to multi-task but academically they were increasingly outperforming their male counterparts at all levels of education. However, the educational underachievement of males compared to females is a relatively recent phenomenon. It is hard to imagine that only in 1948 did Cambridge University accept full membership of women into most of its colleges. It is only since the 1970s that sociologists really focused on the underachievement of females despite the fact that underachievement of girls in schools was a consistent feature of British education until this time. Today, however, women outperform men in most areas of education. This has created a new 'moral panic' concerning the underachievement of males within British schools – a moral panic that many feminists argue did not exist when the situation was reversed in earlier decades.

A number of writers have offered explanations for the historical underachievement of girls in British schools. Sue Sharpe (1976) argued that different aspirations for females at that time explained their lower educational achievement. Her study showed that 'love, marriage, husbands and children' were the main priorities for young women during the 1970s. Sharpe's work was backed up by Angela McRobbie (1978) who argued that females in the late 1970s were influenced by teenage magazines, films and television that often emphasised the importance of romance over career. Deem (1990) has focused on the role of the school curriculum during the late 1970s and early 1980s, and how many teachers encouraged females to take/not take certain subjects, for example, home economics rather than science-related subjects.

However, these studies, while useful, cannot explain why most females are outperforming most males in the classroom today – what is new? Changes in cultural attitudes have influenced the way girls see themselves both inside and outside the school environment. Along with the women's movement in the 1970s, the media has played a role in promoting female individuality and ambition from the 1980s onwards (for example, Hollywood blockbuster movies at that time, such as *Working Girl* and *Erin Brockovich*). But two sets of educational policies introduced by different governments also contributed to the rising rates of female educational achievement. The first was the introduction of the National Curriculum (see Chapter 2) that for the first time made males and females study the same subjects. The second were school initiatives in the late 1980s and early 1990s such as Girls into Science and Technology (GIST) and the Technical Vocational Educational Initiative (TVEI) that actively encouraged the role of females within these traditionally male-dominated vocational areas. No longer would it be socially acceptable or permissible for teachers, parents and learners themselves to use gender as an excuse to inform choice of academic and vocational pathways. Power et al. (2003) have argued that girls are often driven by the school's ambitions to maintain and improve their positions in the league tables and that schools capitalise on this.

Mac an Ghaill (1994) argues that many males experience a 'crisis of masculinity' because of the decline in traditional male jobs or professions over the last four decades. This identity crisis, he argues, allows some males to question the need for qualifications when the jobs they would have traditionally gone into no longer exist. Jobs in the service industries (typically dominated by women employees) increased by 45 per cent from 1978 to 2005 (Social Trends, 2006). This contrasts with a fall by 54 per cent in the male-dominated manufacturing industries over the same period. Jane Clark (1996) argues that males are bombarded with images of the macho or anti-authority stereotypes both within and outside the media. This macho cultural stereotype associated with 'laddism' flies in the face of the image of woman as organiser or woman as carer that young males associate with the role of female teachers. This acts as a disincentive for some males to be seen to focus on their studies within the school environment. Finally, some New Right theories focus on the increase in single-parent families and higher divorce rates in an attempt to explain the lack of role models for males. Blame is often heaped on individuals and families for what is seen as a moral decline in the values of society. The increased determination of women to be economically independent is also blamed, by some more conservative commentators, for recent male underachievement.

However, while it might be tempting to say that the 'glass ceiling' has vanished, this would be an overly optimistic reading of the gendered nature of education, training and employment. The 'glass ceiling' that exists in many firms has been replaced by a 'glass cliff' as women are promoted into positions that men do not want (because they believe they cannot do them) only to be sacked or moved sideways when the unfortunate candidate fails at the tasks they have been employed to carry out. Despite the fact that there are more female teachers than male in Britain, disproportionately more men than women still occupy the senior management levels of schools and colleges. There are also remarkably few black female teachers. Some feminists argue that this creates an expectation that positions of power and authority are automatically associated with men more than women.

Education and ethnicity

When we look at the performance of Britain's ethnic minorities a picture arises in which huge differences exist between the educational performances of one ethnic minority compared with another. In 2005 the Department for Education and Skills reported that Indian and Chinese pupils are more likely to achieve the expected level of educational attainment, whereas black, Bangladeshi and Pakistani learners tend to perform less well than white learners. They suggest one reason for this may be due to economic disadvantage as higher proportions of black, Bangladeshi and Pakistani learners are eligible for free school meals (an indication of lower socio-economic level). Many educationalists explore these differences and how other social variables help to explain why some ethnic groups seem to perform better than others.

Intelligence cannot, as the Swann Committee (a committee appointed by the government to examine the education of ethnic minorities) showed in the mid-1980s, be a reason for differences in educational attainment between different ethnic groupings. The research showed that other social and economic factors were far more important than any differences in IQ (for example, levels of poverty, housing conditions and parental involvement). 'Cultural deprivation theory' states that many black children are deprived of the values needed for school success. The theory represents a group of ideas that claim that working-class and some ethnic minority cultures fail to motivate their children adequately within education systems. As a result they fail to receive the skills and values required to succeed. Douglas (1964) has also tried to use cultural deprivation theory to explain how the lack of parental involvement by many ethnic minorities explains poor educational attainment. Such evidence is based on lack of parental attendance at parents' evenings. However, this view can be criticised because quite often parents who do not attend parents' evenings are either working or feel intimidated by the formal situation. These views can also be attacked by referring to how Ken Pryce (1979) showed that many African-Caribbean parents send their children to voluntary community-run supplementary schools.

Research provides evidence that can lead to both complex and confusing explanations for ethnic underachievement in schools. The Commission for Racial Equality carried out a study in 1998 ('Set to Fail') that showed how Asian students of similar ability to whites were less likely to be entered for GCSEs than their white counterparts. This would seem to show that ethnicity is a significant factor in explaining educational achievement. However, Smith and Tomlinson (1989) argued that the class background of learners was more important than ethnicity in explaining educational attainment. While they argue that ethnic minority groups were allocated in general to lower-level courses and that many ethnic groups did worse in school tests than white students, they also argued that this was because many ethnic minorities come from working-class backgrounds and that differences in class are therefore more important than differences in ethnic background.

A number of classic studies by educationalists have highlighted some factors that help explain ethnic underachievement focusing on the role of the teacher:

- A study carried out in 1998 by the Commission for Racial Equality showed that at 'Jayleigh' school teacher assessment meant that more white learners were entered for a greater number of GCSEs than Asian students. More Asian pupils were also placed in lower sets throughout their time in school.
- Through primary-school classroom observation, Cecile Wright (1992) showed how teachers largely ignored Asian pupils particularly when it came to classroom discussion – wrongly assuming that their levels of English were not good enough.
- The concepts of 'labelling' and a 'self-fulfilling prophecy' show how some teachers label some students as 'troublesome'. The frustration of experiencing this process means that some students develop 'attitude' to counteract the expectation that a teacher will pick on them.

A report into education produced by Gillborn and Mirza (2000) and largely supporting the DfES report mentioned above, shows that while ethnic inequalities still greatly exist in the UK education system, patterns of difference in attainment between various ethnic groups themselves are changing, reflecting differences in gender:

- Indian and Chinese girls often outperform white girls.
- Black African girls are the most rapidly improving group of students.
- There are significant differences between black African and black Caribbean students.
- Black boys are the most excluded groups in the system.
- Girls outperform boys at all levels, within all ethnic groups.
- Bangladeshi and Pakistani boys are underachieving more than white boys.

Research shows that in many cases the underachievment of some ethnic minorities is as a result of institutional racism within English schools. Gillborn (2002) explores the experience of ethnic minority learners at the hands of some teachers. His work has shown that some teachers 'blame' African-Caribbean students more than white students for poor behaviour even when the behaviour is identical. In what he describes as 'the myth of the black challenge' he shows how teachers perceive certain types of behaviour as 'threatening' and then go on to punish students accordingly. He found that these learners were disproportionately placed on report, put in detention or excluded compared with other ethnic minorities in schools. More worrying is that black African-Caribbean boys are seven times more likely to be excluded from British schools than their white counterparts. There is no clear evidence to show that ethnicity itself is a causal explanation for underachievement. What is clear is that the class background and gender of students is highly significant when viewing underachievement in schools along with the labelling processes adopted by some teachers.

 Discussion point

Exclusion is a term that is widely used and little understood. Its usage ranges from the student who is 'excluded' from a particular lesson because of poor behaviour to the suspension or permanent exclusion from a school/college for more serious offences. Quite often these forms of exclusion are related to learners who suffer from emotional and behavioural difficulties. In some cases these learners can be referred to a pupil referral unit (PRU). Such referrals are usually for an agreed short period of time (for example, one term) with a view to reintegrating the pupil back into mainstream schooling. Some schools have an unofficial policy to 'exclude' learners at times of external inspection. To what extent are you aware of your school's exclusion policy?

In-school and out-of-school factors

When examining differences in educational achievement consider 'in-school' and 'out-of-school' factors to explain why learners do well or badly in the particular institution/s you are training in.

   In-school factors include:

- Type of institution – for example, is it selective, urban, rural, post-16?
- Structure – for example, is the institution made up of streams or sets or are the classes mixed ability? How does it cater for learners with disabilities?
- Leadership – is the institution well managed by the head/principal or senior managers?
- Staffing of the school – to what extent does staffing reflect the cultural make up of its learners, that is, if the institution is in a predominantly black or working-class

area, how many black or working-class teachers/managers are employed by the school?

- Funding of the school – does the school/college have enough money for resources (for example, books, desks, rooms, computers, teachers)?
- Entry requirements – does the institution accept learners with a variety of abilities or does it select on the basis of past examination performance?
- Labelling – to what extent do teachers label learners and how might that affect which classes and ultimately which examinations they may or may not sit?
- Self-fulfilling prophecies – as a result of labelling and being placed in a particular set, tier or stream, how might a student start to believe the label and then become the label, for example, gifted and talented (G&T)?

Out-of-school factors include:

- Poverty – to what extent are learners materially deprived (see below) of certain essential requirements if they are expected to succeed within the educational system?
- Parental interest – often (wrongly) more associated with middle-class parents, this might refer to taking an interest in homework, attending parents' evenings, encouragement and support for their child's studies in general and making sure that their child regularly attends school.
- Language differences – whether because of class or ethnic differences, a culture clash can sometimes exist between the language used at home and outside the school with the language found in textbooks and used by teachers.
- Cultural capital – certain forms of cultural capital are rewarded by examination success although in most cases this tends to favour middle-class learners. This, many argue, makes the education system culturally biased in terms of middle-class values often obscuring the potential for success of working-class learners and children of ethnic minority backgrounds.

Poverty as a barrier to learning

It is often very difficult to distinguish why learners in classes might appear listless, disinterested, irritable or disengaged from the educational ethos of the institution they attend. Sometimes, however, this appearance can mask the fact that the extreme levels of low-income, that is, a lack of economic capital, that many young people experience accounts for behaviour often interpreted by teachers as a rejection of the institution. Smith and Noble (1995) outline several factors associated with low income that impede the educational achievement of many young people:

- The lack of finance to pay for school uniforms, home Internet access, school trips, transport, books and so on can lead to bullying, isolation and stigmatisation for the student concerned.

- Low-income families often experience greater levels of ill-health, stress and poor diet, all of which can contribute to poorer performance and attendance in schools and colleges.
- Lack of finances can restrict the sorts of private tuition and education that many middle-class parents can afford for their children.
- Low income can often be at the heart of poor homework submission. It reduces the likelihood of a heated bedroom with a desk and space to do homework, with many children sharing cramped noisy housing conditions.
- The marketisation of schooling in which league tables reward high-performing schools often leads to a situation in which socially disadvantaged children are concentrated into a limited number of increasingly unpopular schools.

Inclusion and special educational needs

The concept of 'inclusion' is a widely debated and historically contested term that embodies Human Rights and Equal Opportunities. The Disability and Discrimination Act 2005 states that schools have a duty to promote disability equality. This is in order to eliminate unlawful discrimination, harassment, and promote equal opportunities and positive attitudes towards disability. Price (2005) argues that the principles of inclusion encompass:

- Valuing diversity – all learners should be valued (regardless of sex, race, ethnicity, class, age, ability, sexuality, physical impairment, religion, cultural and linguistic background and special educational needs).
- Entitlement – all learners, are entitled to receive, with a suitable peer group, a broad, balanced and relevant curriculum.
- Dignity – all learners and their parents, are entitled to be treated with respect and have their views taken into account.
- Individual needs – inclusive practice should not create situations within which individual needs are left unmet.

In the UK, the Special Educational Needs and Disability Act 2001 (DfES, 2001b) enshrines the right to mainstream education for children with SEN. The Office for Standards in Education identifies one in five children needing some form of extra help in class (Ofsted, 2004). The Education Act 1996, Section 312, defines a child as having special educational needs 'if they have a learning difficulty which calls for special educational provision' (DfEE, 1996). The DfES Code of Practice (DfES, 2001a) draws attention to any student having special educational needs if provision is necessary for their inclusion in mainstream education. This is in relation to: academic attainment; special learning difficulties (for example, dyslexia and dyspraxia); emotional and behavioural difficulties; physical difficulties; sensory impairment (for example, hearing and visual difficulties); difficulties in speech and language; and any specific medical conditions (for example, epilepsy). The Code of Practice consists of five principles:

1. Children with special educational needs should have their needs met.
2. The SEN of children should normally be met in mainstream schools.
3. The views of the child regarding his/her education should be sought and taken into account.
4. Parents play a vital role in supporting their child's education.
5. Children with SEN should be offered full access to a broad, balanced and relevant curriculum.

In order for you, the teacher, to be able to facilitate these principles you should have access to a Statement of the child's Special Educational Needs. This annually reviewed document is legally binding and issued by the local authority specifying the type of provision needed. We would strongly advise you to read the Code of Practice and familiarise yourself with the different categories of special education needs. We would advise you to spend as much time as you can in the SEN department of the institution in which you are training. Observe the professionals working there and get to know the learning assistants. If possible run any resources that you create by them and get their advice on how your resources can be improved to meet any SEN requirements.

 M-level thinking: The feasibility of 'inclusion'

In the past it was common practice for children with special educational needs to be taken out of the class and supported on a one-to-one basis by specialist trained staff or to attend specialist schools. Increasingly the practice is for teaching assistants to work alongside learners within the classroom context. While few teachers disagree with inclusion as an educational ideology, many voice resistance to its feasibility in practical terms. Many teachers feel that they have not been trained or possess the skills to teach children with learning, emotional and/or behavioural difficulties. Some argue that children are actually worse off in mainstream schooling because of the lack of specialist staff available. To what extent do you agree with the policies associated with inclusion?

Now that you have read almost all of this chapter you will realise that far from providing equal opportunities of education to all, British education continues, despite valiant attempts, to treat different types of learners differently. The size of the classroom, the region in which the school/college is situated or the type of school that the child goes to, all affect how that pupil might succeed (or not) within any type of formal assessment. Add to that a recognition of the poverty, and the in-school and out-of-school factors this chapter has looked at, and you are left with a variety of often conflicting but nevertheless enlightening explanations for the inequality and difference that exists. This chapter offers you a range of diagnostic lenses for you when considering why some of your learners might not be performing to the standards that you know and expect they are capable of. It also encourages you to be as inclusive as possible as you develop your professional repertoire of teaching skills.

Can individual teachers make a difference?

We hope that this chapter introduces you to many of the discussions and debates concerning why some learners persistently 'under achieve' in education. But we also offer words of warning when reflecting on this chapter. First, be very clear about what you might understand by 'underachievement' as very often the benchmark for 'achievement' is narrowly framed and defined by economic and political conceptions of education determining how 'success' and 'failure' are interpreted by the teaching profession. Secondly, do not let the explanations in this chapter limit the highest expectations you have of *all* your learners. We firmly believe that good teachers can not only 'make a difference' to the lives of all their learners but can often confound the expectations of many of their more experienced colleagues about *their* conceptions of the sorts of learners we discuss in this chapter.

Chapter links →

Themes and ideas explored in this chapter link to corresponding ideas in Chapters 9, 10, 11 and 14.

Suggested further reading

Gillborn, D. and Ladson-Billings, G. (eds) (2004) *The RoutledgeFalmer Reader in Multi-cultural Education.* New York: Routledge.

Tomlinson, S. (2008) *Race and Education – Policy and Politics in Britain.* New York: McGraw-Hill.

References

Ball, S.J., Bowe, R. and Gewirtz, S. (1994) 'Market forces and parental choice', in S. Tomlinson (ed.), *Educational Reform and its Consequences.* London: Rivers Oram Press.

Bernstein, B. (1990) *Class, Codes and Control, Vol. 4: The Structuring of Pedagogic Discourse.* London: Routledge.

Boudon, R. (1974) *Education, Opportunity and Social Inequality.* New York: John Wiley and Sons.

Bourdieu, P. (1993) *The Field of Cultural Production: Essays on Art and Leisure.* New York: Columbia University Press.

Clark J. (1996) 'Insights: gender and education revisited', *Sociology Review,* 5 (4).

Commission for Racial Equality (1998) 'Set to fail', Education and Training Factsheet.

Deem, R. (1990) 'Women and leisure', *Social Studies Review*, 5(4).

Department for Education and Employment (DfEE) (1996) *Education Act*. London: HMSO.

Department for Education and Skills (DfES) (2001a) *Special Educational Needs: Code of Practice*. Nottingham: DfES Publications.

Department for Education and Skills (DfES) (2001b) *Special Educational Needs and Disability Act*. Nottingham: DfES Publications.

Department for Education and Science (DfES) (2005) *Ethnicity and Education – The Evidence on Minority Ethnic Pupils*. Research Topic Paper RTP01-05.

Douglas, J.W.B. (1964) *The Home and the School*. London: MacGibbon and Kee.

Feinstein, L. (2003) 'Very early evidence: how early can we predict future educational achievement?', *Centrepiece*, 8(2): 121–34.

Gillborn, D. (2002) *Education and Institutional Racism*. London: Institute of Education, University of London.

Gillborn, D. and Mirza, H. (2000) *Educational Inequality: Mapping Race, Class and Gender*. London: Ofsted.

Gillborn, D. and Youdell, D. (2001) *The New IQism: Intelligence, Ability and the Rationing of Education*. Basingstoke: Palgrave.

Keddie, N. (1973) *Tinker, Tailor*. Harmondsworth: Penguin.

Mac an Ghaill, M. (1994) *The Making of Men: Masculinities, Sexualities and Schooling*. Buckingham: Oxford University Press.

McRobbie, A. (1978) 'Working class girls and the culture of femininity', in *Women Take Issue: Aspects of Women's Subordination*: Birmingham Womens' Study Group/Centre for Contemporary Studies.

Office for Standards in Education (Ofsted) (2004) *Special Educational Needs and Disability: Towards Inclusive Schools*. London: Office of Standards in Education.

Power, S., Edwards, T., Witty, G. and Wigfall, V. (2003) *Education and the Middle Class*. Buckingham: Open University Press.

Price, G. (2005) 'Inclusion: special educational needs', in V. Ellis (ed.), *Learning and Teaching in Secondary Schools*. London: Learning Matters.

Pryce, K. (1979) *Endless Pressure*. Harmonsworth: Penguin.

Reay, D., David, E.M. and Ball, S. (2004) *Degrees of Choice*. Stoke-on-Trent: Trentham Books.

Sharpe, S. (1976) *Just Like a Girl*. Harmondsworth: Penguin.

Smith, T. and Noble, M. (1995) *Educational Divides: Poverty and Schooling in the 1990s*. London: CPAG.

Smith, D. and Tomlinson, S. (1989) *The School Effect: A Study of Multi-Racial Comprehensives*. London: Policy Studies Institute.

Social Trends (2006) *Social Trends*. London: Office for National Statistics.

Swann Committee Report (1985) *The Report of the Committee of Inquiry into the Education of Children from Ethnic Minority Groups*, Chairman Lord Swann. London: Runneymede Trust.

Wright C. (1992) 'Early education: multiracial primary school classrooms', in D. Gill, B. Mayor and M. Blair (eds) *Racism and Education: Structures and Strategies*. London: Sage.

SECTION 4

PRACTICE

CHAPTER 13

PLANNING AND PREPARATION

Objectives

By the end of this chapter the reader will be able to:

1. understand the importance of lesson planning for effective teaching and learning;
2. understand the features of a good lesson plan;
3. understand the significance of sequencing and planning for pace and variety for good classroom practice;
4. understand the importance of the scheme of work for long-term coordination and planning;
5. recognise the importance of effective preparation for effective learning.

Curriculum planning

The best lessons are performances that are meticulously planned, scripted and resourced. They are enthusiastic and carried out with conviction. Underpinning all these performances – like any good play or piece of theatre – is time spent planning and preparing. This is the hidden work of all good teachers; 'hidden' in the sense that we see the results – the classroom practice – but often are unaware until we enter the profession just what this means in terms of work and effort.

Having said this, planning is a contradictory process – a double-edged sword. The process of planning is essential to good teaching and yet good teachers are also able to be flexible and respond to the many 'in-the-moment' needs of their learners. Equally, good teachers are able to take the seemingly 'set-in-stone' nature of curriculum planning and translate it into what works best for their learners. The thing about all good teachers is that they are able to change their planning as they undertake their teaching performances. Many trainees feel constrained by their plans; they feel almost as if the plans rule over them, and that their practice is dictated by the plans they themselves have made. Certainly, if it was worth careful planning, then presumably it is worth doing (otherwise, why would you have planned it in the first place?), but equally, you need to be sensitive to how each lesson progresses and how the learners are learning.

Things can only get better!

As a trainee teacher you will find that lesson planning and preparation take huge amounts of time. For an hour's lesson, it is not unusual to spend three or four times as long outside of the classroom thinking about the segment of learning time, making the materials and putting together the shape and structure of the learning onto a formal lesson plan pro forma. Do not worry – things do get quicker and easier with experience! Use your colleagues in the team in which you are placed and your mentor who has a responsibility for the development of your own subject-specific pedagogy.

Whereas the majority of this book is about classroom practice – all practice is underpinned by careful and considered planning. Equally, all planning is developed through the insights offered from reflection, both 'reflection-in-action' and 'reflection-on-action' (see Chapter 5). The message here is that teachers are learners too! We need to take what we do, apply it, develop and practice it, and change it over time as necessary. We need to master the sorts of meta-learning and meta-cognition our learners also need to master (see Chapters 14 and 17).

Although this chapter is concerned with lesson planning, planning of the curriculum as a whole is a multilayered phenomenon. Curriculum planning exists at many levels within an educational institution:

- At the uppermost layer, we would have the whole institutional curriculum plan – detailing what programmes are being followed, the awarding bodies and how, strategically, these suit the needs of the learning community as a whole. This level of curriculum planning is drawn up by the senior management team (SMT), monitored by governors and is influenced by legal, national and local responsibilities to policy, national tests and competition.

- Drawing on the whole institutional planning, we have the planning for the cohorts within the learning community – this could be divided by year group, key stage (in secondary schools), learner need or examination/award type.
- Then there are subject-team specific plans, often focused upon teamwork and developing common subject pedagogy.
- From the above team specific plans come the schemes of work for each course or programme being offered at each level of award. This refers to the termly/yearly/module overview of all lessons presented in a brief way.
- Finally, individual teachers within teams write their own lesson plans.

As you can see, planning is essential to the workings of all learning communities and is monitored in a variety of ways. At every level, planning is evaluated and self-assessed, and it is these discussions, documented, that inspectors and funders will need to have access to.

Types of planning and preparation

When thinking about individual lesson planning, there are four important factors to consider:

- Consider the type of learner(s) being taught.
- Consider the course requirements.
- Consider the lesson content.
- Consider the resources and methods to be deployed.

Planning and preparation both take considerable time. These two processes are separate and also related.

1. By planning, we mean the writing of schemes of work and lesson plans – the thinking about the individual lesson components and their place in the overall set of lessons you have with your learners to get to an 'end' result by a specific time of the year.
2. By preparation, we mean the making of the learning and teaching resources and materials and their evaluation.

Furthermore, preparation itself, involves three stages:

1. Collecting and selecting relevant subject material.
2. Preparing material and planning methods to be deployed.
3. Checking and rehearsing.

Lesson planning, as such, takes two forms: the individual lesson plans of the teacher and the scheme of work that the lesson plans draw upon. These are separate documents, and both are important for the self-assessment, monitoring and quality assurance of the institution in which you practice. Normally, individual lesson plans come out of the scheme of work which is usually created first. Rather oddly, many institutions – due to matters of work flow and down time – ask teachers and teams to write and submit for monitoring schemes of work either at the end of the academic year prior to their use, or right at the start of the academic year. This does mean that schemes of work are often created before you actually meet your learners. Therefore, as flexible working documents, it is useful to see them as ongoing and open to change.

With the scheme of work in place, teachers can then draw from this larger picture their own individual lesson plans. Essentially the distinction between these two is:

- Schemes of work – a larger picture; a series of connected learning segments matching together and making up, over time, the whole course of learning for a year, a module or a term (depending how these are organised within the institution in question).
- Lesson plans are individual moments in time; each specific and 'discrete' lesson drawn from the wider picture offered on the scheme of work.

Lesson planning

Although schemes of work are planned before individual lesson plans, this is probably not going to be the case in the experience of many trainee teachers. You join an institution 'already-in-motion' with planning for the year largely set before you arrive. At first, due to the important drip-feed approach of your practice (and the massive learning curve of your own learning), you will probably find yourself teaching a handful of lessons, trying things out, building up to a more substantial block of teaching over time. Due to this, you will end up thinking about individual lessons before you consider the broader picture. Allow your colleagues and mentor to guide you, but always keep in mind that individual lessons are part of a bigger planning process.

Factors in lesson planning

It might be helpful to think about what factors teachers need to take into consideration when planning effectively:

1. Analyse tasks in terms of concepts, principles and skills to be learnt.
2. Know, understand and identify important elements of syllabus/specification.
3. Determine special skills involved for assessment.
4. State relevant learning objectives.
5. Decide prerequisite knowledge required.
6. Set goals for the lesson.

7. Make the lesson content interesting.
8. Relate new knowledge to that already learnt.
9. Build on existing knowledge.
10. Provide continuity.
11. Structure lesson in logical sequence.
12. Integrate learning situation with real-life situations.
13. Encourage participation.
14. Design lessons around learners not teachers.
15. Plan for maximum learner activity.
16. Employ appropriate learning aids.
17. Include question and answering sessions.
18. Provide assessment for learning opportunities.
19. Incorporate note-making, frequent summaries, and reviews.
20. Set homework.
21. Show how you have planned and worked with learning support assistants (LSAs).
22. Show how you have considered Every Child Matters (ECM).

What can we see on lesson plans?

As a physical document/object, lesson plans are usually pro formas with common and agreed headings into which the teacher puts the component elements of their lesson. Most lesson plans are two-sectioned documents with slightly different presentation and information needed in the different sections. As with schemes of work (see below), lesson plans are usually a 'matrix' – a series of boxes, to be completed.

Lesson plan pro formas vary considerably from institution to institution, but they have in common the following elements.

- Group number.
- Subject.
- Module/unit.
- Assessing body.
- Date/week/room.
- Number of learners on the register.
- Aims.
- Objectives.
- Cross-curricular links – key skills, Every Child Matters.
- Differentiation.
- Homework.

There is often a space for the teacher to provide some notes about the group itself, to note any specific support needs, or to contextualise the lesson and provide a rationale for the specific decisions they have made in writing the plan. During your training it is not uncommon to have a section on a lesson plan related to 'areas of development'. This does not refer to areas of development for your learners but is based on your own development from one lesson to the next.

Most lesson plans are essentially two different documents combined. The information above is then combined, often on a second page, with a breakdown of the elements of teaching and learning activity within the time period of the lesson (see Table 13.1). This part of the pro forma usually has headings such as:

- Timing.
- Teacher and learner activity (these may be separated into different columns).
- Assessment.

Table 13.1   Sample lesson plan document

Timing	Learner and teacher activity	Resources	Assessment

How should lesson plans be completed?

Like schemes of work, the best advice is to plan backwards. Think about the outcome – refer to the language of your aims and objectives – and work the narrative of the 'distance travelled' during the lesson back from the final assessment and plenary activity at the end of the journey. At every point, ask yourself, what are the learners doing at this point in the lesson? Ensure that they are active and are learning through doing. Build back from the plenary to the starter (see Chapters 14 and 15).

Planning and using reflective practice

The lesson plan is your chance to think formally and clearly about the choices and decisions you are making. Over time, as a record of your continuing professional development, they can be seen to chart the development of your professional practice – they say something about what sort of teacher you are becoming. Remember, that for each and every minute of the lesson plan you need to have a reason why you have made that choice (even if this reason, as such, does not get documented on the plan itself). Equally, for each decision you make – group work, question and answer (Q and A), buzz groups, jig-sawing and so on (see Chapter 16) – you are at the same time, making a decision not to do something. Make sure you are not using techniques for the right reasons – what you are not doing is just as important as what you are doing.

Aims and objectives

All lesson plans will document both the aims and objectives; these are simply essential to the planning process. The point of planning, is to be planning for learning to take place. As a result, you need to be as clear as possible on what the objectives are, how they fit into broader schemes of work, and you need to find how to communicate your objectives to your learners in a way that makes sense to them. It is certainly the case that observers will be checking carefully the language you have used on your lesson plans. We consider this issue in much greater depth in Chapter 5.

Writing good lesson objectives will help you to plan your teaching and motivate your learners. However, you need to make sure that your objectives are well constructed and are met by the end of the lesson. Your observer will check to see that you have done this. The acronyms SMART and RUMBA are both easy to remember and useful for planning purposes.

What is SMART?

* Specific.
* Measurable.
* Achievable.
* Relevant.
* Timed.

What is RUMBA?

* Relevant.
* Understandable.
* Measurable.
* Behavioural.
* Achievable.

Flagging up your aims and objectives

It is essential that learners themselves know what the points of their lessons are. This is a crucial start to the lesson – settling learners in and knowing what the point of the lesson and the learning is – and certainly one that you will be judged on by observers. Consider the following options and possibilities:

1. You could have the aims and objectives written on a board and have them on display all through the lesson.
2. You could go back to the aims and objectives at the end of the lesson and ask learners to tell you how they have achieved them in the lesson.
3. You could withhold the aims and objectives until after a starter activity which assesses prior learning and then explain to the learners how the prior learning helps with the aims for the lesson they are currently doing.
4. You could have the aims and objectives on display and get the learners to explain in their own language what they mean. In this way they can 'own' the aims for themselves.
5. You could ask learners, once they have understood them, to write down the aims and objectives in their notes, on a handout, in their exercise books or a learning journal so they have a record. If you do this, make sure you go back to it and refer to it, otherwise, like most things, it becomes a little pointless if not really used.

Planning starts and ends

There is a great deal of research that suggests that clear starting and ending activities really help to shape the learning of a lesson (see Chapter 14 for an extended discussion). This is where some planning becomes tricky. While lessons are separate moments in time – and each lesson needs to end 'cleanly' – they are also part of a series of longer and broader learning opportunities (hence the point in having schemes of work). This means that lessons both stand alone and yet connect in series as part of a greater journey at the same time.

In terms of the implications of this for your planning, you need to both:

- treat lessons as discrete elements with clear starts and clear outcomes assessed and evaluated at the end;
- and yet, you need to refer to prior learning and communicate to learners how lessons fit into a broader picture.

The start of the lesson is generally recognised to be a time for (in no particular order):

- registration;
- assessment of prior learning;

- showing how prior learning connects to the new lesson;
- moving learners into a prearranged seating plan if appropriate;
- building relationships (talking, greeting, making them comfortable);
- explaining health and safety issues if needed;
- showing aims and objectives;
- asking learners to make sense of the aims and objectives of the lesson;
- negotiation of rules and activity if appropriate;
- recapping previous lessons;
- posing problems – to then be 'solved' during the course of the remaining parts of the lesson.

The end of the lesson is generally recognised to be a time for (in no particular order):

- questioning learners (although this can also happen all the way through);
- assessment (although as above, this should also happen all the way through);
- answering learners' concerns;
- setting up the next lesson;
- evaluating the lesson;
- recapping main points from the lesson;
- asking learners to recap the aims and objectives.

Often, we speak of ends as being a 'plenary' (see Chapter 14). A plenary is a very important and specific type of end activity – but you could have other ends, or even have a plenary and then still do something else afterwards. Strictly speaking a plenary is a time to bring the class together again. It is a time for reflection and review. A time to ask learners to consider what they have done and learnt in the lesson and see how this connects to their wider programme of study and/or future targets. Further examples of starters and ends are provided in Chapter 15.

Golden rules of lesson planning – from paper to classroom performance

Lesson plans are not abstract – they should not be divorced from the reality of the actual classroom performance. They are there to aid the classroom teaching, not the other way around. Always go back to the teaching at every point in the planning and preparation process. This means, always go back to the learners and their learning: what are they doing? How will they do it? What support will they need?

Be mindful of the following 'golden rules':

- Communicate the aims of the lesson to the learners at the start and have a mechanism in place to check if this has been done at the end of lesson.
- 'Chunk' lessons, making each chunk clear rather than 'seamlessly' drip-feeding bits into the lesson – this can be seen as boring and slow.
- Make sure you have complete silence for clear instructions – do not introduce the lesson with learners wondering around or talking – keep instructions simple.

- Make sure you give clear timed targets for each of the activities – remind learners how long they have left.
- Do not interrupt the lesson with peripheral notices/information as this will encourage off-task chatter.
- Remember to flag up all the good work you do on the plan itself for others to see – mention differentiation, equal opportunities, homework, resources.
- Do not cut and paste from old plans.

Schemes of work

The scheme of work, as the name suggests, is about the flow of the learning over several lessons; it documents the processes teachers and learners undergo over a period of time. The scheme of work is the schedule of the lessons and the learning – presented as a journey from start to finish.

What are schemes of work?

- An overview of topics to be covered.
- A breakdown of the details of each topic.
- A reference guide to resources used.
- A breakdown of learning activities.
- A timescale.
- A guide to the pattern of assessments over time.

Schemes of work are vital documents. We need them so that we can:

- plan time effectively;
- ensure that all parts of the specifications are covered;
- ensure consistency between colleagues;
- enable new teachers to access the curriculum, providing continuity and coherence in the event of staff changes or absenteeism.

Table 13.2   Sample scheme of work document

Week	Aims	Objectives	Learning activities	Resources	Assessment and differentiation	ECM	Mapping againt functional skills	Homework

Schemes of work, like lesson plans (see above) are usually presented as a 'grid' or 'matrix' table (see Table 13.2). Again, like lesson plans, the precise headings used are often due to the institution you practise in. Having said this, it is likely that schemes of work will include the following headings (in no particular order):

1. Aims and objectives (linked to the lesson plans that come out of the scheme of work).
2. Week/date.
3. Learner learning activities (more important than 'teacher activity').
4. Resources.
5. Assessment.
6. Homework.

Some schemes of work might also require you to have separate headings for the following (and even if they do not, these are important factors to consider):

7. Functional skills coverage.
8. Links to Every Child Matters.
9. Differentiation.

What makes a good scheme of work?

- Easy to follow for a new member to the team.
- Comprehensive – fully covers the programme being studied.
- Provides specific guidelines.
- Includes flexibility.
- Includes a variety of teaching and learning strategies.
- It's not 'cut and paste'.
- Takes into consideration the specific needs of the group being taught.

In practice, schemes of work are used:
- As a guide to lesson planning.
- To communicate an outline to learners.
- To evaluate, and then change in the light of experience.

When writing schemes of work try and plan backwards. Many colleagues deliberately under-plan by a couple of weeks, thereby building in time at the end for review and consolidation but also allowing for absence and other derailment. It is common to plan the learning processes in series linked to assessment so you can see how the picture of the learners' learning and your support and monitoring link together and build over time.

Sequencing

Both lesson planning and scheme of work construction are really exercises in the process of 'sequencing': making decisions about the order that learning activities and elements are placed in. Lessons need to flow, although they are best thought of as a series of activities which are 'chunked' together in a logical and progressive order making a learning narrative. Schemes of work also need to flow, building up to the end of the programme or unit/module and usually as a result building up to some kind of summative assessment (see Chapter 10).

In sequencing your scheme of work, consider the following:

1. What activities are the foundation for the programme being studied? What skills or knowledge are needed at the start? Put these first in your planning.
2. What might really capture the interests of the learners, making them engaged and motivated? Maybe these should be planned for early on as a way of getting them involved as quickly as possible?
3. What teaching and learning strategies do the learners like to do and are they those most suited for their learning and this programme? Try and negotiate your way around this so learners find lessons enjoyable.
4. When will formative, summative and ipsative assessments occur (see Chapter 10)?
5. What aspects of the programme are easiest – should they go first?
6. What bits of the teaching programme logically and clearly link to what other bits? Try and arrange a logical progression through the materials. Try and avoid jerking and leaping around.
7. What elements of the programme need more time to be covered than others?

Delivering content verses building skilful manipulators

Do not fall into the trap of seeing schemes of work as planning how course content is delivered to learners. Do not simply see it as an exercise in getting through a load of material. Think about how learners will access and engage in the process of their own learning. Plan and sequence their skills development rather than simply deliver the course content.

To take the planning further, consider how schemes of work enable you as a teacher to enable learning to take place and to maximise every learning opportunity. Think about the following for inclusion on schemes of work:

1. Identify key features of the unit: outline the essential nature and rationale for the unit – include what knowledge, skills and understanding the unit will cover.
2. Identify where the unit will fit in – outline the links with other units, previous and future learning and other cross-curricular aspects (for example functional skills).
3. Identify your expectations: what will learners be able to know, do and understand on completion of this unit?

4. Identify your expectations for all learners including those who will attain levels above and below the required level.

5. Consider inclusion strategies which will ensure all learners are able to achieve the expectations.

6. Consider prior learning: what has been the learners' previous experience in relation to what has been learned through previous units and how have they been taught, that is, teaching and learning styles.

7. Identify aims and objectives of the individual lessons that make up the shape of the overall scheme.

8. Outline the knowledge, skills, and understanding that learners will learn by the end of the unit including assessment criteria.

9. Select and identify the content: state how the material is to be developed from the initial starting point to the end result. The intention is to show progression.

10. Identify learning across the curriculum: set out the relationship between the lessons and the embedment of functional skills. How can you enhance these aspects of learner learning?

11. Identify links with PSHE, ECM and citizenship where appropriate.

12. Identify health and safety issues where appropriate.

13. After you have taught the scheme of work you need to evaluate it for its effectiveness and improve on it for the next year.

This last point is important. Try and evaluate the scheme as you go along. If you deviate from the scheme, make annotated notes both for your records, and as information/evidence for line managers and inspectors – help them to see that you are tracking the changes as you go along, in line with the needs of the group that you are studying. If you deviate considerably and work as part of a larger team, ensure you speak to your colleagues and keep them as fully informed as possible.

Rigidity verses flexibility in curriculum planning

It should be possible to pick up your scheme of work, identify the week in question, go and observe the lesson and see the connection between what is written on the scheme of work and what goes on in the classroom. But then again, life often does not work like this. Most teachers will tell you that schemes of work are 'ideal' documents that then get applied, evaluated and changed as the learning process is undertaken by each new group. The scheme of work used last year will not necessarily meet the needs for the next year since the learners are different year on year. Having said this, in institutions where common year and cohort schemes are in place for all classes and all teachers, it still might be the case that schemes need adapting and changing – one group might need different support and more time than another.

For these reasons, you need to approach schemes of work with a degree of flexibility. Yet, having said this, you still need to ensure that all aspects of the programme are covered and that all learners have been stretched to the best of their ability – and are then moved forward. Remember, you are planning to enable learning to take place. This is the whole point of any planning process.

Chapter links →

Themes and ideas explored in this chapter link to corresponding ideas in Chapters 5, 6, 7, 10 and 14.

CHAPTER 14

HOW TO ENGAGE LEARNERS

Objectives

By the end of this chapter the reader will be able to:

1. understand what is meant by 'learner engagement';
2. see the relationship between engagement and motivation;
3. understand the relationship between motivation and classroom management;
4. explore the importance of questioning for pace, engagement and assessment;
5. understand the relationship between assessment, feedback and motivation.

'It is all a question of engagement'

If asked 'what makes a good lesson?' our reply, simply enough, would be that learning has taken place (see Chapter 6). To elaborate on this simplest of views, a good lesson is when appropriate learning has taken place relative to the needs of the learners and the requirements of the programme under study. This learning should be both supported and yet challenging, and all learners should be on task. In other words, it is all a question of learner engagement. This is also true for classroom management (see Chapter 11): engaged and motivated learners are easier to teach, and what is more, there are less opportunities for derailment and distraction, thus pre-empting some potential classroom management issues.

Thinking about 'engagement'

By 'engaged' we mean that learners are clearly:

- 'on task';
- intrigued and curious to know more;
- enjoying the classroom experience;
- asking questions;
- welcoming challenge;
- stretching themselves.

Motivation refers to what triggers an individual to do something, and to want to do it. Engagement and motivation comes at the point where learners are successful and at the same time, challenged. Where they can see what they have done and where they are, and have appropriate feedback to move forward. Such engaged learners are a pleasure to teach. We also firmly believe that all learners can become engaged providing that:

- they are enrolled on the correct programme suitable for their needs;
- they are enrolled on the correct programme suitable for their interests and goals;
- they have a sense of their own development and where they need to progress to next;
- they feel their learning is worthwhile;
- they feel they are making progress and are supported in this development.

The trick for the classroom teacher is to get to know their learners so that they can fulfil the criteria above. But, more importantly, learners need to see for themselves that their teachers care and are taking seriously their learning, development and well-being. How you communicate this depends upon what sort of teacher you wish to become and what the ethos is of the institution you are working within. But you must find a way to communicate to your learners that you have the highest expectations of them, and ensure that your lessons challenge and enthuse.

Challenging and enthusing teaching is characterised by:

- a classroom environment that values learners' work through wall displays;
- lessons that are fast paced, with variety;
- lessons where learners feel the learning is worthwhile – they can see how it connects with skills or knowledge they need for examination/employment/programme completion;
- tasks which require thought – from both the teacher and the learner;
- unusual and varied routines which capture the interest of the learner;
- regular ipsative assessment (see Chapter 10);
- all learners being included and feeling that they are included;

- all learners feeling safe to take risks and try out new ideas/solutions/ways of working;
- teachers being on top of all potentially disruptive and derailing behaviour and situations (often called 'with-it-ness');
- teachers being lively and energetic;
- teachers being clear and focused communicators;
- teachers being flexible where needed and yet having a clear planned structure at all other times.

Think about the impression of your professional self

Think about what you say to learners about what sort of teacher you are, and about what you really want to say. Think about how you communicate what sort of teacher you are to learners – it is not always through verbal and intended communication. For example, if you can present a professional self which is largely motivated – your learners will be motivated too. Make it show that you want to be there and want to be teaching your classes. This means a great deal to learners.

Try to communicate that you are: upbeat, planned and organised, in good humour, taking learning seriously but not taking yourself too seriously, approachable, strict, flexible, still a learner yourself and, above all, that you have high opinions and high regard for your own learners.

Motivation

The starting point for much discussion on the role of needs, drives and motivation in education is often found in the classic work of Abraham Maslow (1970) (see Chapter 9). For Maslow, needs can be expressed on a hierarchy ranging from basic needs such as the physiological need for food and air, through more emotional needs for love and relationship, and ending with the high-order need for 'self-actualisation', in other words, for self-fulfilment. Maslow points out that the higher level needs cannot be fulfilled without the lower needs at the bottom of the hierarchy having been met. Thus, starving people cannot appreciate aesthetic beauty until they have the base physiological need or 'drive' for food met.

Post-Maslow, motivation is frequently seen to be characterised into two types:

1. Intrinsic motivation – self-reward; pleasure found within the task itself being undertaken. Motivation comes from within.
2. Extrinsic motivation – motivation resulting from what the task might lead to. Motivation comes from external rewards.

Intrinsic motivation is 'deeper' than extrinsic – it is also longer lasting, but harder to develop in the first place.

Extrinsic motivation derives from variables outside the actual task being completed. For example, in a lesson, intrinsic motivation might be found in the pleasure for learning the individual has found within mastery of the task, whereas extrinsic motivation might be managed (or mismanaged) by how the teacher responds to the learners.

Medals and missions: the role of feedback in motivation

Central to the work of the Assessment Reform Group (2002) is the notion of the role played by formative assessment in motivating learners (see Chapter 10). Formative assessment is assessment that is ongoing and provides both teachers and learners with a sense of where learners are within a wider journey. Formative assessment then points the way with targets for the learners' future development.

The Assessment Reform Group advocates the use of a 'medal and mission' approach to the feedback resulting from formative assessment. This type of feedback is seen to be highly motivating for the learners involved.

Medal = what is done well – that is, the praise
Mission = what the learner needs to do next in order to further improve.

Thinking about praise

Be mindful of when and how you use praise. Too often and you can devalue your intended outcomes – not enough and many learners can become disheartened. Drawing together the literature we can suggest the following points to consider when thinking about praise and its role in motivation:

P = punchy delivery, not long winded
R = received as a clear message by the learner – they need to know exactly what was good/exactly what they are being praised for
A = articulated through both verbal and non-verbal (body language) communication
I = ignore rule-following – only praise learning
S = space your praise – do not do it too often or you will devalue it
E = expressed naturally – it needs to seem authentic and genuine to the learner

It is not just the case that we need to be mindful, as teachers, of how we shape and express praise. It is also the case that learner motivation is seen to be shaped by the deeper values and attitudes held by the teacher about learners and about learning.

Discussion point

Many behavioural psychologists are wary of praise being used in what they see as the wrong context. From this perspective, praise and reward are highly effective motivators if they are used to praise learning, and not used to praise rule-following or compliance. Compliance should be expected – and therefore as such it should not be praised. If it is, this then creates the wrong message, and ultimately undermines praise given to learning and effort. Have you seen colleagues fall into this trap? Have you done it yourself?

Developing the 'motivation to learn'

The Assessment Reform Group (2002) uses the phrase 'motivation to learn' which is seen, in many resects, to be parallel to the 'assessment for learning' techniques the group advocate (see Chapter 10). The group identify eight key factors that can affect the learner's 'motivation to learn':

1. How do learners see their worth?
2. Do learners feel they can actually succeed at a given task?
3. Can learners self-evaluate their actions and performance?
4. Does the purpose of the learning make sense to the learner?
5. Does the learning hold interest? Does it give pleasure?
6. How much effort is the learner prepared to put in before they give up?
7. Does the learner feel in control of their own learning? Do they feel they can affect it?
8. Are learners confident in the actions they are taking? Do they see the potential outcome?

While challenging tasks often are highly motivating, they are also risky. What we mean by risk is that they could lead to learners feeling like they have failed and as a result be unwilling to take risks in the future. Challenging tasks are therefore risky since if a learner fails, this would be highly unmotivating. And yet, on the other hand, low-order ('easy') tasks are often not motivating due to their very ease of completion. We can apply these ideas to Bloom's taxonomy of learning (see Chapter 13). Low-order tasks (identify, explain, comprehend, define, list, recite) are easy, low risk, and relatively simple, whereas higher-order tasks (synthesis, apply, evaluate) are more of a challenge but more of a risk as a result.

This poses some interesting problems for the classroom teacher – to try and set challenging tasks, yet support them in appropriate and differentiated ways (see Chapter 17) so that learners can feel the benefit of effort and its reward, and yet, at the same time, the task is not too impossible.

A risky business?

The relationship of good teaching and learning to risk is an interesting one. Learners – and teachers as learners too – need to take risks. And yet, by their nature, risks are sometimes uncomfortable. You will need to develop a good positive relationship with learners to get them to take risks in the very public space of the classroom, but then again, 'safe' teaching is often dull which then brings with it problems of its own. Create an atmosphere where it is OK to get things wrong.

Making learners no longer able to learn!

Psychologist Johnmarshall Reeve (2005) uses the concept of 'learned helplessness' to think about the dangers of overly structured and 'risky' teaching and activities. Learned helplessness means to give up responsibility for learning in the face of feeling that effort is pointless since the outcome is fixed and beyond change.

Some teachers do not allow learners to discover for themselves, and to feel that they have a say over the direction their learning takes. Given this, why would learners want to take part and engage with what teachers are asking them to do?

There is a tension here – teachers do need to assess and they need to direct and frame learning, but at the same time, they need to ensure that learners feel they are being consulted and informed about the choices teachers are making. There is also a compromise to be made in listening to the learner voice (see Chapter 19), providing opportunities for ipsative assessment (see Chapter 10) and allowing learners to learn by doing so in an 'active' fashion (see Chapter 16).

One way to think about your classroom tasks and activities is to put yourself in the learners' shoes, and think about the following questions:

1. Can learners complete the task – is it possible given their prior learning and performance?
2. Which individuals need more/extra/different support from others?
3. What barriers might there be to completing the task?
4. Is the task relevant – and how do learners get to see that it is relevant?
5. Is the task doable in the time given?
6. Are the instructions clear and unambiguous?
7. What will learners find hard; what can be done about this?
8. Are resources, or the task itself, stimulating and pleasing?

The research surveyed by the Assessment Reform Group points to the conclusion that tests as a form of assessment are often highly unmotivating or, to express it more strongly, often demotivating. They argue that since tests are often an 'exposure' of the learner, the risks are too great for the effort to be put in, only to risk failure. To make things worse, the results of tests are often made public to whole groups of learners, making the likelihood for demotivation even higher.

The rules of engagement

Learners will be engaged and will be prepared to put in a lot of effort if:

- the task is stimulating;
- resources are well presented and at an appropriate level;
- teacher support is offered;
- the task is challenging – but not too much;
- instructions are clear;
- the point of the learning and its value is made clear to the learner at all times.

---

ch and Moon (2008) argue that motivating and engaging learning is only possible gh developing a sense of 'participatory' learning. This is achieved through learn-king charge and having a voice in the direction(s) their learning takes. Equally, ding to Leach and Moon, teachers need to see themselves as learners too, and to ct and present that image to their learners – to offer themselves as a learning role l. Finally, on an intuitional level, teachers and learners need to agree on what ngful learning is – what it looks like and how it takes place – and everyone needs : learning in as transparent terms as possible. This view – that learners need to ow their own learning works – brings us to the idea of meta-cognition.

eta-cognition

tivation is sometimes linked to the development of a very particular 'thinking skill' thinking process' referred to as 'meta-cognition'.

Meta – above, over and beyond the surface.
Cognition – thinking.

Meta-cognition, or as it is sometimes known, meta-learning, is 'thinking about think-ing', or rather, 'thinking about how we think'. This is a reflexive process seen to enable learners to develop their learning even further – to own the processes they follow when they are learning as a means to maximise each opportunity. This comes through very strongly from the views of both Leach and Moon and the Assessment Reform Group that we looked at earlier in this chapter.

Bruner offers the following statement:

> The child is not merely ignorant or an empty vessel, but somebody able to reason, to make sense, both on her own and through discourse with others. The child ... is capable of thinking about her own thinking, and of correcting her ideas and notions through reflection – by 'going meta', as it is sometimes called. (Bruner, 1996: 56)

As we can see here, meta-cognition is the ability to own the processes through which one applies thinking – to really know the processes and stages that our own learning passes through. It is usually seen to be both reflective and also applied – in the sense that we use it in an active fashion to develop our learning and thinking further. Meta-cognition is therefore ongoing.

All this means we have to motivate learners to develop their meta-cognition, and in turn, develop their meta-cognition to help motivate them! This is often what educational theorists and theories mean when they speak about the importance for learning to be (a) transparent, (b) meaningful and (c) 'owned' by the learners.

McGregor (2007) suggests that questioning can help to develop practical meta-cognition – both questioning of learners by teachers (asking 'why did you do that?', 'how would you do it again?', 'why did you make those choices?'), and the encouragement of learners to ask reflective questions of themselves and each other. In this way, meta-cognitive processes allow ownership and they also allow a supportive dialogue between the teacher and the learner. They allow for reflective thinking and also lead to ipsative (self-)assessment (see Chapter 10).

Think about your own learning!

In order to develop a critical and evaluative approach to your own teacher education, you might wish to think about your own learning. Teachers need to develop meta-cognition as much as their learners – they need to understand their own professional learning and to see why they approach tasks in the way they do.

This criticality is essential for postgraduate study in general, and also important for the new M level in teaching and learning (see Chapter 19).

Learner-centred teaching and learner engagement

Meta-cognitive processes are often closely linked with two schools of educational and pedagogic thought: constructivism and social learning theory.

- Constructivism suggests that learning is built upon older learning. Learning processes are seen to involve the manipulation of bits and pieces of a greater whole using puzzles and problem-solving and applying previous knowledge.

Learning is active – learners are doing something – and also communal; learners need to talk and interact with each other and the teacher (see Chapter 9).

• Social learning theory emphasises the need for interaction for learning to take place. Learning is seen to be at its most productive when learners learn with and from each other (see Chapter 9).

What these philosophies have in common is a commitment to what we can call 'learner-centred teaching' and to 'active learning' (see Chapter 16). Learner engagement and motivation is seen to lie within the social and 'playful' pedagogic practices and strategies these theories deploy, resulting in learners being social, working with others, talking as a means to learning and building meaning which they feel they themselves own.

Pace

Engagement can also be enhanced through the 'pace' of the lesson. By pace we mean the tempo of the lesson – how the experience and social encounter flows from start to end. This is an essential issue to consider when planning lessons (see Chapter 13). Good lessons are 'pacy' if:

• learners are on task, and there is always something for them to do that is appropriate and meaningful;
• lessons have variety within them;
• everyone is doing something from the very start;
• the teacher is able to explain why learners are doing what they are doing – to demonstrate the purposefulness;
• time for each activity is judged so that learners can complete but others have not finished too soon;
• extension activities are provided for those that do finish early;
• the lesson has a sense of 'start', 'middle' and 'end' about it (see Chapter 15).

One trick is to plan backwards in your lesson plans (see Chapter 13). Ensure that lessons are a journey or have a narrative – where the sections of the lesson build on top of each other over the duration. Another trick is to plan the learner activities foremost – to think about what learners will be doing, rather than what you as the teacher will be doing. This is very hard at first, but to see the lesson from the learners' point of view is essential. If learners are not working on a task – doing something – then pace will be lost. Equally, if activities are given too much time (or too little) then this will also disrupt the flow.

Get the pace right, and you will often avoid minor disruptions and distractions. Lessons should not be always run at a breakneck speed (sometimes learners find this confusing and unsettling), but learners should feel that they are being swept along and have not a moment to think apart from fully immerse themselves in the learning tasks on offer.

Effective questioning techniques

One aspect of learner engagement that is often linked to pace in the classroom is the role played by teacher 'questioning'.

Questioning is hugely significant for teaching – it is something we do all the time, often without thinking about it, and this therefore makes it even more important that we reflect upon the sorts of questions we ask, the reasons for asking questions and the ways of asking and answering.

There are many reasons why we might ask questions in the classroom:

- to check learning;
- to assess prior learning;
- to encourage learner reflection;
- as a teacher, to check our own instructions make sense;
- to offer support;
- to enable meta-cognition (see above);
- to settle everyone in by getting everyone to say something;
- as a classroom management technique – to check that learners are on task and paying attention;
- to provide feedback;
- to illustrate that we value the contributions and opinions of learners;
- for differentiation purposes.

Your questioning technique will really make a difference to how learners respond to you, and to how you can quickly move through the pace and tempo of your lesson – good questioning adds flow and that all-important 'relational' quality between the teacher and the learners. Done in the wrong atmosphere or at too great difficulty, questioning can lead to learners feeling unmotivated.

Having said this though, by varying the use of closed/open/multilayered questions, you can gradually build the confidence of learners who, although they might get questions 'wrong', can see that by answering them learning is taking place. This is what we mean when we say that questioning should not just assess but should stretch, and that learners should learn from your questioning of them.

Ten common questioning pitfalls

Avoid the following, they occur more often than you might think!

1. Asking rhetorical questions (some learners will not realise).
2. Asking a question and then giving the answer away within the question itself.
3. Asking a question of the same few learners each time.
4. Giving too little time between the question and asking for the answer.
5. Asking such open questions that they are vague and meaningless.

6. Asking questions to the whole class that no one will answer.
7. Answering your own questions seconds after asking them – without allowing time for the learners to consider a response.
8. Asking a long-winded question where the answer is a simple one-word response.
9. Asking leading questions where the answer is obvious – for example, 'don't you think that ...'
10. Provide the answer as a 50/50 choice, and thinking it is a genuine learning experience, for example, 'What is happening here? Is it 4 or is it 8?'

Some teachers favour a 'thinking time' approach to questioning – especially among younger learners. The teacher asks a question and learners have a prearranged common time-period in which to think and reflect about the question and its answer before they are allowed to answer or before the teacher asks for answers. Sometimes this thinking time can be used to consult with a peer, but this would be up to the teacher to set the framework within the thinking time.

There is often a tendency for teachers when using questioning to want to rush and move on. Although pace and tempo are clearly important, there is a negative consequence to rushing questioning, leading to learners often becoming demoralised, unwilling to provide answers – in turn leading to difficult classroom moments when teachers wish learners to speak out loud and learners 'refusing' or not being comfortable doing so. Over time, if a learner is given time to answer – and that answer is correct – then they will gain confidence and motivation over a series of lessons.

Make a good start

Try to get all learners comfortable and used to saying something right at the start of the lesson – every lesson. Asking learners to recite, chant, list low order concepts at the start, maybe building up to harder questions later – makes a difference to pace, engagement and learner confidence. It is important to start this process early on, so it becomes an accepted part of a normal routine, otherwise sometimes it has the opposite, demotivating effect since it is threatening if suddenly adopted mid-year.

When thinking about questioning, here are some techniques to try:

1. Socratic questioning – try to draw out answers from learners rather than fill them up with content – 'what do you mean by that?', 'can you explain that?', 'why do you think that?'

2. Rolling questions – build questions on top of other questions, each learner response leads to another question from another learner, picking up on words used in the previous response.

3. Traffic-directing – get learners to ask questions of each other; your role simply becomes managing the interplay between them as if you were directing traffic rather than being involved in asking actual questions yourself.

4. Bloom's questioning – move your questions up through Bloom's cognitive hierarchy (see Chapter 6). Start with recall, then define, then apply, synthesise and, finally, evaluate. Each part could be asked of one learner or of different learners.

5. Low-order questioning as a starter and plenary – simple recall questions can still have lots of value at the start and end of a lesson to get everyone involved as either a 'warm-up' or 'warm-down'.

6. Teacher mobility and questioning – aim to ask questions standing by each wall of your classroom (preferably in the centre of that wall). At each point where you stand 'sweep' the classroom from left to right choosing two or three learners to fire questions at. This is an efficient and effective way of making sure that the whole class feels like you may ask any learner questions and, as such, is a valuable classroom management strategy.

'Question banks'

You might wish to get learners to make, collectively, their own 'banks' of short, snappy questions which are then pulled together into as large a resource as possible. This is an excellent revision tool and allows learners to feel engaged in the process of their own revision.

Questioning: the 'dos' ✓

Good questioning can lead to pace and can make learners feel engaged in classroom activity.

1. Try to make sure that your questioning assesses learning.
2. Try to make sure that you assess and include all learners in your questioning.
3. Ensure that questions are able to be answered by those you are asking ...
4. ... but at the same time, try and stretch learners.
5. Encourage learners to ask questions of you.
6. Encourage learners to ask questions of each other.
7. Use questions at the start of the lesson to settle learners into the learning.
8. Build an environment and ethos where it is okay to get questions wrong.
9. Use questions at the end of the lesson to show learners what they have done.
10. Ensure that your questioning extends learning as much as it assesses it.

Know your learners!

In order to have engaged and motivated learners you need to engage them! Learners, over time, will need to find their own intrinsic motivation, but perhaps it helps to see the role of the teacher – at the start of their relationship with a group of learners – as directing, supporting and framing their future motivation. Learning is hard, and all too often schools and colleges can be alienating and damaging places. Many learners might feel they are unable to succeed, or might feel that 'have to be there' and have no choice. If you can help learners to develop a sense of purpose, develop meta-cognition and to see the value in what they do, your job and theirs will be much easier and more rewarding for all concerned.

Chapter links →

Themes and ideas explored in this chapter link to corresponding ideas in Chapters 13, 15, 16 and 17.

Suggested further reading

Assessment Reform Group (2002) *Testing, Motivation and Learning*. Cambridge: University of Cambridge.

Leach, J. and Moon, B. (2008) *The Power of Pedagogy*. London: Sage.

References

Assessment Reform Group (2002) *Testing, Motivation and Learning*. Cambridge: University of Cambridge.

Bruner, J.S. (1996) *The Culture of Education*. Cambridge, MA: Harvard University Press.

Leach, J. and Moon, B. (2008) *The Power of Pedagogy*. London: Sage.

McGregor, D. (2007) *Developing Thinking, Developing Learning: A Guide to Thinking Skills in Education*. Maidenhead: McGraw-Hill.

Maslow, A.H. (1970) *Motivation and Personality*. New York: Harper and Row.

Reeve, J. (2005) *Understanding Motivation and Emotion*. Hoboken, NJ: John Wiley.

CHAPTER 15

CLASSROOM IDEAS THAT REALLY WORK

Objectives

By the end of this chapter the reader will be able to:

1. use a variety of activities for starting lessons;
2. deploy a variety of activities during the main section of the lesson;
3. use a variety of activities to end lessons;
4. introduce activities for lessons with a new class of learners;
5. judge the appropriateness of classroom ideas against the time taken to prepare and how repeatable the technique is.

Why teaching is like being a magician?

Shortly before he died in 2009, iconic British magician William Wallace argued that in reality, there were only 10 magic tricks in the world that had ever been invented and that all modern magicians do is to find new ways of presenting these same 10 tricks. We would argue that this is not altogether dissimilar from the world of teaching. The 'trick', however, is to find exciting ways to initiate these teaching ideas, reflecting the creativity, charisma, enthusiasm and personality of the teacher who 'works' them. The teaching strategies in these next two chapters are influenced by the educational theories, concepts and inspiration of those we have encountered as well as a few ideas of our own.

Ease of use?

This feature allows the reader to judge for themselves the potential usefulness of the classroom techniques this chapter makes available. The individual reader will need to balance, as all teachers do, the time it takes to make a resource/plan against the learning benefits derived. The task also needs also to be judged against how simple the instructions might be for the learners.

Ideas to start lessons

While we agree that it is very important for learners to understand the aims and objectives of all lessons, have you ever stopped to wonder how many classes start in exactly the same way, that is, learners copy down aims and objectives and the teacher calls out the register? Is it any wonder then that some learners might not be overly worried if they were to miss the first 3–4 minutes of some of their classes? The following starter activities set the mood, pace, energy, high expectations and dynamism you require to ignite the minds of those you teach and have learners rushing to your lessons – on time!

Total recall: Ease of use ***** 5 stars

Time to prepare:	Time to set up:	Ease of instruction:	Student or teacher centred?	'Repeatability':
moderate	moderate	simple	student centred	once per term/module

Put a complex picture on the board that relates to the lesson you are about to teach and ask learners to study it carefully to remember as many features as possible from the picture (you could 'up' the competitive element here by offering a 'prize' for the best memory). Remove the picture and get learners in two minutes of silence to write down as many elements of the picture as they can recall – use the elements they remember to launch the lesson.

Quiz ball: Ease of use ***** 5 stars

Time to prepare:	Time to set up:	Ease of instruction:	Student or teacher centred?	'Repeatability':
none	none	simple	midway	often

Scrunch up a bit of paper (or buy a juggling ball) and throw it to a pupil and ask them a question, when they answer correctly they can throw to someone else asking them their next question. All questions must relate to the previous lesson you taught them.

Question master: Ease of use **** 4 stars

Time to prepare:	Time to set up:	Ease of instruction:	Student or teacher centred?	'Repeatability':
none	none	simple	student centred	occasional

Each person thinks (and writes down) five questions to which they know the answers from last lesson, then in groups they test each other. Can be made more fun by getting the groups to bang an imaginary buzzer before they have to answer a question.

Anagram fun: Ease of use **** 4 stars

Time to prepare:	Time to set up:	Ease of instruction:	Student or teacher centred?	'Repeatability':
none	none	simple	midway	occasional

Write the title of the lesson and ask learners to make as many words from the title in 3 minutes.

Stand up/sit down: Ease of use **** 4 stars

Time to prepare:	Time to set up:	Ease of instruction:	Student or teacher centred?	'Repeatability':
none	none	simple	midway	occasional

All learners stands up and can only sit down when each has said one key word from the last lesson – no repetition allowed.

Jackanory: Ease of use **** 4 stars

Time to prepare:	Time to set up:	Ease of instruction:	Student or teacher centred?	'Repeatability':
none	none	simple	midway	occasional once per term/module

A collective story where the teacher starts the story and asks each pupil to add a bit to it, for example, 'In 570AD in Arabia a man called Muhammad was born. He lived his life …'.

DJ: Ease of use **** 4 stars

Time to prepare:	Time to set up:	Ease of instruction:	Student or teacher centred?	'Repeatability':
moderate	moderate	simple	midway	once only

Have a piece of music playing as learners enter room. Stop the music and ask them to identify key lyrics, artist name and song title. Teacher links the song to the lesson topic.

Jigsaw puzzle: Ease of use **** 4 stars

Time to prepare:	Time to set up:	Ease of instruction:	Student or teacher centred?	'Repeatability':
moderate	moderate	simple	midway	once only

Make a quick jigsaw puzzle (cut out images from magazines and so on) and get images/objects from lesson in pack on each table. Ask learners to look at these, put them together and try to identify things they will cover in the lesson.

Spymaster: Ease of use **** 4 stars

Time to prepare:	Time to set up:	Ease of instruction:	Student or teacher centred?	'Repeatability':
moderate	moderate	simple	midway	once only

Write the lesson title or key word in code and ask the learners to crack it. For example: Slavery = 19 – 12 – 1 – 22 – 5 – 18 – 25 (clue Z = 26).

Key word clue: Ease of use **** 4 stars

Time to prepare:	Time to set up:	Ease of instruction:	Student or teacher centred?	'Repeatability':
moderate	moderate	simple	midway	occasional once per term/module

Each paired pupil has an envelope on their desk with a key word inside. The other person is allowed to ask three questions to find out the word.

Square bashing: Ease of use **** 4 stars

Time to prepare:	Time to set up:	Ease of instruction:	Student or teacher centred?	'Repeatability':
moderate	moderate	simple	midway	once only

Four rectangles on a PowerPoint slide, each with a drawing which represents a key word for the lesson. Four key words represent the objectives/aims of lesson – learners in groups decode the drawings and guess the objectives of lesson.

Sift and sort: Ease of use **** 4 stars

Time to prepare:	Time to set up:	Ease of instruction:	Student or teacher centred?	'Repeatability':
moderate	moderate	simple	student centred	once per term/module

Simple sorting exercise to match 10 key words to definitions – these are printed, laminated and left in envelopes for start of lesson (ideal in pairs or solo).

True/false dilemma: Ease of use ***** 5 stars

Time to prepare:	Time to set up:	Ease of instruction:	Student or teacher centred?	'Repeatability':
none	none	simple	student centred	once only

Display a contentious statement on the board. Ask learners to move to one end of the class if they feel the statement is true and to the opposite end of the class if they believe the statement is false. Explain to the class that they need to be able to, in one sentence, justify why they have moved to that position. Choose two learners from each end to feed back their reasons to the class.

Collective mind-map: Ease of use *** 3 stars

Time to prepare:	Time to set up:	Ease of instruction:	Student or teacher centred?	'Repeatability':
moderate	moderate	simple	midway	occasional

This works best if you have access to one of the many mind-mapping programmes available to download. However, it can also work well if smart-board technology exists in your classroom. Ask learners for key ideas from the last lesson (with books closed) and collate as a collective mind map on the smart board. This activity can be extended into a homework by asking learners to create their own mind-map based in this activity.

Humpty Dumpty: Ease of use **** 4 stars

Time to prepare:	Time to set up:	Ease of instruction:	Student or teacher centred?	'Repeatability':
moderate	moderate	simple	student centred	once per term/module

Cut up an exemplar essay intended to stimulate discussion and related to the lesson being taught. Distribute to learners in envelopes. They have to work together to reconstruct the paragraphs in the order that the essay was written.

Diamond-9: Ease of use ***** 5 stars

Time to prepare:	Time to set up:	Ease of instruction:	Student or teacher centred?	'Repeatability':
moderate	moderate	simple	student centred	once per term/module

Using 'word' or 'publisher' on your computer create nine squares that can fit together in the shape of a diamond. In each square produce a contestable statement. If possible laminate and put in envelopes. Learners in pairs are asked to rank statements in a diamond shape according to if they agree/disagree with them.

Multi-choice challenge: Ease of use ****** 6 stars

Time to prepare:	Time to set up:	Ease of instruction:	Student or teacher centred?	'Repeatability':
none	moderate	simple	student centred	once only

Using multiple choice questions and answers made up by learners from their home-work (see below) get learners in pairs to test each other with their own true/false questions. This can also be adapted in the form of the game show *Who Wants to be a Millionaire?*

The five Ws: Ease of use **** 4 stars

Time to prepare:	Time to set up:	Ease of instruction:	Student or teacher centred?	'Repeatability':
moderate	moderate	simple	midway	once only

Choose an evocative photograph (for example, Napalm child running on street). Ask learners what they think is going on by focusing on the five Ws (What? Where? When? Why? Who?) to which you can also had an 'H' with the question 'how?' Target the questions at named learners in your classes and scatter the questions across the classroom (that is, front, back and sides).

Arty-fact: Ease of use **** 4 stars

Time to prepare:	Time to set up:	Ease of instruction:	Student or teacher centred?	'Repeatability':
moderate	moderate	simple	midway	occasional

Show them an object that relates to your subject area (for example, in Religious Education bring in the rosary) and ask learners to devise five questions to ask that when answered will explain what the object is.

These starter activities are useful when planning your lessons and developing your 'schemes of work' (that is, short-, mid- and long-term planning). Consider the 'repeatability' feature we include in this chapter and in Chapter 16. This particular feature will help you create a balanced repertoire of teaching strategies that differentiates for the wide variety of learners that you will encounter.

Ideas for middles of lessons

We hope you find the following activities useful when planning the main sections of your lessons. These activities could form all of the main section or a segment of it depending on the length of the lesson. Remember to read Chapter 16 as well when considering the most efficient ways of moving learners and organising some of the group work strategies required.

Kinaesthetic quiz: Ease of use *** 3 stars

Time to prepare:	Time to set up:	Ease of instruction:	Student or teacher centred?	'Repeatability':
moderate	moderate	simple	student centred	occasional

Using flashcards that you have prepared, put a pack of different coloured cards on each table. Each card contains information, for example, key terms, dates, images, and so on. Each table has five minutes to learn these before you remove all the sources. Jigsaw the groups (see Chapter 16) and then each student explains their sources to another table. Reconvene the groups and set a competitive quiz based on all the sources with a prize for the winning group.

Google Earth tour: Ease of use *** 3 stars

Time to prepare:	Time to set up:	Ease of instruction:	Student or teacher centred?	'Repeatability':
significant	significant	moderate	midway	once only

You will need access to a number of computers for this activity. Using Google Earth/Street tour get pairs/groups to carry out an e-expedition somewhere that your learners could not be taken to (jungles in South America, inner-city slums in Mexico, and so on). Get each pair/group to work on a different theme/destination/concept depending on what is appropriate for your subject area. Learners report back to the class what the outcomes were.

Chief examiner: Ease of use **** 4 stars

Time to prepare:	Time to set up:	Ease of instruction:	Student or teacher centred?	'Repeatability':
moderate	moderate	complex	student centred	once only

Obtain from examination boards exemplar passed papers with known marks and the accompanying mark scheme (you can always create your own if you prefer). Make sure you have three papers (photocopied in different colours) that represent high, mid and low marks. Each student gets a set of the three exemplars and the mark scheme. Learners have to agree on the marks they would award. Their job is to get as close as possible to the correct marks you have already decided.

Revision cards: Ease of use ***** 5 stars

Time to prepare:	Time to set up:	Ease of instruction:	Student or teacher centred?	'Repeatability':
none	none	simple	student centred	occasional

In earlier homework activities (see below) get learners used to creating their own case studies/revision cards that relate to their subject areas and that they can use to revise for examinations (for example, cards could contain key names, concepts, evidence, dates). In class get them to memorize five of their cards in silence (in 5 minutes) and then they can test each other in pairs or in groups). Each week get them to choose the three cards they know least and then swap and test in pairs on their weakest cards.

In your zone: Ease of use **** 4 stars

Time to prepare:	Time to set up:	Ease of instruction:	Student or teacher centred?	'Repeatability':
significant	moderate	complex	student centred	occasional

Create table zones where each table has a theme. For example, in a history lesson about the causes of the Cold War one table could be Russia, one table America, and so on. Arrange learners in groups of four and assign them a table. Create/leave sources/artefacts, text, images on each table. Have a buzzer/bell and allow learners 5 minutes at each table before sounding the buzzer and moving them on. The job of the groups is to research the causes and then feed back to the class their findings after all tables have been visited.

Time-line: Ease of use *** 3 stars

Time to prepare:	Time to set up:	Ease of instruction:	Student or teacher centred?	'Repeatability':
moderate	significant	complex	midway	once only

Create a time-line: for example, split class into four groups giving each group a time span to cover (for example, 40 years). The task is to investigate the lifetime of a significant person related to the subject being studied (for example, Karl Marx for sociology; Thomas Hardy in English). Learners can map out a time-line on the wall/floor/ceiling of significant events that happen directly and indirectly in the life of the character chosen.

Who wants to be a millionaire? Ease of use **** 4 stars

Time to prepare:	Time to set up:	Ease of instruction:	Student or teacher centred?	'Repeatability':
moderate	moderate	simple	midway	once only

Based on the television quiz, this activity works well towards the end of any unit/module and requires the teacher to put two chairs at the front of the classroom. Give learners 10 minutes to create the quiz questions. If possible record the soundtrack of the show. Pick one pupil to be the contestant and one to be the host and use the questions that learners have created. Like the television show give learners three lifelines; 50:50; phone a friend (ask someone in the class) or ask the audience (everyone in the class write answer on blank paper and holds it up). Swap the contestant and host.

Bridget Jones: Ease of use **** 4 stars

Time to prepare:	Time to set up:	Ease of instruction:	Student or teacher centred?	'Repeatability':
moderate	moderate	simple	student centred	once only

Get learners to complete diary entries putting themselves in the shoes of someone else. Give learners a range of resources (for example, textbooks/newspaper cuttings). What events do they write about and what advice would they give themselves. Choose learners to read out their entries.

Key concept quizball: Ease of use **** 4 stars

Time to prepare:	Time to set up:	Ease of instruction:	Student or teacher centred?	'Repeatability':
none	moderate	simple	student centred	once only

Get learners in groups to devise as many key concepts related to their subject as they can. Get them to memorise them in five minutes. As a whole class or in smaller groups learners chuck the ball from one person to the next. Whoever the ball is thrown at has to remember a concept (and explain it). That person then throws the ball to the next person, and so on.

Wall displays: Ease of use **** 4 stars

Time to prepare:	Time to set up:	Ease of instruction:	Student or teacher centred?	'Repeatability':
moderate	moderate	complex	student centred	once only

At the end of a topic use the entire lesson to design a wall display. Use a previous homework for learners (in groups) to collect items for the display/collage and so on (for example, photos/artefacts). Give the learners the materials (scissors, Velcro, and so on) allocating a section of the wall for each group and allowing them the freedom to decide how the display should look. The role of the teacher will be to mediate between the learners to ensure that they reach a compromise. Ask senior members of staff to come in and award a prize for the best display.

Hide the word: Ease of use **** 4 stars

Time to prepare:	Time to set up:	Ease of instruction:	Student or teacher centred?	'Repeatability':
moderate	none	simple	student centred	occasional

Remove key words from any text (can be done by scanning and editing or good old-fashioned correction fluid) placing those words jumbled at end of text. Learners in silence have to work out where words go in the text. In pairs they can compare their answers finally defining those key words.

Agony aunt: Ease of use **** 4 stars

Time to prepare:	Time to set up:	Ease of instruction:	Student or teacher centred?	'Repeatability':
moderate	none	simple	midway	once

This activity works well when confronting sensitive issues (for example, abortion, relationships, job interviews, and so on). Cut out (or create) problem scenarios and allocate these to different groups. Each group has to construct reply letters which can be read out to the class. Teacher needs to closely monitor ethical content of discussion and written output.

Envoy: Ease of use **** 4 stars

Time to prepare:	Time to set up:	Ease of instruction:	Student or teacher centred?	'Repeatability':
moderate	moderate	complex	student centred	occasional

Split the class into groups and allocate different information to each group (for example, pages from textbook, magazine article). Each group to study the information and discuss the relevant key issues. Choose one person to act as 'envoy' by moving to other groups and exchanging information before returning to the original group.

Ends of lessons

The final few minutes of your lessons should be dynamic, fun and allow learners to 'recap' what they have learnt in your lesson. It is an opportunity for learners and teachers to evaluate how successfully the aims and objectives of the lesson have been met. We hope that the following activities provide efficient ways for you, the teacher, to evaluate the success of your lessons.

Speed-dating: Ease of use *** 3 stars

Time to prepare:	Time to set up:	Ease of instruction:	Student or teacher centred?	'Repeatability':
moderate	moderate	moderate	midway	once only

Arrange the room in the fashion of a speed-dating scenario, that is, one long line of tables with chairs arranged so that two people will always be seated opposite each other. Make sure that you have five or six themes that you wish learners to discuss. Call out the first theme and give the class two minutes to discuss – blow the whistle. Keep *one* side of the class seated in the same seats but make sure all the others move down one person. Launch your second theme and blow your whistle. Continue till you have used all themes up.

BT – phone home! Ease of use ***** 5 stars

Time to prepare:	Time to set up:	Ease of instruction:	Student or teacher centred?	'Repeatability':
none	none	simple	student centred	occasional

Project the lesson objectives up on the board. In pairs, learners write down three questions they would like to ask as a result of what they have learned in the lesson relating them to the objectives of the lesson. Learners are then selected by the teacher to 'phone a friend' in the class who then attempts to answer a question.

Mad hatter: Ease of use **** 4 stars

Time to prepare:	Time to set up:	Ease of instruction:	Student or teacher centred?	'Repeatability':
none	none	simple	student centred	occasional

Ask learners to write one question on a piece of paper and scrunch it up putting it into a hat that you have brought into the lesson. Shake the hat around and then ask each pupil to take one question out of the had. Each pupil has to read out the question and answer it.

Last one standing: Ease of use ***** 5 stars

Time to prepare:	Time to set up:	Ease of instruction:	Student or teacher centred?	'Repeatability':
none	none	simple	student centred	occasional

All members of class stand up. Each student to think of one fact they have learnt in the lesson and then that student can sit down (or leave the class).

The domino effect: Ease of use **** 4 stars

Time to prepare:	Time to set up:	Ease of instruction:	Student or teacher centred?	'Repeatability':
significant	moderate	simple	student centred	once only

Create a set of dominoes on paper/card (for example, half of an A4 sheet with a key word/ concept and half with a definition). This can be done manually by you or you can download software that enables this to be done quickly. Give each group of four learners a pack of the dominoes (making sure that you never have the correct definition and key word on the same card). The winning group is the one that correctly lines up the dominoes.

Don't mention it! Ease of use **** 4 stars

Time to prepare:	Time to set up:	Ease of instruction:	Student or teacher centred?	'Repeatability':
moderate	none	simple	student centred	once only

Learners choose, from a bag, a term they have learnt during the lesson. They should attempt to describe, in a maximum of 30 seconds, the term to the other members of the class without using the word itself. Learners put their hand up as soon as they know the answer.

Just-a-minute: Ease of use *** 3 stars

Time to prepare:	Time to set up:	Ease of instruction:	Student or teacher centred?	'Repeatability':
moderate	moderate	complex	student centred	once only

Based on the BBC Radio 4 programme, learners have to talk for one minute on the subject taught without repetition, deviation or hesitation. This activity can be done as a whole-class or group activity. If possible find a buzzer/bell that learners can use to challenge when there is repetition and so on.

Hangman: Ease of use **** 4 stars

Time to prepare:	Time to set up:	Ease of instruction:	Student or teacher centred?	'Repeatability':
none	none	simple	student centred	once only

The class have to defeat the teacher by guessing the key concept/phrase before he/she can draw the hangman on the gibbet. The teacher draws a series of dashes (each dash corresponds to a letter in a word/phase that learners have to guess). Every correct letter they guess is written in the correct position but each false guess allows the teacher to draw the first part of a 'hangman'.

Who am I? Ease of use **** 4 stars

Time to prepare:	Time to set up:	Ease of instruction:	Student or teacher centred?	'Repeatability':
none	none	simple	student centred	once only

Each group is given a set of Post-it notes. Each member of the group writes the name of a famous person related to the subject taught and sticks in on the forehead of the person next to them. That group member is allowed up to 20 questions to find out the name of the person stuck to their head.

Cubism: Ease of use ***** 5 stars

Time to prepare:	Time to set up:	Ease of instruction:	Student or teacher centred?	'Repeatability':
moderate	none	simple	student centred	once only

Create or get hold of a large cube that you can write on. On each side write a generic question (for example, one thing I learnt today? One key concept I learnt today?). Create enough die for each group. Let the members of the groups role the dice in turn and answer the questions.

Put a sock in it: Ease of use **** 4 stars

Time to prepare:	Time to set up:	Ease of instruction:	Student or teacher centred?	'Repeatability':
moderate	none	simple	student centred	occasional

If possible buy four or five brightly coloured socks. Type up and laminate as many definitions/key concepts as relate to your lesson/s. Put them in the socks and give the sock to each group. One member starts by picking a concept from the sock and explaining it to the group without using the same word they have chosen. Whoever guesses the word correctly is given the sock and chooses a new word, and so on.

House of cards: Ease of use ***** 5 stars

Time to prepare:	Time to set up:	Ease of instruction:	Student or teacher centred?	'Repeatability':
none	none	simple	student centred	once only

Use a normal pack of cards and deal one card to each member of the class. Ask them to remember their card and give the cards back to you. Only use the cards that you have given out and ditch the rest. Read out a card and whoever 'was' that card has to recall one fact from your lesson. Read out the next card and that person has to remember a new fact from the lesson *and* the previous person's 'fact', and so on.

Just a minute or two: Ease of use ***** 5 stars

Time to prepare:	Time to set up:	Ease of instruction:	Student or teacher centred?	'Repeatability':
none	none	simple	student centred	once only

Either in groups/pairs/solo, give the class 60 seconds to come up with as many terms/facts/pieces of information they can in the 60 seconds. The winner is the one with the most.

The ideas above are meant to be fun and provide a lively ending to your lesson. But remember too that there are other ways of finishing lessons that are also really useful for learners (for example, in silence highlighting any new bits of information they have learnt, updating their subject diaries, arranging their folders). While such activities may be less 'dynamic' they nevertheless are a vital element to your repertoire and provide useful balance to the more extrovert ideas listed above.

Those first few lessons with a new class

Throughout your training you will invariably be taking over new classes and will want to create a good impression. But remember that you also want to create a sense of high expectation, not only about the sort of teacher you want to be with them but also the sorts of activities you want to do with learners throughout the year. Remember that it is much harder to attempt to move learners in fun group-based activities later on in the year if they are not used to you doing it from the start. We hope that these activities help you forge the sorts of relationships and classroom atmosphere that enables many of the activities that this book offers you.

Don't blame the DJ: Ease of use ***** 5 stars

Time to prepare:	Time to set up:	Ease of instruction:	Student or teacher centred?	'Repeatability':
significant	moderate	simple	midway	once only

Put together a CD of 12 songs related to the subject you are about to teach. Edit down to 5 seconds for each song (or just play the first 5 seconds). The class, arranged into teams, has to guess the group/song title or both. We suggest a box of chocolates or similar for a prize for the winning group. Use song themes to launch topic.

Jigsaw pieces: Ease of use ***** 5 stars

Time to prepare:	Time to set up:	Ease of instruction:	Student or teacher centred?	'Repeatability':
moderate	moderate	simple	student centred	once only

Cut up a picture or article related to the lesson. Use large pieces. Give each student one piece of the puzzle and ask them they to walk around to complete the puzzle. This activity is really good at getting learners moving and talking to people they would not normally talk to and is good for kinaesthetic learners.

Vision on: Ease of use ***** 5 stars

Time to prepare:	Time to set up:	Ease of instruction:	Student or teacher centred?	'Repeatability':
moderate	none	simple	midway	once only

Each student is given play-dough/plasticine or equivalent. Give them 2 minutes to create a model of anything that represents their feelings at starting a new course with you, their new teacher. Ask them to feed back to the class their thoughts. This activity works well for breaking down barriers in a fun and non-threatening way, and is great for giving you a quick insight into your learners.

Broken glass: Ease of use **** 4 stars

Time to prepare:	Time to set up:	Ease of instruction:	Student or teacher centred?	'Repeatability':
moderate	moderate	simple	student centred	once only

Get learners to individually reassemble an emotive image of a person/people cut into pieces. Ask them to discuss in pairs what people in the picture might be thinking or feeling. Get feedback from the class on what they would think or feel in their place.

Guess what! Ease of use ***** 5 stars

Time to prepare:	Time to set up:	Ease of instruction:	Student or teacher centred?	'Repeatability':
moderate	moderate	moderate	student centred	once only

Split the class into two teams. Choose three or four members from each team who, in turns, will come up to the front of the class facing their team mates. Behind are images/key words that the class has to explain to their team member who has to guess the image/word. Explanations must not directly refer to the picture/word (chose pictures/concepts that relate to the lesson you are about to teach). The winning team is the one that takes the least time in guessing all the images/words.

Line up: Ease of use *** 3 stars

Time to prepare:	Time to set up:	Ease of instruction:	Student or teacher centred?	'Repeatability':
moderate	moderate	simple	student centred	once only

Prepare pin-up cards that each student can wear. Each card will have on it a symbol/keyword/date/picture (whatever is appropriate to your lesson, for example, key events in world history). Ask the entire class to line up into a logical line at the front of the class (this creates high-spirited mayhem so be prepared to follow up immediately with a contrasting activity to calm learners down).

Film critic: Ease of use **** 4 stars

Time to prepare:	Time to set up:	Ease of instruction:	Student or teacher centred?	'Repeatability':
moderate	moderate	simple	midway	once only

Show a film clip relevant to the subject you are going to teach. Produce (preferably laminated) summary cards, some of which are true and some which are false. Brief the learners that they will receive cards *after* the film and that they need to decide if the cards are true or false. Run the clip and then give the packs of cards to paired learners to decide which are true and which are not.

Remember that on the morning of your lessons photocopiers, laminators and so on are often being used (either by other teachers or, if very early, probably by other teacher trainees like yourself). Having your own computer and printer at home is, we argue, an essential 'tool' of the trade. Remember, too, that in the bigger high street stationers, small laminators are incredibly cheap. Although some of the activities in this chapter may take longer to prepare than others, once these are done you can use them again and again. With both sets of equipment, you can 'knock up' professional long-lasting resources that will impress your tutors and raise your profile and respect with the most important 'stake holders', that is, your learners.

Chapter links →

Themes and ideas explored in this chapter link to corresponding ideas in Chapters 14, 16 and 17.

CHAPTER 16

IDEAS FOR ORGANISING LEARNING: GROUP WORK, REVISION AND HOMEWORK STRATEGIES

Objectives

By the end of this chapter the reader will be able to:

1. understand the conditions in which successful group work can take place;
2. deploy strategies to move learners around the classroom;
3. enhance group dynamics when taking over new classes;
4. introduce active learning strategies that encourage classroom discussion;
5. possess a range of homework strategies that can be fed into classroom teaching;
6. introduce successful examination-based revision strategies.

All ideas contained in this chapter draw on the many theories and concepts that this book has examined. For successful classroom teaching we firmly believe that focused and challenging classroom 'talk' is an essential component to mixed-ability teaching. Not only can this enthuse learners and boost the confidence of all learners, but it also provides a rich environment for you, the teacher, to monitor and assess the real learning that is taking place. However, successful classroom discussion and 'group work' are not activities that can just be thrown together on a whim. They require careful planning and orchestration on the part of the teacher, but in turn lead to 'buzzy', productive and exciting learning environments if done well. We passionately believe that noisy classrooms are classrooms where good learning is taking place, as long as the teacher manages and harnesses student interaction. We hope that this chapter offers you a variety of ways in which that orchestration can take place.

Moving learners around the classroom

There are many benefits and reasons for moving learners around the room during a lesson:

- As a means of classroom management, learners can be active and involved physically in the lesson.
- Moving and re-grouping learners enables effective differentiation through the strategic grouping of learners based upon characteristics and needs.
- Moving can stop learners from feeling bored and tired.
- Re-grouping might lead to a variety of strategies for peer working, discussion and peer assessment.
- Re-grouping can enable learners to mix and thus build a stronger sense of group identity over time.
- Re-grouping enables the teacher to place emphasis (in the planning and delivery processes) upon student talk and interaction as a prime vehicle through which learning takes place.

Five strategies for moving learners around the classroom

1. Jigsaw – this is a great method to ensure you are moving learners to sit with different members during the course of any lesson. It also is an extremely efficient method to disseminate large amounts of material to be learnt. Make sure tables in your class are arranged in groups of between three and five people. Ensure that these 'home' groups are reading and taking notes with different information (for example, different articles, sections or articles). After an appropriate time number each student on each group ('Group A, remember your numbers: 1, 2, 3, 4'; 'Group B, remember your numbers: 1, 2, 3, 4' and so on). Make sure the class can see you allocate a number to the original 'home' group tables ('Ladies and gentlemen this table is now "table 1", this table is "table 2"' and so on). Once *all* learners are clear

which table is which, move learners according to the number you allocated to them ('All number 1s please move to table 1, all number 2s to table 2' and so on). You now have re-formed groups with completely different members – ideal to bring together views gathered from the original home tables. If necessary you can then ask all learners to return to their home groups to summarise key ideas, themes, and so on.

2. Envoying – form 'home groups' at the start of the lesson. Learners in these groups will be working on tasks set where information-gathering is crucial. Each home group will be working on different information. Give groups time to summarise and then choose one person (the 'envoy') from each group to go to another group and transfer the information as well as pick up new information from the group they visit; then send them back to home groups.

3. Lollipop sticks – arrange and clearly number tables in groups before the lesson. Have a collection (enough for each member of your class) of lollipop sticks with a number on (make sure that the number corresponds with the amount of grouped tables you have arranged in the class). As each student comes into your class give them a lollipop stick and ask them to sit at that table.

4. Snowball – learners are asked to do an activity on their own for five minutes (for example, thinking of three questions they wish to ask about the subject studied). Learners pair up then to answer their own questions. Learners are then formed into fours where they identify key issues/concepts ideas that need to be further explored. Finally, one member is chosen from each group to bring up issues/ conclusions/suggestions useful to the class as a whole.

5. Circuit training – the classroom is arranged in a series of 'islands' each with a different activity on. You can label each table with a coloured title describing to learners what the nature of the activity is. As they arrive, they put their bags and coats to the side so that they are not an obstacle as they move, and in pairs or threes sit at a table of their choice. Each activity is short, lasting maybe between 10 and 20 minutes (depending on the length of your lesson) and afterwards learners move to the next task. If you vary the number of seats around the activities and ask learners not to move them, this forces the learners – over time – to re-group, leading to new combinations.

Activities to create group dynamics when taking over new classes

When taking over new classes it is important to break down barriers as quickly as possible so that you can create the right sort of classroom dynamics for learning to take place. It is also important for your learners to see you confidently manipulating the classroom in imaginative and creative ways. The following activities are suggestions for ways to create the rapport, empathy and good humour required for the ideas used in this chapter.

Game for a name: Ease of use **** 4 stars

Time to prepare:	Time to set up:	Ease of instruction:	Student or teacher centred?	'Repeatability':
moderate	moderate	simple	student centred	once only

Arrange seating in one large circle facing inwards. Going first anti-clockwise and then clockwise, ask each person to call out their name. Ask one volunteer to run to the chair of somebody else calling their name. This person must leave their chair calling the name of somebody else who, in turn, must leave their chair, and so on. This is a highly energetic way of breaking down barriers in new groups.

Back to back: Ease of use **** 4 stars

Time to prepare:	Time to set up:	Ease of instruction:	Student or teacher centred?	'Repeatability':
moderate	moderate	simple	student centred	once only

Learners sit back to back – one person has a picture or information and must describe it to the other. They must guess in words or draw what they think it is.

Square deal: Ease of use **** 4 stars

Time to prepare:	Time to set up:	Ease of instruction:	Student or teacher centred?	'Repeatability':
moderate	moderate	simple	student centred	once only

Give to each member of your class a sheet of paper that is made up of one large square with four smaller ones within. Learners should be sat in groups of three or four. Instruct the class to write down four bits of information about themselves, three of which must be lies, and one of which must be true. The group must tease out from each member which piece of information is correct.

Triangular interviews: Ease of use **** 4 stars

Time to prepare:	Time to set up:	Ease of instruction:	Student or teacher centred?	'Repeatability':
moderate	moderate	simple	student centred	once only

This activity works well the first time you take over a new class that has never met before and serves as an 'introduction'. Tables are not necessary for this activity and, if possible, move them to the sides of the classroom. Seat learners in groups of three numbering each student '1', '2' and '3'. Get the 1s to interview the 2s while 3s take notes. These interviews are short biographical details to be fed back to the class by way of introduction. Keep interviews short (3 minutes) and then ask the scribes to feed back to the whole class. Repeat, changing the roles until all learners have been introduced.

Popcorn: Ease of use **** 4 stars

Time to prepare:	Time to set up:	Ease of instruction:	Student or teacher centred?	'Repeatability':
moderate	moderate	simple	student centred	once only

Sit everyone in a circle with one person standing in the middle of the group. The person in the middle works around the circle naming each person either 'pop' or 'corn'. The person in the middle can call out either 'pop' (if this happens all the 'pops' have to change seats) 'corn' (all the 'corns' have to change seats) or 'popcorn' (everybody has to change seats). With one chair short one person will always be left in the middle, whereby they decide what to call.

The survival game: Ease of use **** 4 stars

Time to prepare:	Time to set up:	Ease of instruction:	Student or teacher centred?	'Repeatability':
moderate	moderate	simple	student centred	once only

Get your new class to sit in groups of four or five learners. Inform them that they are flying as passengers on a jumbo-jet over the pacific. By chance a nuclear war takes place during their flight disrupting the aircraft's instruments forcing the captain to ditch close to a small island. Shortly before crashing the captain learns from the radio that they are about to become the last remaining survivors on the planet. The job of each group is to decide what sort of society they can create on the island. Questions that might help the groups in deciding could include: what needs to be arranged immediately? How will tasks be arranged? How will decisions be made? How will children be looked after? How will family life be sorted? What happens to rule-breakers?

Strategies for classroom discussions

Unless classroom talk is tightly managed it can quickly dissolve into low (and sometimes high) level off-task behaviour. The following strategies will enable you to energise the classroom providing all learners the opportunity to engage in targeted conversation. This in turn will embed the learning affording learners the opportunity for greater recall as and when they require this information. It also provides invaluable opportunities for you to monitor and evaluate to what extent your teaching has been successful.

Rank statements: Ease of use **** 4 stars

Time to prepare:	Time to set up:	Ease of instruction:	Student or teacher centred?	'Repeatability':
moderate	moderate	moderate	student centred	once only

Initially seat learners in pairs. Give each pair 10 contentious statements related to your subject. Each pair have to rank these in order of agreement. Once agreed move two sets of paired learners together (class now in fours) and let the two pairs argue for the correct ranking. Repeat doubling up each time the numbers of learners, until you have a noisy debate between two halves of the class.

Jerry Springer: Ease of use *** 3 stars

Time to prepare:	Time to set up:	Ease of instruction:	Student or teacher centred?	'Repeatability':
significant	moderate	moderate	midway	once only

Based on the television show, give five learners a brief synopsis of their character. They then talk to other panel members in front of the class. The audience must ask questions and can also swap places with a character if they have something important to say.

Agree/disagree: Ease of use **** 4 stars

Time to prepare:	Time to set up:	Ease of instruction:	Student or teacher centred?	'Repeatability':
moderate	moderate	moderate	student centred	once per term/module

Write a statement up on the board with a line drawn down the middle of the class-room floor – pairs of learners move to whichever side they agree with. You then ask them to justify their position.

Debating pairs: Ease of use **** 4 stars

Time to prepare:	Time to set up:	Ease of instruction:	Student or teacher centred?	'Repeatability':
moderate	moderate	moderate	student centred	once only

Tables are not used in this lesson so move them all to the sides. Arrange chairs in pairs but so that each chair faces each other on one long row down the length of class. Choose two articles that offer opposing views on an issue and give one article to one half of the pair and one to the other. Allow them 5 minutes to prepare their case and then allow them to debate for 5 minutes. Once done, move half the pairs on clockwise to the next pair and get them to repeat but to a different partner (each time they are sharpening their arguing skills but also getting a different line back from their new partner).

BBC Question Time: Ease of use *** 3 stars

Time to prepare:	Time to set up:	Ease of instruction:	Student or teacher centred?	'Repeatability':
significant	significant	moderate	midway	once only

Based on the BBC programme ask for five panellists to represent the views related to any topic you are teaching – give them a week to prepare. Ask every member of the audience to prepare a question for the panel. Use the programme music (BBC website) to introduce the panel to the audience. Members of the audience put their hand up if they want to ask a question. Panel members must be allowed to finish what they were saying. This activity requires a strong chairperson.

What's changed? Ease of use **** 4 stars

Time to prepare:	Time to set up:	Ease of instruction:	Student or teacher centred?	'Repeatability':
moderate	moderate	simple	student centred	once only

Learners identify differences between two pictures or photographs. They must explain what has changed and why it has changed. For example two pictures showing differences in an environment (for example, a supermarket where there was once a park).

Games for learning

While some of the games below might require slightly more preparation they are well worth the extra effort. Games allow learners to take risks and experiment with knowledge in the full understanding that being 'wrong' is socially acceptable in the eyes of you their teacher. They provide wonderful ways for learners to revise concepts learnt and apply these ideas in different contexts. Finally, they break up what, at times, can be a monotonous curriculum experience and they enjoy their lessons all the more.

Pass-the-prop: Ease of use **** 4 stars

Time to prepare:	Time to set up:	Ease of instruction:	Student or teacher centred?	'Repeatability':
moderate	moderate	moderate	student centred	once only

A variation on the radio show, *Just a Minute*, with the learners in groups of three or four. Give them a topic to talk about (this could be a revision topic or a means of introducing a new topic). The aim is for the group to talk for a minute (or two) about the topic. One pupil is chosen to start talking; he/she will need a prop to pass round (for example, a pencil case). As soon as the pupil runs out of things to say or begins pausing, he/she should pass the pencil case to another pupil to continue. Learners in the group can offer to take the 'prop' and continue talking when they feel someone is drying up.

Swat the key word: Ease of use **** 4 stars

Time to prepare:	Time to set up:	Ease of instruction:	Student or teacher centred?	'Repeatability':
moderate	moderate	moderate	student centred	once only

Write items of subject vocabulary previously introduced on the board. Divide the class into two teams. One pupil (rep) from each team stands at the front of the class. Give each a fly swat or long ruler. Read out the definitions of the words. The teams call out the answer to their reps. The first pupil to swat the correct word claims it for their team.

Noughts and crosses: Ease of use **** 4 stars

Time to prepare:	Time to set up:	Ease of instruction:	Student or teacher centred?	'Repeatability':
moderate	moderate	moderate	student centred	once only

A version of the traditional game of the same name. Draw a grid on the board and write a number in each box numbering them 1–9. Divide the class in half and label them noughts or crosses. Team 1 chooses a number from the grid. The teacher reads a previously prepared question/definition which corresponds with the number on the board. If learners respond correctly, they win their team a 'O' or 'X'. For incorrect answers, the other team wins the 'O' or 'X'. It is then team 2's turn. The first team to get three 'O's or 'X's in a line wins.

Pass the parcel: Ease of use **** 4 stars

Time to prepare:	Time to set up:	Ease of instruction:	Student or teacher centred?	'Repeatability':
moderate	moderate	moderate	student centred	once only

While playing music, pass around a box filled with statements about the topic you will be studying in the lesson. When the music stops, the student with the box must pick out a statement, read it and decide whether it is true or false.

My other half! Ease of use **** 4 stars

Time to prepare:	Time to set up:	Ease of instruction:	Student or teacher centred?	'Repeatability':
moderate	moderate	moderate	student centred	once only

Divide the class into two halves, with one half given questions and the other given answers to those questions. Learners must go around the room trying to find out who their partner is.

Crosswords: Ease of use **** 4 stars

Time to prepare:	Time to set up:	Ease of instruction:	Student or teacher centred?	'Repeatability':
moderate	moderate	moderate	student centred	once only

Using crosswords (create your own or search online) get learners to do these under timed conditions and perhaps with a box of chocolates for the team that completes first (This also can make a fabulous homework to give to learners close to revision time.)

Bingo: Ease of use **** 4 stars

Time to prepare:	Time to set up:	Ease of instruction:	Student or teacher centred?	'Repeatability':
significant	moderate	simple	student centred	once only

Create bingo cards with a mixture of key concepts on each card but varying the assortment so that no one board is the same. Teacher reads out the definitions and learners have to cross out the appropriate key word. First one to complete board cries out 'bingo'.

Blockbusters: Ease of use *** 3 stars

Time to prepare:	Time to set up:	Ease of instruction:	Student or teacher centred?	'Repeatability':
significant	moderate	simple	student centred	once only

Based on the television game show and prior knowledge of this game vital. Split the class in two and give each a colour (red and green). The red team has to get from the top to the bottom and the blue team from left to right of the board. The teacher asks questions, for example, 'what M is a term for'. Learners need to put a hand up and not shout out (if they shout out, the point goes to the other team). The correct answer wins the team a blob of their choice and choice of the next letter. The first team to get from one side to the other wins.

Seven 'golden rules' when deploying group work

As firm believers in group-based learning we also recognise that, if not tightly managed, learners can quickly go off task. Adhering to the following 'rules' should enhance the effectiveness of any group-based teaching strategy you deploy.

1. Learners must have complete silence in any activity when they are memorising or reading material.
2. You must be able to move around the classroom with complete freedom – to troubleshoot but also to keep learners on task and be seen to be keeping them on task.
3. You must be able to listen to all learners in groups so that if at any time you need to stop the activity in order to clarify something, you can!
4. You must have complete eye contact with all members of the groups.

5. The activities must not go on for too long, but long enough for them to be able to gain confidence to engage – remember they actually love the challenge that these tasks pose.
6. Try if possible to photocopy handouts/resources onto different coloured paper – it makes the whole activity look more fun, it engages more people (differentiates) and in complex group work allows you to see easily which groups/pairs are working on what.
7. Seating for group work is essential: for example, try to split up all males in the class, get them working with females where possible; and make sure groups have a lively assortment of different learner abilities in them at the start, allowing weaker learners to gain confidence from picking up their ideas.

'Active learning' strategies

By 'active learning' we mean classroom strategies that enable learners to be engaged, usually through talk and peer interaction. These strategies are often rooted in a theoretical base of constructivism (see Chapter 9) and are often seen to help learners to develop higher order evaluation skills through learning and discovering together (see Chapter 15 for a fuller theoretical explanation of the notion of 'active learning').

The five Ws: Ease of use **** 4 stars

Time to prepare:	Time to set up:	Ease of instruction:	Student or teacher centred?	'Repeatability':
moderate	moderate	moderate	student centred	once per term/module

Show the class a mystery object or photograph. Ask them to come up with five W questions (who, what, when, where, why) which, when answered, may tell them what the object is.

Framing the picture: Ease of use **** 4 stars

Time to prepare:	Time to set up:	Ease of instruction:	Student or teacher centred?	'Repeatability':
moderate	moderate	moderate	student centred	once only

Give learners one photograph in groups (for example, a war photograph). Ask for suggestions as to what the 'bigger picture' might be – what is going on that we cannot see?

Learners then create the 'bigger picture'. You can use the five Ws (who, what, where, when, why?) to enhance the frame.

Matchmaker: Ease of use **** 4 stars

Time to prepare:	Time to set up:	Ease of instruction:	Student or teacher centred?	'Repeatability':
moderate	moderate	simple	student centred	once only

Clear large space in the classroom. On stickers and in large letters write key words and definitions. Give each sticker to a student and then get them to move around the class to find their 'partner' word or definition.

Shopping for ideas: Ease of use **** 4 stars

Time to prepare:	Time to set up:	Ease of instruction:	Student or teacher centred?	'Repeatability':
moderate	moderate	simple	student centred	once only term/module

Learners are given a 'shopping bag' of ingredients, for example, lollipop sticks, paper, pens, string. They have to plan an activity in five minutes in which they use the ingredients to teach something, for example, explain a solar eclipse, or how an electoral system works. This can also be set has homework where learners bring in their 'bags'.

Pig-in-the-middle: Ease of use **** 4 stars

Time to prepare:	Time to set up:	Ease of instruction:	Student or teacher centred?	'Repeatability':
moderate	moderate	simple	student centred	once only

Learners should be in threes. The teacher names a topic and two learners take it in turns to say words relating to the topic, keeping going until one person cannot go. The third pupil notes down the words. These are then fed back to the whole class.

Call my bluff: Ease of use **** 4 stars

Time to prepare:	Time to set up:	Ease of instruction:	Student or teacher centred?	'Repeatability':
significant	moderate	simple	student centred	once only

Based on the television game show, provide learners with a number of envelopes. Each envelope contains one term and three definitions, only one of which is correct. Pairs need to work to decide which definition is the correct one.

Jigsaw memory: Ease of use **** 4 stars

Time to prepare:	Time to set up:	Ease of instruction:	Student or teacher centred?	'Repeatability':
moderate	moderate	simple	student centred	once only

Take any article and split it into sections; then jigsaw it (see above), that is, split the class into three or six groups and give each group a section to read and memorise! Do not allow them to keep the articles. Collect them in, then get them to compare what they have remembered, taking notes. Split the groups up (this can be done by numbering them to re-form new groups) and get them to share the information. Finally, send them back to home groups teasing out issues by concepts, theories, and so an.

Question relay: Ease of use **** 4 stars

Time to prepare:	Time to set up:	Ease of instruction:	Student or teacher centred?	'Repeatability':
moderate	moderate	simple	student centred	once only

Make up a box or basket in which you have put lots of questions on strips of paper. Split the class into small groups. One member from the group runs to the front to get a question and goes back to the group to confer. When they have conferred, he/she returns to the teacher and explains the answer. If it is correct, the runner picks out the next question; if it is incorrect, the runner returns to the group to confer. The winning group is the group that answers most questions.

Effective revision ideas

We would argue that revision periods are often the most enjoyable phases of the teaching year. In most cases learners have covered all the material and should have some understanding of most of it. Their motivation levels will be heightened as they draw nearer to their final assessment. What greater opportunity could you ask for to introduce a range of fun-based activities to identify those examination based skills. The following activities should go some way in helping you do this.

Post haste! Ease of use **** 4 stars

Time to prepare:	Time to set up:	Ease of instruction:	Student or teacher centred?	'Repeatability':
moderate	moderate	moderate	student centred	once only

Give each group a theme to summarise and then each member of the group summarises one point on a Post-it note – all Post-its are put up around the class. Learners can then copy these down for later revision.

Station-to-station: Ease of use *** 3 stars

Time to prepare:	Time to set up:	Ease of instruction:	Student or teacher centred?	'Repeatability':
moderate	moderate	moderate	student centred	once only

Move all desks/tables to the side of the class and set up five or six 'stations' around the classroom (chairs can all be moved to the centre of the class or slid under tables as no chairs are used during the lesson) with important information at each station and on different coloured (preferably laminated) paper. Split the class into five or six groups instructing them to take notes for a maximum of five minutes at the particular station they arrive at (for example, key theories, key debates, key people).

Exemplar question: Ease of use **** 4 stars

Time to prepare:	Time to set up:	Ease of instruction:	Student or teacher centred?	'Repeatability':
moderate	moderate	simple	student centred	once only

Set the room up with four or five grouped tables with giant rice paper/flip chart paper on each. At the top of the paper write down an examination question (each table has a different question). Allocate one group to each table, giving them five minutes to write down their model answer to the question. Move the groups on to new tables, instructing the groups to add *new* material to the answer they see written down. Continue so that all groups circulate the room. Collate their answers and give them back to learners the next time you see them.

Using model answers: Ease of use *** 3 stars

Time to prepare:	Time to set up:	Ease of instruction:	Student or teacher centred?	'Repeatability':
significant	moderate	moderate	student centred	once only

Make sure you have lots of model questions and answers prepared in advance. As homework, give learners three questions for which they have to make essay plans. In the class the following week get them to compare their plans (five minutes per plan) with a view to writing under timed conditions, but do not tell them which question they are actually going to answer. Afterwards 'reward' them immediately with the model answer to the question they have written about *and* the two to the questions they prepared for. Get them to highlight anything in the model answer that does not appear in their own answers.

Folder blitz: Ease of use ***** 5 stars

Time to prepare:	Time to set up:	Ease of instruction:	Student or teacher centred?	'Repeatability':
none	none	simple	student centred	once per term/module

Do this activity three to four times a year. Instruct learners that for homework they are to prepare their folders to look immaculate, for example, labelled dividers, maximum of two handouts in each clear plastic wallet. It is essential that this is rigorously followed up if not carried out.

Card sort: Ease of use **** 4 stars

Time to prepare:	Time to set up:	Ease of instruction:	Student or teacher centred?	'Repeatability':
moderate	moderate	simple	student centred	regularly through revision period

In previous homework throughout the year learners will have been asked, on a regular basis, to prepare their own revision cards based around the key concepts, ideas and names related to your subject (see 'Homework strategies' section). Use these cards in the revision period. For example, learners can memorise their own cards choosing their weakest 10 cards, or test each other by asking their partner to pick out five cards from their set, and so on.

Card board: Ease of use **** 4 stars

Time to prepare:	Time to set up:	Ease of instruction:	Student or teacher centred?	'Repeatability':
moderate	moderate	simple	student centred	once only

Prior to the lesson, think about the revision cards your learners have created. On A4 paper (landscape) create blank boxes (similar to those on a Monopoly board game) where learners can place their revision cards. Make sure that you allocate a category to each of the blank boxes (for example, key words, key people, key theories). Photocopy the A4 page onto A3 paper and laminate the boards. Give these out in class and get learners in their pairs/groups to discuss where they should place their cards in the boxes you have created.

Fool the examiner: Ease of use **** 4 stars

Time to prepare:	Time to set up:	Ease of instruction:	Student or teacher centred?	'Repeatability':
moderate	moderate	simple	student centred	throughout revision period

After any timed writing that learners do for you, make sure they read through their own answers. Before giving the answers to you, instruct them to highlight key words, names, evidence, and so on. Make sure they also highlight the first three words of any new paragraph and their conclusions. Provide for them a list of key phrases (for example, 'in contrast', 'following on from this', 'returning back to the question') and get them to identify which phrases they could have substituted in their own answers.

Samson and Delilah: Ease of use **** 4 stars

Time to prepare:	Time to set up:	Ease of instruction:	Student or teacher centred?	'Repeatability':
none	none	simple	student centred	once only

Give learners two pieces of paper getting them to write their strongest topic on one piece and weakest on another. Match the learners accordingly so that they can teach each other according to strengths and weaknesses.

Homework strategies

The following suggestions for homework strategies are underpinned by the variety of theories on learning that this book has introduced you to. We have tried to include suggestions that provide a variety of assessment opportunities and that can be fed back into the following lesson. We hope you find them useful.

1. Use a mobile phone/camera to take photos/movies of places or people (for example, film an interview).
2. Google Earth can be used in variety of ways. Try setting a particular destination and get learners to write up what they see.
3. Put together a photo montage on a theme.
4. Get learners to make their own podcasts.
5. Make protest banners about an issue.
6. Take photos of anything that could represent an aspect of British culture/identity.
7. Design a poster/leaflet/booklet on a theme using work/Publisher.
8. Use Windows Moviemaker to make short 10-minute 'movie'/presentations.
9. Early in the year get learners to regularly create their own flash cards for revision.
10. Design a 'Microsoft PowerPoint' presentation *but* only using pictures and no words – learners present explaining why the pictures are important (this avoids monotonous reading out of slides).
11. Measure the photographic space of images in newspapers (for example, compare pictures of women and men in sports) – write up their findings.
12. Ask learners to find and bring in pictures linked to the next lesson.
13. Design a T-shirt logo on a theme related to your subject.
14. Design a quiz/true–false for your partner. You must make two sheets, one with the questions and the other with the answers. This can be the starter for the next lesson. Pairs swap quizzes and complete.
15. Write a diary entry from the perspective of a character or personality that you are studying.
16. Design a board game around a topic you are studying.
17. Record music/song extracts that can highlight different themes (could be edited five-second extracts that other learners have to guess, and then guess the reason they have been chosen).
18. Interview parents/grandparents/people about a specific historical issue and play back to class.
19. Write and record a speech made by an imaginary politician on a particular theme.
20. Use 'YouTube' to download speeches by famous people.
21. Make a model at home (for example, medieval castle/Roman forum).
22. Create a game (could be done in pairs/solo/group) that other groups have to play.
23. Search a supermarket for Fairtrade goods, writing down the name of the goods and where they come from.
24. Make a themed cake on any issue related to your subject.

25. Visit a library, museum, park – obtain specific information/research.
26. Learners are given photocopies of a modern map and the corresponding area on an old map. Their task is to imagine that they are in the modern world and find a hole though which they pass into somewhere which turns out to be the same place but back in time. Instruct them to write up the adventure and try to include things their character(s) notice from the maps that are the same and changed.
27. Write an essay but include in the margins the page numbers and textbook references of exactly where sources have been used.
28. Summarise key text/article but attach summary to key text having highlighted key words in text.
29. Find, recommend and review a particular website on a theme related to your subject.
30. Using Microsoft Publisher, produce a newspaper article on a topic.
31. Read subject-related text and turn it into a tabloid/broadsheet story.
32. Produce plans for three/four examination papers/questions on the assumption that one of these will be chosen to do in class.
33. Write a letter to a politician about an issue of concern.
34. Write a letter to a famous person in the past or someone in the future.
35. Write letters to an agony aunt.
36. Write a poem/song/play/script/advertisement using key words from the subject being studied.
37. Write a diary entry from a famous historical person.
38. Write a job application/CV for yourself in 10 years' time/50 years' ago.
39. Write a television/sports/film review.
40. Write a short 150-word description of your own identity using key concepts from the subject (this is great for you to read as a teacher to get to know your learners).
41. Create crosswords/true false/anagrams and so on to then be given to others in class.
42. Write a mini-proposal for a piece of research.
43. Using an existing song, write new words on a theme related to your subject.
44. Make up an advertising jingle about a key concept in a subject.
45. Create a top 20 set of songs related to a particular theme.
46. Bring in newspaper articles on a theme.
47. Bring in music that looks at different named issues.
48. Using Word and clip art, produce names of key researchers and then draw a line to the photo of a suitable image that represents their work.
49. Produce a revision schedule at home and provide it along with a photo of it taken of it on the wall at home.
50. Produce spider diagrams of issues/themes/revision.
51. Draw a picture of a key person.
52. Bring in a picture of a historical source that reflects a particular period. Talk to the class about the reasons you have chosen it.
53. Print off information from a given website.
54. Conduct a survey/questionnaire.
55. Design a time-line.

56. Bring in a religious symbol and explain its significance using key words/concepts related to your subject.
57. Assemble all homework chronologically since the beginning of the year.
58. Design newspaper headlines.
59. Compile a list of favourite or most useful websites on particular topics.
60. Revise for a mini-test.
61. Create a wall display.
62. Collect several versions of the same news item.
63. Cooperate with the media and ICT department at your school to get learners access to film equipment. Ask learners to make a documentary about a topic they are studying. Allocate roles (for example, newsreaders, on-scene reporter).

We hope these are ideas that you can put into practice. Experiment with them and adapt them to your own emerging identity as a teacher. Creativity, energy and an openness to try out new ideas are the hallmarks of a great teacher. They are also, we suspect, the hallmarks of the types of learners you are trying to cultivate. This chapter should go some way to helping you achieve that goal.

Chapter links →

Themes and ideas explored in this chapter link to corresponding ideas in chapters 14, 15 and 17.

CHAPTER 17

TEACHING THINKING SKILLS: EXAMINATION, EVALUATION AND DIFFERENTIATION

Objectives

By the end of this chapter the reader will:

1. understand the relationship between thinking and learning;
2. be able to apply differentiation strategies to classroom practice;
3. be introduced to the importance of the notion of meta-cognition;
4. understand the role played by evaluation in thinking;
5. be able to apply evaluation and thinking skills to classroom choices and strategies.

What is thinking?

While being highly contested and often ambiguous, much of the literature on 'thinking' suggests:

- it is a cognitive process – something to do with the 'mind';
- it is possible to improve thinking by practising it – thus, it is a 'skill' rather than an 'ability';
- the need for stretching and challenging lessons and activities for the development of opportunities to expand and extend thinking skills.

In a review of the literature, McGregor (2007) highlights the importance of:

1. Open tasks to encourage creativity and individual responses.
2. Learning built on the previous learning that has gone before.
3. Meta-cognition ('thinking about thinking') in helping learners to see how and why they arrive at the answers they do.

Thus, while no single adequate definition of thinking exists, we are able to say that it is based upon learners being able to:

- manipulate old and new knowledge;
- apply knowledge in different situations;
- link pieces of knowledge learned in different contexts together;
- assess what is useful and valuable about ideas;
- identify the processes and steps they have taken to arrive at the conclusions they have;
- combine in creative ways ideas to produce something new.

What we have here is essentially another way of expressing what we have extensively referred to in this book as the cognitive domain (Bloom, 1956) (see Chapters 6 and 13) – the stepped progression through specific thinking skills based upon their level of difficulty:

- knowledge;
- comprehension;
- application;
- analysis;
- synthesis;
- evaluation.

Anderson and Krathwohl (2001) have taken the notion of a hierarchy or taxonomy of 'thinking skills' and instead offer:

- remembering;
- understanding;
- applying;
- analyzing;
- evaluating;
- creating.

Working within the cognitive domain

In considering the cognitive domain, it is often useful to think about the sorts of words that we might use to describe the various levels on the taxonomy. It is useful perhaps to note that all of these words are verbs: thinking is therefore a process of doing. It is not possible to be passive in the process.

In no particular order (drawing on both Bloom, 1956, and later, Anderson and Krathwohl, 2001), thinking is therefore a matter of:

linking;
combining;
relating;
outlining;
separating;
predicting;
defending;
justifying.

Many teachers use these (and the vast range of such words possible) to help them to pin down and clarify (another 'thinking word' itself):

1. What the point must be behind the activities and resources they make.
2. The aims and objectives of the lessons they have.

In this way, teachers need to be thinkers in order to plan lessons where learners can be thinkers.

Can we teach thinking?

Many teachers might ask 'can we teach thinking?' To answer this question what is important to recognise is that thinking is a skill and not an ability. This means it can change over time and develop with practice.

- Skills are learned and the competence can be improved upon with the right sort of training.
- Abilities are more innate and are less easy to develop.

'Thinking' – the processes of connecting, deconstructing and applying knowledge and of building new knowledge onto old knowledge – is innate in the sense that it is a natural part of human cognition. However, our effectiveness at thinking is a matter of practice. Many such as McGregor (2007) and the Assessment Reform Group (see Chapter 14) argue that thinking about thinking is itself a powerful means by which to, first, understand how we learn and, secondly, to develop our learning further.

McGregor (2007) draws upon the available research literature to provide a really useful summary of strategies to adopt in a 'thinking lesson':

1. Pose interesting and thought-provoking questions at the start of the lesson to stimulate intellectual curiosity. You could do this along with the aims of the lesson at the very start.
2. Always get learners to think about the contrary view to the one they might assume/expect/hold themselves. McGregor refers to this as 'cognitive conflict'.
3. Get learners to become reflective: get them thinking about why they think what and how they think – you need to set this up carefully with structured parts of the lesson devoted to such opportunities.
4. Always seek to engage learners in discussions of why they think what they do. Get them to think about the steps they have taken to arrive at the views they hold.
5. Use collaborative learning strategies to ensure that learners can share their thinking.

This last point – the role played by peer support and peer learning in enhancing thinking skills – is central to a large part of the research literature on this topic. For example, Leat (2000) has suggested that using mixed-ability groups working on a collaborative and common task is a highly successful strategy to adopt when encouraging thinking skills, since it places the learning firmly in a shared context and this is most readily able to then be transferred and owned by all.

What is evaluation?

Evaluation often is seen to have a special place in education, and in thinking; it is a 'high-order thinking skill' – the very pinnacle of the cognitive taxonomy of learning. In examination it is often the hardest assessment area for many learners to meet and do well in. And yet, like all thinking processes and skills, we can improve with practice.

This means, in order to be better evaluators, we need to give learners the opportunity to evaluate and, while doing so, illustrate to them how the skill works so they can better understand what it means.

Getting learners to understand what 'evaluation' is and to then apply their understanding is probably one of the hardest skills for any teacher to master. Evaluation means critically weighing up evidence for and against a particular viewpoint, questioning how data behind any argument is gathered and when. This can involve:

* thinking through the eyes of theories/principles/concepts;
* using one set of theories/principles/concepts to attack another;
* drawing attention to historical precedents to endorse/challenge theories/principles/ concepts;
* criticising the methodology/evidence that writers use to argue their points;
* comparing and contrasting one set of ideas with another;
* identifying bias and/or logical incoherency in ideas;
* drawing attention to the dated nature/historical specificity of some ideas;

- drawing attention to the ethnocentricity of some ideas;
- pointing out the positive and negative 'contributions' of a particular idea;
- drawing attention to the 'usefulness' (useful for whom?) of a particular idea.

To do this you might need to train learners to critically question to what extent empirical data can be 'verified' for its accuracy. You might wish your learners to analyse an argument to see if it 'holds together' logically and to identify to what extent the theory, study or claim is/is not 'comprehensive', that is, that it can/cannot be used to explain other situations in a different culture, time or place. These are high-order skills and require both time and a diversity of strategies for them to be developed.

Starting to 'teach for evaluation'

A possible starting point when thinking about your own teaching, is to look at your own subject and identify five 'magic ingredients' that we argue are the backbone of evaluation for any subject:

1. Theories/explanations/principles.
2. Concepts/key words/language.
3. Key names/writers/important people.
4. Key events/historical moments.
5. Evidence.

Get your learners unpacking all areas of the syllabus using these ingredients and you are well on the way to teaching them what successful evaluation is.

Understanding what examiners are looking for

Examiners in most subjects argue that many learners make the following three errors:

1. They write too much for short answer questions leaving not enough time to write more developed evaluative answers for questions worth higher marks.
2. They write pre-prepared answers to essay questions instead of focusing on the exact wording of the question in the examination.
3. They write answers that illogically and incoherently drift from one point to the next.

Your starting point for understanding the evaluation skills associated with your subject will be to go to the examination or assessment board for which your subject will be formally assessed. Accessing this information is easy and materials are usually available free on the examination board website. Your job as a teacher is to get inside the mind of the examiner and then be able to communicate these thoughts to your own learners. Learners are quick to respect those teachers that clearly and confidently can talk not only about their subject but the specificities of examination content, skills and requisite marks. To do this you need to make sure that you have access to the following:

1. The specification (syllabus). This will be available on the website and in most cases in printed form. Use this not only to inform schemes of work but specifically to identity the particular skills and the associated marks awarded for those skills in your subject examination (be it coursework or sat examination). Note that often different parts of the examination are testing different sorts of skills (including those associated with evaluation).
2. Past examination papers and model answers. These are invaluable and are available in most subjects on the examination board website going back several years. Make sure, however, that you are aware of curriculum changes and that you do not confuse examinations that predate a specific curriculum change. Model answers are usually available to download with each examination paper.
3. Copies of mark schemes. Not only are these invaluable to you when setting and marking 'mock' or practice papers, but they are an excellent resource to give to your learners to peer mark the work of others. There is no better way to introduce your learners to the evaluation skills required at examination level than to work with these documents. In most cases they indicate how marks are allocated and how much should be written for each answer. Specifically they signpost the sorts of skills that are being tested in each answer.
4. Examiner's report on each subject. Many teachers underestimate or ignore this exceptionally useful document. After each examination the chief examiner has to write a report on how learners performed thus providing a useful source of hints about their thinking and the way papers are marked. They tend to indicate not only what they are looking for in answers, but also the more common errors made by learners in previous examinations.

When sitting an examination it is essential that you train your learners to be mindful of four golden rules:

- The importance of reading/highlighting key words in each question/instruction.
- Ensure that they understand the significance of so-called 'command words' (for example, 'compare and contrast', 'discuss').
- To guarantee that they understand which specific skills are being assessed in each particular question.
- To understand that their biggest enemy on the day of the examination is time. They must be able to allocate the correct amount of time to each element of the question (usually in direct proportion to the marks awarded).

Many teachers tend to leave a focus on the importance of examination-based skills till relatively late in their courses or in some cases only in the revision period. We argue that good teachers instil awareness of *all* of these issues from the very start of their courses. By doing this early you will minimise the extent to which learners go into panic in the final stages of their courses and you will help 'short-cut' much of the revision process for them.

Command words

In most cases it takes anything up to a year for public examinations to be written, that is, once the chief examiner has written the paper the examination is scrutinised by key individuals on the examination board to check for consistency, understanding, accuracy and an adherence to the skills associated with each subject discipline. Examinations in most subjects are worded in such a way as to be able to provide a spread of answers that cover the range of marks awarded on the mark schemes. This means that each and every word in the examination has been meticulously thought through before being chosen. Your job, as a teacher, is to 'sensitise' your learners to the subtleties of the wording in each examination. So-called command words are your starting point and we include some of the more common ones below:

- Evaluate – judge the importance or success.
- Compare – are things alike/similar or are there important differences?
- Contrast – look for differences.
- Criticise – use evidence to support your opinion on the value or merit of theories, facts or views from others.
- Define – give the meaning.
- Describe – write in detail.
- Differentiate – explain the difference.
- Discuss – write about the important aspects of the topic, are there two sides of the question? Consider the arguments for and against.
- Distinguish – explain the difference.
- Explain – make clear.
- Illustrate – give examples which make your point clear.
- Interpret – explain the meaning in your own words, for example you may be asked to interpret a graph.
- Justify – give reasons to support an argument or action.
- Outline – choose the most important aspects of a topic and ignore minor detail.
- Relate – show the connection between things.
- State – write briefly the main points.
- Summarise – bring together the main points.

Introduce learners to these command words by creating a simple sorting exercise where they match the command word to the correct definition. You can then follow this activity with one where you have created a variety of answers to questions using these command words. Learners have simply to match the command word to the correct type of answer. This is a simple but hugely effective way of introducing learners to these sorts of skills.

High-order evaluation categories

The following four categories are actually very easy for learners to grasp but are relatively unused by teachers when getting them to critically evaluate the concepts, viewpoints, events and so on associated with their subject.

- Empirical adequacy – that is, what evidence is there to support the particular argument/ theory/principle/idea being discussed?
- Comprehensiveness – that is, can the particular argument/theory/principle/idea be used in all cases under all conditions?
- Logical coherency – that is, does the argument/theory/principle/idea 'logically' hold together?
- Historical perspective – that is, how might views have changed over time about the specific argument/theory/principle idea?

Evaluation skills associated with coursework and research projects

Although many subjects no longer contain research projects as part of their formal assessment, the language of methodology remains. Remember that many learners can opt for an extended project where research evaluation skills are critical. 'PETS', as an easy-to-remember acronym, stands for 'practical', 'ethical', 'theoretical', and 'sensitive' issues that must be considered when evaluating anything to do with methods of research or methodology.

- Practical problems – include issues related to access, cost, time, equipment and so on.
- Ethical problems – is the research considered morally defendable and in what way might people be physically or emotionally harmed during the research process?
- Theoretical issues – in what way can theories/principles and so on inform, influence, criticise the particular method of research and its findings.
- Sensitivity – what is the relationship between the sensitive nature of the research topic and the design and choice of research.

Learners should be able to answer the following three questions when looking at any claim made by researchers:

1. How reliable is the research data? This refers to whether the same results could be achieved if the research was to be repeated: at a later point in time; if the research was carried out by different researchers; by using different methods; by using different samples.

2. How representative is the data? This refers to the ability for generalisations to be made from the sample used in the study, and is more associated with quantitative methodology rather than qualitative research.
3. How valid is the data? Despite many textbooks arguing that this is only associated with qualitative research, it actually refers to the ability of research data (both quantitative and qualitative) to reflect the true nature, attitudes, behaviour or characteristics of whatever the researcher claims is the case.

Asking learners to evaluate stories or pictures in magazines, books, diaries, newspaper articles, historical records and so on can be really challenging. The following four categories are easy for them to remember.

- Authenticity – are the documents really what they say they are?
- Credibility – to what extent can you believe the content of the documents?
- Meaning – what do the documents claim to state?
- Representativeness – to what extent can you make generaliseable claims based on the evidence contained within the documents?

Improving essay skills for public examinations

Getting learners to write critically evaluative essays under timed examination conditions is a challenging task for the most experienced of teachers. The next time you set timed written work get learners to carry out a self-evaluation checklist of their own completed work before they submit their answers to you. Some of the questions that you might like them to consider in that checklist are:

- Did you have a watch on the table?
- Did you check your watches every five minutes to guarantee you have enough time for each answer?
- Did you run out of time?
- Did you circle key words in the question so you could return to them in your conclusions?
- Did you read the questions before reading any additional items included in the paper?
- Did you check the source of the item (for example, date, author, type of publication)?
- Did you read the questions/items at least twice?
- Did you offer examples/evidence to back up your points?
- Did you start a new paragraph with an evaluation word/phrase (see below)?
- Does your introduction refer to the question?
- Does your introduction outline the following argument?
- Do all your paragraphs use the key words/concepts/names/principles/theories associated with your subject?
- Does your conclusion refer back to the question?

- Does your conclusion offer a new piece of information taking your points in the essay forward?
- Did you revise sufficiently for today's timed written answer?
- How much time did you spend revising (hours/minutes)?
- Would you revise in the same way for the real public examination?
- Could you improve your whole approach to revision?
- Are you clear how you might improve this approach?

Signposting evaluation

Learners often find writing structured logically coherent paragraphs one of the most difficult skills to master. Once they have carried out the above checklist, get learners to highlight the first word/words in each paragraph of their answers (and, if you really want to ram home the point, get them to identify a midpoint in each paragraph). Then get them to choose one or more of the following evaluation phrases to add/substitute with the words they have highlighted:

The relevance of this; This indicates; This is similar to/different from; Thus; So; Therefore; This means/does not mean; Hence; A consequence of; The implication of; The contrast between; Put simply; Illustrated by; Support for this; As shown by; This can be seen in; For example; This can be applied to; This is associated with; This leads to; This touches on; According to: The same applies to; This is confirmed by; In defence of this; A strength of this is; The value of; A benefit of; The usefulness of; An argument for; An advantage of; The importance of; This contributes to; This provides a balance to; This is significant because; This does take account of; However; Alternatively; A criticism; Another view; I disagree because; A different interpretation; On the other hand; The problem with this is; It is debatable; This is questioned; An argument against; A disadvantage of; Although; This assumes; Whereas; This cannot be explained by; This does not stand up because; This lacks support because; On the contrary; It makes little sense because; It is not true/valid because; To sum up; Having weighed up; The balance of the argument suggests; The weight of evidence suggests; The conclusion is; I agree because; Returning back to the question.

Make sure that you get learners to use different evaluation phrases each time they commit new written work to you. Make sure, too, that before they hand their work to you they write five targets they need to work on in order to improve the quality of their work. The joy with this form of ipsative assessment is that you are training learners to diagnose their own work and set their own targets freeing you up to provide altogether more constructive feedback on their own evaluation.

Differentiation

Differentiation is a key aspect of all teaching and learning, and one that certainly causes confusion and frustration for many teachers – experienced and inexperienced alike. Since the point of teaching is learning, and learning can only really be effective if it takes into consideration the needs of the learners themselves, differentiation is hugely significant in what makes a lesson successful.

When we use the word 'differentiation' we refer to the way in which difference between learners needs to be recognised, planned for and supported. In other words, we need to match the skills and needs of the learners to the lesson and materials we plan.

When we talk about differentiation, what we mean is:

- recognising equality and diversity;
- recognising that learners might learn differently;
- seeking to understand learners as individuals;
- planning to enable all to access the learning in the most productive fashion;
- coping with difference.

Planning for differentiation

When setting lesson and learning objectives, many teachers use the following sentence rubric to help ensure they are thinking about and beginning to plan for the divergent needs of their class:

By the end of this lesson ...
all learners will have XXX.
most learners will have XXX.
some learners will have XXX.
a few learners will have XXX.

The needs of *all* the learners must be met. Often teachers might tend to concentrate on those considered to be of a lower ability, and sometimes teachers might try and stretch those considered most able, but the key to getting differentiation right is to cater for all needs.

Traditionally, the teaching profession has thought about differentiation as a tension between two poles:

1. You can differentiate through the outcome of the learning.
2. You can differentiate through the tasks learners do.

For the first approach, open tasks are set where learning can take place at a variety of levels. For the second, different tasks are given to different learners based upon an assessment of their skills.

Many teachers (trainee or otherwise) find the second approach difficult since it is both hard to manage different learners doing different things at the same time and also it takes increased time in preparing different tasks and activities. Despite being harder work, differentiation by task is often a more effective method to directly target divergent needs and skills.

However, there are a myriad of ways through which differentiation can be achieved as the following list indicates:

1. You can ask different learners different questions or ask the same questions in different ways.
2. You can give different amounts of time to complete the same tasks depending upon need.
3. You can set up peer groups differently according to either mixing abilities or matching needs of learners.
4. You can vary the length of time you support different learners for, and,
5. You can vary the nature of the support you offer learners.
6. Different learners can choose what tasks they do (with your guidance and support).
7. Different learners can choose how they present or undertake a task.
8. You could even chose to let learners make choices.

As you can see, differentiation comes down to your own sensitivity for what is appropriate for your learners based upon your assessment of them and, at the same time, the choices and decisions you are making about how best to support their needs to help them develop. The purpose of differentiation then, is to move learners from where they currently are to extend their learning and thinking.

One step at a time

Differentiation strategies are really key for how you support learning and, therefore, for how the learning takes place. You are best advised to try new strategies one at a time, isolating each new step and reflecting upon the results: which learners have benefited? Which have not? The adoption of new differentiation methods could be the source of experimentation along the lines of practitioner action research as discussed in Chapter 20. You could set yourself a schedule to experiment with different differentiation choices and log what you think the outcomes are. If you do this, make sure you involve the voice of the learners (see Chapter 19) in providing you with feedback on what they thought worked. You could also share your findings with colleagues, disseminating the knowledge.

Differentiation is essential and it is vital that you plan for it and illustrate this on lesson planning. You are almost completely guaranteed that the observers of your teaching practice sessions will be looking out for differentiation strategies and their effective and obvious deployment. Consider the checklist in Table 17.1 as a source for the structuring of possible differentiation strategies.

Table 17.1   A variety of approaches to differentiation

You can differentiate ...

Teacher response
The learning object (the resource)
The content
The level of questioning
Extension activity and task
The amount of teacher support
The level of teacher support
The type of teacher support
How challenging you are of individual learners
How you structure group-work tasks
How you structure group-work membership
How you encourage peer support and whom you encourage to work together
The degree to which you allow learners to choose tasks
The degree to which you negotiate with learners their choices
The length of time of support
What other resources learners can have to help support them to complete a given task
The way in which you feed back
The role you give to learners in the class
The role you give to learners in groups
How learners are allowed to record and document their learning
How you scaffold learner's support

Barriers to differentiation

Differentiating and doing it well is essential, but not easy. You literally do need to try to please all of the learners all of the time. There are a number of barriers that might make differentiation harder for some teachers working in some contexts, rather than others:

- size of class;
- frequency of contact with the group;
- lack of materials for extension and support;
- lack of specialist staff to support and guide.

We recommend three key strategies when faced with some of these challenges:

1. Build a 'class profile' in discussion with other colleagues teaching the same class based upon skills and abilities. Review this profile from time to time, updating.
2. Always inform senior staff about concerns if you think some learners' needs are not being met. Seek help and advice and ask for support from training and external agencies where applicable.

3. Always talk to learners themselves on a regular basis asking them about their views on their needs and what is and is not effective support.

Specialist provision

Differentiation covers all learners, irrespective of whether they have a special learning need identified or not. Differentiation recognises that different people learn in different ways. If you have learners who have a recognised and diagnosed specialist need then you must seek the support and guidance of specialist staff. They will be able to refer you to training, books, useful websites and also will help you to plan for the use of learning support assistants, if available, in your classroom.

Specialist differentiation: the case of dyslexia

According to the 2008 research report 'Research for teachers: strategies for supporting dyslexic learners' issued by the General Teaching Council (GTC), up to 1 in 20 learners are approximated to have dyslexia. To support dyslexic learners, this report, which surveys various literature reviews in the field, recommends the following strategies:

1. Get learners to see connections between things.
2. Help learners to remember learning as a journey with a pattern so the connections between bits of knowledge are clear.
3. Patterns are more important than mere sequences.
4. See the larger patterns – think holistically.
5. Apply learning to practical experience so the point of the learning is made clear (GTC, 2008: 2).

In addition, the charity Dyslexia Action note that teaching for dyslexic learners should:

- adopt multi-sensory methods;
- be highly structured – with clear plans that learners have access to and can follow;
- value cumulative learning – learning builds up over time and learners are clear what they have done and what is coming next;
- place emphasis upon repetition;
- adopt short and varied routines – injecting pace;
- illustrate to learners what the point of the learning is and how they can apply it (http://dyslexiaaction.org.uk/).

What is significant, is that these strategies would work with a variety of learners in a number of different contexts.

Thinking about the thinking

In all, the various elements that have been discussed in this chapter (while being concerned with examination technique, evaluation skills and practices and differentiation) have been tied together by the notion of meta-cognition: the thinking about thinking and the learning about learning (see Chapter 14).

If we want learners to be able to manipulate and apply their knowledge – and to enjoy the rewards that come from understanding that they are being creative, imaginative and effective thinkers – then these learners need to understand their own thinking. We need to support learners to reflect upon their learning and learn from their experiences. Lessons which cater for the techniques, ideas and strategies presented here will enable the teacher and the learners to start to play with the pieces of knowledge, building more and more solid foundations each time.

Chapter links →

Themes and ideas explored in this chapter link to corresponding ideas in Chapters 13, 14 and 16.

Suggested further reading 📖

General Teaching Council (2008) 'Research for teachers: strategies for supporting dyslexic pupils', www.gtce.org.uk

Useful website

See the pages for the charity Dyslexia Action: http://dyslexiaaction.org.uk/

References

Anderson, L.W. and Krathwohl, D. (eds) (2001) A Taxonomy for Learning, Teaching and Assessing: A Revision of Bloom's Taxonomy of Educational Objectives. New York: Longman.
Bloom, B.S. (1956) Taxonomy of Educational Objectives, Handbook I: The Cognitive Domain. New York: David McKay.
General Teaching Council (GTC) (2008) 'Research for teachers: strategies for supporting dyslexic pupils', www.gtce.org.uk
Leat, D. (2000) Thinking Through Geography. Cambridge: Chris Kington.
McGregor, D. (2007) Developing Thinking, Developing Learning: A Guide to Thinking Skills in Education. Maidenhead: Open University Press.

CHAPTER 18

USING TECHNOLOGY TO TEACH: E-LEARNING, M-LEARNING AND BLENDED LEARNING

Objectives

By the end of this chapter the reader will be able to:

1. understand the conditions under which successful e-learning can take place;
2. understand the key e-learning tools at a teacher's disposal and their possible uses;
3. recognise key debates concerning the appropriate use of e-learning;
4. identify a range of strategies that can be used to take advantage of 'Web 2.0' technologies;
5. review strategies for using e-learning tools as a means to support learning needs.

What is 'e-learning'?

It is best to start with a definition:

> e-Learning can be defined as 'learning facilitated and supported through the use of information and communications technology'. It can cover a spectrum of activities from the

use of technology to support learning as part of a 'blended' approach (a combination of traditional and e-learning approaches), to learning that is delivered entirely online. Whatever the technology, however, learning is the vital element. (Joint Information Systems Committe (JISC), http://www.jisc.ac.uk/, accessed June 2009)

So, within this, what exactly does the 'e' stand for? When the term first became popular we used the 'e' to mean, quite simply, electronic. Recently, there has been a move away from this use of the term to place emphasis upon the fact that technology is only the answer if it is the appropriate learning tool. In this sense, e-learning could also stand for:

- enhanced learning;
- emergent learning;
- effective learning;
- empowered learning;
- enriched learning;
- experiential learning;
- maybe even, enlightened learning?

These are quite some claims! But the idea is that the use of digital and electronic technologies adds to the learning in some way. Alongside e-learning, we now hear increasingly of the term 'emergent technologies' to refer to new and developing technology and communication tools as they gain popularity, but are still in their early stages of 'adoption'. It is certainly true to say that the teaching and learning landscape is rapidly changing, with many choices and tools available for teachers and learners alike. This choice is sometimes quite bewildering at first.

As with any type of learning, there is no single type of e-learning but rather the phrase is used to cover a wide range of pedagogic practices and resources. E-learning could be:

- on-demand – a bag of collected content sitting on a website available 'on demand' as and when needed by learners;
- live chat – live real-time distance learning using chat rooms for virtual discussion where learners are not in the same place;
- online mentoring and coaching – where experienced learners support the practice of others through email, chat, resource development and swapping;
- simulation learning – where technology is used to re-create case studies for learners to safely practice within;
- knowledge archives or banks – where databases are held for learner access with search facilities to help support research and investigation.

As a basic distinction, e-learning is usually referred to being either:

- synchronous – in real time, or
- asynchronous – outside of real time

E-learning 2.0?

The term e-Learning 2.0 is currently being used to refer to new ways of thinking about e-learning inspired by the emergence of Web 2.0 technologies and platforms. This new e-learning places increased emphasis on social learning and the use of social networking and social software such as blogs, wikis, podcasts, and virtual worlds such as second life – these are tools that have risen both with and contributing to the rise of Web 2.0. Put simply, the original Internet (Web 1.0) was based on having easily available content for users. Over time, the web has changed and, in particular, it has led to user-generated content. What this means is that those who use the tools construct, create and connect content and individuals and groups together. Thus, you can 'tag' a location on a map with a picture and share it with others or upload a video to YouTube. Alternatively you can join a wiki and help edit someone else's content, maybe as part of a large community. This Web 2.0 is interconnected and the networking behind it means it is social. Many of these tools can be adopted for educational use as the list below indicates.

Adopting Web 2.0 tools for teaching

There is a wide and ever-changing range of Web 2.0 tools that teachers can use in their classrooms and beyond, outside the traditional walls. Most of these require Internet connection and rely upon user-generated content, and many are good at building communities of learning among peers:

- YouTube – useful for stimulating archive materials or for learners showcasing their work.
- Wikis – excellent means by which learners can collaborate on a final document, working together, sharing and collectively editing.
- Blogs – where learners can keep online diaries showing development and reflective practice.
- Delicious – or other bookmarking or 'tagging' sites which allow learners to build and develop research notes and bibliographies and webographies with some ease.
- Facebook – or any social networking site which allows learners opportunities to interact with each other.
- Twitter – a 'micro-blogging' site – could be used (as could text messaging for the same effect) to get learners to record answers to quizzes or for teachers to present questions, essay and homework titles or even a 'daily learning message' for their classes.
- Second life – could be used to provide learners with an online real-time virtual community to work within, encouraging social learning.

Safer children in a digital world

The Byron Review (DCSF, 2008) identifies codes of safe practice for parents and educators supporting children learning within digital and virtual worlds. This report was written in the light of understandable anxiety concerning high-volume Internet, social networking and SMS (text messaging) usage among the young. The report concludes that digital and virtual words offer enriching and learning experiences, but only if managed correctly. The report also recognises what it refers to as a 'generational digital divide' – whereby parents and many teachers feel anxious and threatened by children and young people's digital skills, seeing them as alienating. Equally, the report notes that while children and young people have a huge capacity for quickly developing confidence with emergent technologies, their critical skills need further support to help them make appropriate decisions regarding safety in the digital worlds they inhabit.

The full review 'Safer children in a digital world' can be downloaded from www.dcsf.gov.uk/byronreview.

Blended and mobile learning

More recently, we speak of 'blended learning'. This is in part a recognition that e-learning opportunities cannot replace traditional methods. Instead, we should choose our teaching tool kit based upon fitness for purpose. In other words, the choice to use e-learning or not must fit into wider pedagogic decisions. We should be ready to adopt what works best and what most suits – in this way merging together or 'blending' old and new ways of learning.

We also now speak of 'M-learning', or of mobile learning. This is a recognition that the spaces within which we learn have changed. It is now possible to listen to recorded lectures on a mobile phone or surf the Internet while travelling on public transport.

O'Malley et al. (2003) define mobile learning as: 'Mobile learning is any sort of learning that happens when the learner is not at a fixed, predetermined location, or learning that happens when the learner takes advantage of the learning opportunities offered by mobile technologies' (O'Malley et al., 2003, quoted in Savil-Smith et al., 2006: 2). Mobile learning therefore redefines the space of the traditional classroom – it is anytime, anywhere learning. It is a combination of e-learning and distance learning.

Savil-Smith et al. (2006) offer a report on the outcomes of the m-learning project which ended in September 2004 and was funded through the European Commission's Information Society Technologies (IST) initiative. In this research project, a mobile learning tool kit was established and then piloted in FE colleges. The report found:

1. Most of the teachers who took part developing and using the mobile quizzes and games felt that m-learning could easily be integrated into the curriculum with not much more preparation than normal.
2. Teachers felt that the m-learning they experimented with broadened learning in their classrooms.
3. Many felt that the adoption of mobile technologies was a much more 'subtle' way of introducing difficult and challenging learning, engaging young people much more quickly than might otherwise be the case.
4. On a negative note – many teachers found that young people enjoyed using the mobile technology so much that they became distracted and off task quite easily.
5. Tutors noted that the mobile technology become a 'hook' to draw otherwise demotivated learners into lessons.
6. Learners themselves reported that the mobile technology was useful in breaking up their normal routines.
7. Equally, learners felt that mobile technologies were especially useful for plenaries – helping them confirm that their learning had taken place.
8. Finally, many teachers experimenting with the m-learning tools noted that it was absolutely essential to have a traditional back-up in the case of technical problems.

There are various strategies and tools a teacher could adopt if interested in m-learning. Some suggestions include:

• The use of text messaging (SMS) for quizzes, reminders and short messages.
• The use of downloadable PDF files with short course notes that learners might store on portable devices such as third-generation mobile phones and portable multimedia players with video screen capability. These could be revision notes or materials to be considered on a field trip for example.
• Teachers could record audio files – podcasts – for learners to listen to anywhere they had a mobile device and headphones. Learners could record these for each other too.

All these strategies make sure of mobile devices that many young people already have and understand how to use, making them quite accessible.

'Digital natives' and e-learning

The term e-Learning 2.0 is used to refer to new ways of thinking about e-learning inspired by the emergence of Web 2.0 technologies. This emergence of new technologies, some claim, has also lead to the emergence of a 'digital native' – someone totally at home with learning from and using this technology to then extent that they know no different. This new e(nhanced)-learning places increased emphasis on social learning and the use of social networking. Web 2.0 is a recognition that the virtual world of high-speed communications technology has moved on – and it has moved on due to changes in the technology itself: how it maps together, how it works outside of 'real time' and how users adopt tools with fluidity and 'intuitive' flair, the more exposed we become. The growth of users, increased interconnected interactivity of new Internet tools and the affordability and availability of broadband 'always-on' Internet connections, has led to what we refer to as Web 2.0.

The Teaching and Learning Research Project (TLRP) refers to four distinctive features of the value of Web 2.0 technologies (Selwyn, 2008). They can be:

- playful;
- expressive;
- reflective;
- exploratory.

Within the literature, there are claims made by some that we are experiencing the rise of the 'digital native' (Prensky, 2001). Based upon factors such as accessibility, affordability and submersion, it is the post-1993 generation who are most often seen to be the first true 'digital natives'. There is also some talk of the 'new actor' within cultural and educational dynamics and global change (Veen and Vrakking, 2006). Equally, it is claimed that we are witnessing the 'rise of the homo zappien': a mouse in one hand, a keyboard/PDA/MP3 player in the other. Clicking and zapping their way through a media-saturated reality where learning is fast paced, immediate and social in nature (see Veen and Vrakking, 2006).

This is not to say, however, that Web 2.0 tools are to be treated uncritically: These claims might exaggerate the picture but it is true to say that technology plays a part in young people's lives in an ever-changing and increasing way. Perhaps this is something that educators need to take into account when they make their choices over the tools and resources of learning?

A pedagogic warning!

Jackson and Anagnostopoulou (2001) offer us a warning about the claims that seem to characterise the view that 'all digital and electronic learning must be good'. This is clearly not the case. They argue that in order to make e-learning work, teachers need to plan very carefully and ensure they are adopting the right tool for the right job. They argue that e-learning works in a very specific context:

1. Learners value online learning in proportion to how much 'orchestration' the teacher has done around the learning resource and object.
2. Technologies that can be used in a variety of ways, as decided by learners themselves, are more readily adopted.

3. The teacher's effort and enthusiasm is largely responsible for the 'richness' of the e-learning experience.
4. Any use of learning technologies should try to accommodate as many different learning theories as possible for maximum effectiveness.

In echoing the spirit of this warning, Beetham and Sharpe (2007) use the phrase 'Pedagogy before technology'. Equally, the Joint Information Systems Committee (JISC) notes that 'successful innovation' is dependent upon the technologies adopted being chosen due to their link to the learning outcome (JISC, 2005). In this manner, e-learning opportunities, like any teaching and learning tool, is but one choice among many, and not always the right/best/most suited choice at that.

With these warnings in mind, it is possible to make explicit some tentative 'rules' of e-learning:

1. Technology is not always the answer.
2. The pedagogic reason for the resource and learning tool always comes first.
3. E-learning takes tremendous set-up and management by the teacher (at least initially), despite what assumptions one might hold about 'young people and technology'.
4. When thinking about e-learning, do not allow the learning to take second place to the medium of transition of the learning object.

Using e-learning appropriately

The skill in using e-learning platforms and resources is not the technical skill required to make the learning object but, as with any teaching, the application of appropriate pedagogy to the lesson content and learners. It is the matching of the learning resource to the learners' needs that makes for an e(nhanced) experience. It is not always best, just because it is new and electronic! With this in mind, the teacher wishing to adopt or experiment with e-learning strategies needs to try and identify e-learning tools that are most appropriate.

VLEs

The acronym VLE stands for virtual learning environment. These are platforms which work securely within an institution offering teachers the opportunity to upload documents and embed learning games and objects for their classes to log on and download or use. Virtual learning environments, while needing an institutional login and password, can nonetheless be accessed remotely outside of the college environment and can also provide teachers with the means to group-message whole classes and cohorts of learners and to assess learning through online quizzes.

In the 2009 Ofsted report, *Virtual Learning Environments: An Evaluation of their Development in a Sample of Educational Settings*, the usage of VLEs was surveyed across 41 educational institutions covering primary and secondary schools and colleges. This report concluded:

1. VLEs offer a rich opportunity for learners to access learning.
2. Most educational institutions are investing considerably in the use of a VLE.
3. And yet, too often VLEs are not used as powerful learning tools but are simply the repository for course notes and traditional lesson resources.

The criticism that Ofsted applies to the use they have seen of VLEs is that they are not really being used to enhance learning. Learners are not active within the environment but, rather, they are being used as online storage systems. This is not to say that this does not have a use (far from it, it is extremely useful) – but this does not mean that learning is taking place. They are virtually no learning environments. Equally, it does nothing to take advantage of the unique features of a VLE as described earlier. What most institutions do with VLEs could be done with a simple shared folder of files. The report also notes that where e-learning was most apparent through VLEs this was largely due to the enthusiasm and effort of the teacher to popularise the technology with their learners and blend it into classroom and normal learning activity.

Pedagogic theories of e-learning

There are really no models of e-learning per se – only e-enhancements of models of learning. That is to say, using technology to achieve better learning outcomes, or a more effective assessment of these outcomes, or a more cost-efficient way of bringing the learning environment to the learners. (Mayes and de Freitas, 2004: 4)

In the quote above we begin to see the genuine challenge in adopting e-learning for the teacher. While, as a profession and certainly in your training, we focus upon theories of teaching and learning, the use of digital and emergent technologies often takes place seemingly in a theoretical vacuum. It is almost as if the adoption of e-learning tools is itself a pedagogic theory of learning, which it is not. Instead, e-learning offers us access to a wide variety of tools and strategies but we would nonetheless still need to apply our pedagogic theories to their use in order to justify our choices and explain our decision making. We need to be as reflective about e-learning as any other sort.

Mayes and de Freitas (2004) have attempted to map existing theories of pedagogy (see Chapter 9) onto e-learning practices to see which has the greater fit. Most notably the conclusion to the mapping exercise carried out by Mayes and de Freitas is that while there are seemingly lots of links in the literature to e-learning offering opportunities for situationist and constructivist learning (see Chapter 9), there is no real evidence that e-learning adoption within educational institutions has led to a significant increase in constructing communities of learning. It does support peer learning but the wider development of whole integrated communities is somewhat lagging behind.

E-learning for accessibility and equal opportunities

A number of teachers and institutions are investing time and funds in e-learning due to the possibilities that flexible digitalised and mobile resources and learning have for equal opportunities provision.

JISC offers a range of suggestions and training resources on this issue – often presented through some very helpful case studies of best practice in a range of educational institutions. There are some broad areas to consider when thinking about e-learning and its potential for enabling increased accessibility for learners:

1. Portable document format (usually shortened to PDF) files are often very helpful for learners who find reading text and following and scanning difficult. This is because PDF files come with a series of 'thumbnail' indexes and bookmarks to the structure and headings of the document which can help some learners navigate their way through the text and, in doing so, follow more easily and find their place again if distracted. The IT support team in educational institutions can help with this, but an alternative would be to download the open source package, Open Office, which is both free and comes with a PDF converter. (You would need to seek permission of the institutional IT team for this and we also recommend that you never download any programme unless you are sure of the source of the file and that the programme will not have a disadvantageous affect on your system).

2. PDFs also allow a variety of means to magnify text and to change text and background colours without editing and losing the original – this is very useful for some partially sighted learners and for some learners on the dyslexic spectrum.

3. Many learners find the use of hyperlinks in text a useful way to navigate large documents (such as guides and course handbooks), making them more accessible and inclusive. You can set up a hyperlink from any section to any other point within a digital document, making it easier to find your way around as the reader.

4. You might also consider the use of the Document Map feature if using Microsoft Word. The Document Map is a means, rather like the bookmarks on a PDF, to view the internal structure of a document, giving you the headings presented as a list. If you construct documents using the 'headings' feature (usually found within format/ styles) you are able to set categories for headings using different fonts and sizes for different levels of headings – sections, subsections, and so on. Thus a hierarchy is then reproduced for the reader in a tool bar making it easier for them to find a particular section (providing your headings make sense!).

5. Many institutions, as we have noted elsewhere, have invested resources in what we call virtual learning environments. Despite their criticisms, having your teaching and learning resources easily accessible, available and transferable (downloadable) for learners is a genuine means to support them. It adds to the options the learners have to manage their own access to course content.

6. For learners who are partially sighted or for those who prefer working aurally, many textbooks are available in audio form. These usually require a subscription

or cost more than a traditional text would, but the benefits in making content more accessible through this medium are significant.

7. Teachers can also record their own audio content in the form of podcasts. These are relevantly simple to create and can be downloaded to learners' home computers or streamed wirelessly to laptops. They can be uploaded onto most VLE platforms and, equally, can be transferred by learners onto mobile devices such as MP3 players and accessed while travelling.

Further details on some of these ideas and many more are available from the various publications issued by JISC.

Smoke and mirrors – have things really changed?

The claims of the digital native are largely exaggerated. And yet, learning and learners are changing, as is teaching. Classrooms are no longer the places they were. With the means to be connected to the Internet comes access to a rich range of tools and resources, provided they are used appropriately. The criticism of much so-called e-learning is that teachers have tended to think about the 'e' more than about the actual learning itself. It must be recognised that digital learning technologies are not a panacea for all educational ills. But, if used well, they can offer rich mobile learning and social learning opportunities and, as part of a well-chosen blended delivery, can truly enhance the learning experience.

Chapter links $\rightarrow$

Themes and ideas explored in this chapter link to corresponding ideas in Chapter 9.

Suggested further reading 📖

Joint Information Systems Commission (JISC) (2004) *Effective Practice with e-Learning: A Good Practice Guide in Designing for Learning*. Bristol: JISC.

Savil-Smith, C., Attewell, J. and Stead, G. (2006) *Mobile Learning in Practice: Piloting a Mobile Learning Teachers' Toolkit in Further Education Colleges*. London: LSN.

Useful websites

The Joint Information Systems Committee (JISC): www.jisc.ac.uk/

References

Beetham, H. and Sharpe, R. (2007) *Rethinking Pedagogy for a Digital Age: Designing and Delivering e-Learning*. London: Routledge.

Department for Children, Schools and Families (DCSF) (2008) *Safer Children in a Digital World*. The Report of the Byron Review. Crown Copyright. Nottingham: DCSF Publications.

Jackson, B. and Anagnostopoulou, K. (2001) 'Making the right connections: improving quality in online learning', in J. Stephenson (ed.), *Teaching and Learning Online: Pedagogies for New Technologies*. London: Kogan Page.

Joint Information Systems Committee (JISC) (2004) *Effective Practice with e-Learning: A Good Practice Guide in Designing for Learning*. Bristol: JISC.

Joint Information Systems Commission (JISC) (2005) *Innovative Practice with E-Learning: A Good Practice Guide to Embedding Mobile and Wireless Technologies into Everyday Practice*. Bristol: JISC.

Mayes, T. and de Freitas, S. (2004) *JISC e-Learning Models Desk Study Stage 2: Review of e-learning Theories, Frameworks and Models*. www.jisc.ac.uk

Office for Standards in Education (OfSTED) (2009) *Virtual Learning Environments: An Evaluation of their Development in a Sample of Educational Settings*. London: Crown.

Prensky, M. (2001) 'Digital natives, digital immigrants part 1', *On The Horizon – The Strategic Planning Resource for Educational Professionals*, 9(5).

Savil-Smith, C., Attewell, J. and Stead, G. (2006) *Mobile Learning in Practice: Piloting a Mobile Learning Teachers' Toolkit in Further Education Colleges*. London: LSN.

Selwyn, N. (2008) *Education 2.0? Designing the Web for Teaching and Learning. A Commentary by the Technology Enhanced Learning Phase of the Teaching and Learning Research Project (October, 2008)*.

Veen, W. and Vrakking, B. (2006) *Homo Zappiens: Growing Up in a Digital Age*. London: Network Continuum Education.

SECTION 5

REFLECTION

CHAPTER 19

DEALING WITH M-LEVEL CREDITS: ACADEMIC DEBATES AND ISSUES

Objectives

By the end of this chapter the reader will be able to:

1. engage with a number of key contemporary educational issues;
2. understand the significance of key educational issues;
3. apply the relevance of theoretical debates to their own practice;
4. possess a range of theoretical vocabularies to enable further consideration of educational issues and debates;
5. comprehend the significance and challenge that an M-level profession might raise for teachers.

Flagging M-level possibilities

While this chapter aims to introduce you to some wider issues and themes around education and educational practice which you might find useful on an M-level programme, it is not the only place in this book where you will find useful issues

(Continued)

(Continued)

and strands of key concerns and debates to take your reading further. All through this book you will find, from time to time, various suggestions for ideas, themes, concepts and research that little by little might help point you in interesting directions for your own M-level work. We conclude this chapter on page 281 with a complete list of these (Figure 19.1) for you.

In many parts of Britain teachers in training are now being required to take (or consider taking) Masters (M)-level credits. The reasons why and how this development has emerged in teacher education is not something we tackle in this book, although we do consider this worthy of 'M'-level exploration itself. There is little in the way of harmonisation across HE institutions in terms of what 'M'-level accreditation actually means. Some institutions have amended the title of their award to 'Professional Graduate Certificate in Education' rather than introducing M-level learning. What we can be certain of is that teacher training courses are demanding enough without the additional burden of having to study at M level. However, we also acknowledge that studying at M level provides an exciting opportunity for teachers in training to engage critically with the debates, theories and professional stocks of knowledge that make up this wonderful profession.

M-level teaching: Making a case for reflection?

M-level study allows the practitioner an opportunity to begin to explore the research and academic literature in more depth. A great deal of initial teacher education (and, consequently, a great deal of this book) places key emphases upon the role that reflective practice plays in the ongoing formation of classroom skills. Added to reflective practice – and something that the issues in this chapter illustrate – is the need to try and engage with the research literature – and most importantly of all, to link the theory and your own practice together. Without the context of your own reflective practice many of these issues and themes in the academic study of education might seem slightly obscure or abstract. But, linked to your practice, they hopefully provide you with some powerful tools to begin to think about your own teaching and classroom experiences in more depth.

This chapter cannot possibly offer the in-depth levels of reading required for Masters accreditation. What we do offer, however, are brief forays into some of the big educational issues worthy of 'M'-level writing. The following sections introduce you to some (not all) of the key debates that we consider relevant for teachers in training.

We have chosen these particular debates because of the relative ease in which each can be further researched by you during your training.

Teacher socialisation

The first year in teaching is an important phase in any teacher's professional growth because 'the school and classroom experiences of beginning teachers may either catalyze or inhibit a lasting commitment to effective teaching' (Ginns et al., 2001: 111).

Burden (1982), in describing the first year of teaching as a 'survival' period, maintains that this induction period can involve feelings of inadequacy, stress and confusion on the part of the teacher. This, it is argued, evolves over the next two to three years into what he describes as an 'adjustment period' in which 'reflection' on what works and does not work in the classroom takes place and teachers become more comfortable with their teaching. Furlong and Maynard (1995) identify five broad patterns of development within the early years of teaching. These range through early idealism; personal survival in an attempt to cope with the reality of teaching; dealing with difficulties in which you cope with more problems; attainment of most initial teacher education competencies and the move to extending knowledge and understanding of teaching and learning.

In discussing to what extent teachers change as a result of the work that they do, Lacey's work on the autonomy of teachers (1977) has been highly influential. He proposes three types of strategy: strategic compliance, in which an individual complies with an authority figure's definition of the situation but retains private reservations; internalised adjustment whereby an individual complies with a situation in both action and belief; and strategic definition in which the individual brings about change within the formal power. Some of the teachers he studied demonstrated 'strategic compliance', that is, they deliberately went along with the overall norms and values of the school but never fully accepted or believed everything that they pretended to.

Bottery and Wright (2000) argue that teachers are being 'de-professionalised' by the loss of control over what and how they teach. Work is seen as increasingly routinised and de-skilled. Teachers are increasingly controlled and the existence of the autonomy of the professional is denied. They argue that the UK experience is not unique but does encapsulate post-Fordist trends in which control over education is centralised while implementation is devolved through market mechanisms. Hargreaves (1994) notes certain characteristics of this 'intensification thesis'. These include less time for relaxation during the day, lack of time to keep up with one's field, and chronic and persistent overload, which reduces personal discretion. This fosters dependency on externally produced materials. Corners are cut to save time, which in turn leads to enforced diversification of expertise to cover personnel shortages. This may then create further dependencies on externally produced resources and cutting of corners.

The nature of professional socialisation raises a number of questions for teachers carrying out research. First, to what extent can the professional identity of a teacher change, that is, are the identity traits of teachers fixed or do they change as a result of professional socialisation. Secondly, do teachers experience the autonomy that some definitions of 'professionalism' imply or are they 'de-professionalised' as some of the literature above has suggested? Thirdly, to what extent does the 'intensification' process that many writers argue for, take place within the early careers of teachers.

 M-level teaching: The two worlds?

The Masters requirement for some teachers is an interesting phenomenon – and one that to a great extent divides the 14–19 agenda in two. The spirit of the 14–19 agenda (see Chapter 4), which this book has been written to address, is to try to examine the commonalities between learners within the 14–19 age range – irrespective of whether the location of their learning is a school or college. What the Masters requirements for secondary school teachers do is to illustrate just how different the compulsory and post-compulsory professional teaching worlds are. Teachers and lecturers in college, if they teach vocational subjects, might not be graduates, let alone need to do a Masters. Therefore the M-level requirement for school teachers is highly devisive.

Student/pupil voice

Student (or 'pupil') voice has been the subject of considerable academic debate and is now, since the government's Every Child Matters policy initiative, grabbing the attention of policy-makers, examination boards, government ministers and journalists. Driving forces for this relatively new institutional initiative and movement in Britain include the United Nations Convention on the Rights of the Child, the UK Healthy Schools Initiative, Building Schools for the Future (BSF) and, increasingly, School Self-Evaluation (SEF).

Lodge (2008) notes that there has been a shift in the way we perceive children today compared to nineteenth- and early twentieth-century perceptions of childhood. The notion for many that 'children should be seen and not heard' has been rapidly replaced by a child-centred philosophy in the domestic sphere and a marketised more consumer-based mentality in some schools, in which the learner voice agenda fits cosily. While many schools are still reluctant to 'listen' to the voices of those that make up its majority, there are many benefits to be gained. Halsey et al. (2008) argue that these include:

- improvements in learner services (for example, changes in school dinners; improving toilet facilities);
- improvements in decision-making (for example, giving learners more of a say in the financial decisions taken by schools);

- greater democracy for learners (for example, allowing learners a say in which teachers are employed; how long lessons run for; influencing subjects offered);
- fulfilling legal requirements within schools (for example, in terms of 'citizenship' and Every Child Matters legislation);
- enhancing children's skills (for example, allowing learners to run meetings with staff; including learners on interview panels);
- empowering child self-esteem (for example, increasing self-confidence and status when learners are consulted by their peers and teachers).

Teachers, heads and administrators gain access to the specialist (and largely untapped) knowledge that learners have about their schools. As a result Fielding (2001) has argued that many learner voice projects act as a catalyst for change in schools including improvements in teaching, the curriculum and, most importantly, learner–teacher relationships. Yet Fielding is also highly critical of some of the ways that student voice is articulated:

> Are we witnessing the emergence of something genuinely new, exciting and emancipatory that builds on rich traditions of democratic renewal and transformation? ... or are we presiding over the further entrenchment of existing assumptions and intentions using student or pupil voice as an additional mechanism of control. (Fielding, 2001: 100)

McMahon and Portelli (2004) identify three theoretical perspectives on student voice that are useful when embarking on 'M'-level research:

1. Conservative – a relatively uncritical view that regards learner engagement and consultation as a means to improving learning. In particular it focuses on the strategies, skills and procedures that teachers need to develop.
2. Liberal – a more holistic view of the child that goes beyond the academic and takes into consideration learner–teacher relationships and the emotional well-being of children.
3. Critical/democratic – a view that challenges the nature of, and status quo in, many schools in ways that the above two approaches ignore. Young people and adults are perceived as engaging together in ways that question the processes, purposes and procedures in schools and classrooms, with empowerment for all as an ideal outcome.

These three perspectives can be used to frame any research project that you might wish to embark on at M level. Consider, for example, the fact that in many schools where learner voice runs, only a minority of learners have an opportunity to voice their opinions. In many cases, these opinions are used to endorse policies the school had planned to put into place in any case (for example, the provision of new computers). Schools are, in most cases, hierarchical structures (for example, power rests with the board of governors, the head and the senior management of the school). They are also hierarchical in terms of learners, that is, older learners tend to have greater 'voice' and status within most schools. Quite often segregation by age, class, gender, ethnicity and ability restricts the 'voices' of many learners in schools where learner voice operates. This presents numerous opportunities for in-depth qualitative interviews with those whose 'voice' might not be heard.

Values in education

As a focus of research in education, the role of values in relation to teachers' work, has gained momentum in recent years. Values associated with people wishing to become teachers have included a commitment to children's welfare, justice, equality and intellectual growth. By teachers' 'values' we refer to what teachers regard as worthwhile. These values are constructed over time, through social interaction in the home, school, community and wider social setting. Values are carried by people but they can change, be extended and elaborated on through life experience. Teachers' values can come into tension and conflict with the values that circulate within the institutions in which they work. This in turn can create dissonance for teachers if these values differ from some of their own.

Research related to new teachers suggests that the first few years of teaching are significant in relation to influencing teachers' values and, for many, the decision whether or not to remain within the profession (Kelchtermans and Ballet 2002). The first few months of teaching have been described as a period of 'sink or swim', a term used by Hatch (1999) to describe the isolated conditions of teachers' work. Referring to this initial period as one of 'survival', Shindler et al. (2004) argue that this time can involve feelings of inadequacy, stress, confusion and disillusionment. In the UK, Tickle is similarly pessimistic about many aspects of the transitions from teacher training to classroom teaching, arguing that many classrooms are sites where 'the crucifixion of teachers' learning occurs' (Tickle, 2003: 2). However, not all accounts of this transition, are painted in this negative light. Writing about Australian teachers, Carter (2000) has suggested that the processes of becoming a teacher involve varying degrees of personal and professional growth. Serving as carer, role model, guide and teacher of life skills had become key aspects of their work which they valued.

The complex experience of being a newly qualified teacher is frequently subject to chance placement in employment; institutional conditions of service; the views of senior teachers about their own roles as professional tutors and mentors, along with assessors, and managers and their conceptions of newly qualified teachers (Tickle, 2000). Turbulence may exist for many newly qualified teachers when the values that drive them are at odds with the values of the schools in which they gain first employment. For many newly qualified teachers this period involves a transition from some of the idealism and the theoretical input they have received during training to the relative isolation of being a full-time teacher. This transition can provide a variety of value tensions that emerging teachers encounter once into the 'reality shock' (Veenman, 1984) of the classroom. Researching the value tensions between the different 'communities of practice' (Wenger, 1998) that teachers engage with can provide a rich source of research material worthy of 'M'-level accreditation. It can also provide invaluable reflection on your own practice and the ideas that inform what it means to be a 'good' teacher.

The academic/vocational debate

Vocational training supposedly refers to any type of training that is preparing people for the world of work; a point worth dwelling on when considering differences in status between, for example, teachers, doctors, nurses and plumbers. In many countries in Europe throughout most of the twentieth century, vocationalism was very much part of the school curriculum. However, in many parts of Britain up until the 1960s, vocational training was viewed by successive governments as something that should be tackled in the workplace rather than in school. A discursive shift in thinking during the 1970s meant that 'New Vocationalism' referred to the change in view by the government that vocational training should also take place in schools and colleges. Debates surrounding vocationalism continue to dominate thinking in schools, colleges, universities and employers, organisations, and have, in part, led to the introduction of Diplomas. Time will tell if this is the panacea required to heal the academic/vocational rift that characterises British education.

Nineteenth-century state education came about primarily as a result of a realisation by governments that there was a direct relationship between education and the economy. By teaching children how to read they were being prepared to be efficient workers at a time when international economic competitiveness was of national concern. This concern has constantly remained seen with the conception and gradual introduction of New Vocationalism during the period of economic decline during the late 1970s and 1980s. Under the international glare of the Organisation for Economic Co-operation and Development (OECD) accompanied by frequent condemnation of British schooling (particularly in England) by employers and universities, vocationalism continues to be a source of embarrassment and concern for successive British governments in their attempts to boost the staying-on rates of British teenagers, many of whom feel alienated in schools and colleges.

Stephens et al. (2001) argue that in Britain there has always been a class snobbery between those that are 'trained' and those that are 'educated'. They argue that in many other countries no such snobbery exists. Such snobbery, they argue, accounts for why, in the UK, employers, parents, learners and universities see A levels as being socially more acceptable than vocational qualifications. British class snobbery has also led Richard Pring (2005) to ironically refer to a 'New Tripartism' consisting of those with A levels, those with vocational training and those who have received some sort of work-based learning. At each level he draws correlations relating to class, occupation and pay. You might like to consider how those with power have the ability to effectively control the destiny of so many young people through the decisions they take, be they teachers, career guidance counsellors, parents or, indeed, other learners. Teachers effectively 'stream' children when they advise that they either take an academic or vocational route in education. Many schools, worried about their league table positioning, effectively 'exclude' some children from their schools through their sixth form admissions policy by not offering them vocational pathways. Teachers may well have fixed ideas about the type of learners that may fit better in academic rather than vocational subjects, and vice versa. Such fixed ideas can have identifiable and in some cases disastrous impacts related to class, gender and ethnic identities of young people. These are worthy debates to explore at M level, as is the question, to what extent is this lack of parity of esteem between the vocational and the academic purely a British phenomenon?

Every Child Matters (ECM)

In February 2000, after months of physical and mental abuse, Victoria Climbié, aged, eight was murdered by her great aunt and her great aunt's lover in the London Borough of Haringey. Published in 2003, the Laming Report concluded that at every stage child protection arrangements had failed the child. Lord Laming, former chief inspector of social services, called for a fundamental reconfiguration of care for children, integrating child protection with health, education and children's services more generally. Nationally the administration of children's services was brought under the control of the Department for Education and Skills (DfES), which in 2004 published a Green Paper entitled *Every Child Matters*.

The paper acknowledges that learner performance cannot be separated from their well-being. *Every Child Matters* identifies five outcomes for children and young people that are central not only to the well-being of children, but to a policy that unites children's services with education, health and social care. These outcomes aim to ensure that children:

- are healthy;
- stay safe;
- enjoy and achieve;
- make a positive contribution;
- achieve economic and social well-being.

Husbands (2007) notes that this programme is one of the most ambitious cross-government agendas of change for children anywhere in the world and is rapidly reshaping the professional world of teachers and schools. However, he also notes three negative consequences in the early stages of the implementation of ECM:

1. School inspections focus their attention on individual schools, which means that schools still have a tendency to focus individually on their ability to meet the five outcomes rather than working in collaboration with other agencies.
2. Linked to the inspection framework many teachers are asked to link lesson plans to the five ECM outcomes, creating an unrealistic expectation on teachers.

3. This tendency for addressing ECM also places an unrealistic expectation on the role that the school curriculum plays in the delivery of the five outcomes. Whereas, in fact, much of what ECM attempts to do is beyond the scope of any formal taught curriculum.

Nevertheless ECM continues to impact in a variety of ways on the teaching profession, its associated institutions and the range of 'paraprofessionals' that make up the world of education. Two developments are worth noting in this section. The first is the development of, at the time of writing, 3,800 'Extended Schools'. Developed since 2003, most stay open from 8.00 a.m. till 6.00 p.m. and, in addition to offering a core-curriculum, provide a range of activities including breakfast clubs, after-school clubs, sports and community-based projects. Husbands (2007) notes that these schools are impacting on parental expectations, not only of their own children but also of the roles schools play in children's lives. The second development has been the rapid transformation of workforce development in schools. The numbers of non-teaching staff (for example, learning mentors, teaching assistants) continue to grow. In many institutions the roles formally carried out by teachers (tutorials, liaising with parents, and so an) are increasingly carried out by these 'paraprofessionals'. Reduced exclusions, lower absentee rates and better behaviour are amongst the benefits that many schools report as a result of this transformation. Every Child Matters is a new initiative and one which begs exploratory research by teachers new to the profession. Its aims are bold and to be welcomed. How it is played out in different schools and the consequences for learners and staff, be they positive, negative or both, are bona fide objectives for any research project at M level.

Well-being and 'therapeutic education'

The Every Child Matters initiative refers, as we have seen above, to five key aims or outcomes. Within these we see the phrase 'achieve economic well-being' but that is not the sort of 'well-being' that this M-level issue is concerned with. By looking more closely at the language used to describe the other outcomes, we see reference to healthy, safety and enjoyment; in other words, a more complete notion of 'well-being' as an emotional and physical state that enables learners to function in society and within education. This well-being is seen as an entitlement for all.

In the 2008 Department for Children, Schools and Families (DCSF) research report *What Do We Mean by 'Wellbeing'? And Why Might It Matter?* Ereaut and Whiting (2008) argue that 'well-being' far from being a simple and achievable concept, is both ambiguous and unstable. They suggest that policy concerns such as ECM seemingly centred around notions of well-being, as if it has a single stable and identifiable meaning, are merely 'discourses' – they are ways of thinking which are being presented by policy-makers as 'truths'. Well-being is seen by these authors as a 'cultural construct' – with little recognition that the term shifts in meaning over time. Ereaut and Whiting suggest that the contradictory ideological media representation of children – as both in need of protection and also as out of control at the same time – is the guiding logic behind the focus of well-being within UK policy agendas.

According to Ecclestone and Hayes (2009) concerns with well-being give rise to what they see as a 'dangerous' tendency for much education to become 'therapeutic'. By this Ecclestone and Hayes point to the increasing use of pseudo-therapeutic and counselling practices in education and within the classroom at the expense of learning. Examples of this include sitting in circles, discussing feelings and emotions within the learning process, making rules for comfortable classroom conduct and for speaking and listening to each other. For Ecclestone and Hayes these therapeutic tendencies in education give way to an increased dependence of the learner on the teacher and a learned helplessness which ultimately limits creativity. They describe the rise of this ethos as a 'silent ascendancy' whereby teachers uncritically have adopted these techniques dramatically within the past 10 years.

Notions of well-being, as with any discourse construct the group that is being discussed. By this we mean that the very language used to talk about the issue or group of people is an act of power, controlling and limiting how we might otherwise see them and how they see themselves. This question – do debates about well-being protect, enable or limit children and their identity? – is an interesting question for teachers and certainly worthy of further M-level study.

Globalisation and teachers

Broadly speaking it is possible to identify three themes within discussions about the nature of globalisation that are significant to the teaching profession. The first sees globalisation in terms of the convergence and uniformity it produces in political, economic, cultural and social terms. The second is to consider the influence of globalisation on the nation state and its education systems. The third theme examines how a combination of both a 'global' and 'local' understanding of the processes of globalisation has particular resonance for teachers.

Much literature has been generated about globalisation that explores the dynamic interrelationship that is said to exist among economic convergence and integration, education systems, institutions and social actors at local levels (for example, Hirst and Thompson, 2002). Explanations that connect the processes of globalisation to what takes place in the classroom abound. Ritzer refers to the 'McDonaldisation of society' which leads to the 'dehumanisation of education, the elimination of a human teacher and of human interaction between teacher and student' (Ritzer, 1993: 142). Ball (1999), referring to 'northern countries' describes a move towards a 'single paradigm' that 'reworks' or 'remakes' teachers within the context of converging educational systems. He points to the existence of the post-modern 'reformed teacher' who is 'accountable, and primarily oriented to performance indicators, competition and comparison and responsiveness' (Ball, 1999: 26). Globalisation is thus typically presented as an external phenomenon which results, at the school level, in such neo-liberal features as managerialism, competition and market arrangements (Angus, 2004) to the detriment of the teaching profession.

However Green et al. (1999) argue that while there is certainly evidence of widespread educational policy borrowing at an international level and that some convergence of national policies is taking place (for example, institutional linkages between work and education, emphases on adult education and training, and competence-based assessment, to name but three), nevertheless, education still fulfils primarily national objectives. And while it would be foolish to ignore the role of international agencies such as the OECD or reports such as those carried out in 2001 and 2003 by the Programme for International Student Achievement (PISA) (OECD, 2001, 2003) in the formation of national policies on education, much of the literature on globalisation overemphasises the degree of convergence in the identities and values of teachers in these globalising times. Furlong et al. (2000) ask us to consider 'contextual specificities' when making any cross-national comparisons and generalisations. Research over the last decade has attempted to demonstrate that while globalising tendencies may well be at work at influencing the world of teaching, national cultural traditions can influence the system of schooling in general, on national curricula, and on teachers' values and classroom practices in schools.

Notions of 'paradigm convergence' (Ball, 1999) within Northern countries, mentioned at the beginning of this section, are left wide of the mark when understanding the work that teachers do in different national locations. Such an understanding is important when convergence and homogenisation of the teaching profession is not only implied but lies at the heart of the European agenda (European Commission, 2005) for teacher mobility across all European countries. Debates surrounding the nature of globalisation raise questions for educational researchers. These include the extent to which teacher identities and their values are mediated by the national policy contexts, institutional settings and the variety of other professionals that teachers engage with. Such discussions are significant when teachers trained in one country consider how problematic it might be to teach in another, and lie at the heart of a European agenda on teacher mobility.

Global citizenship and teaching

Like student voice, 'global citizenship' is rapidly becoming a buzzword in many schools across Britain. The concepts and principles it promotes include multiculturalism, anti-racism and environmental education linked specifically to an understanding of poverty, both at the local and global level. This particular take on globalisation places schools firmly at the heart of targeting the knowledge, skills and values that learners are likely to need in what is hoped will become a more equitable and sustainable world.

Global citizenship as a cross-curricular theme fits comfortably into three recent developments in teacher education and the school curriculum. First, in September 2007 the current Professional Standards in teaching were introduced in which three new elements were brought under their gaze: Every Child Matters, personalised learning and new professionalism. Secondly, new National Curriculum frameworks were implemented in 2008 with an emphasis on cross-curricular collaboration. Finally, the overarching themes of the new KS3 curriculum in particular focus on identity and cultural diversity, the global dimension and sustainable development. However the notion of 'cross-curricularity' continues to cause tensions among many teachers (and some of their trainers) as they try to juggle timetable constraints, large class sizes and the requirements to deliver their own subject.

Without realising it, most young people in schools are eager recipients of the eight concepts that make up the global dimension (conflict resolution, social justice, values and perceptions, sustainable development, interdependence, human rights, diversity and global citizenship). In a 2006 poll conducted with over 2,300 learners aged 11–16, on behalf of the Department for International Development, 83 per cent wanted to know more about what is happening in developing countries, 56 per cent thought they should learn about these issues in school and 66 per cent were concerned about poverty in developing countries (MORI, 2006). A captive audience awaits in schools but, as in the case of mainstream subject areas, there is a danger of falling into the trap of delivering these themes in ways that seem divorced from the complexities, ambiguities and tensions that make up the lives of young people. In evaluating the success of 'global citizenship' as a cross-curricular theme in both initial teacher education (ITE) and school curriculum development in general, it is important to acknowledge this trap and two of its victims, that is, those trainee teachers who believe global citizenship to be irrelevant to their subject areas and those ITE subject tutors who believe that global citizenship has little to do with their roles as teacher educators.

There is sympathy for both teachers and teacher educators who feel under pressure in the delivery of their core subjects. However, that sympathy, while understandable, can easily stultify the creativity that is such an essential element to teaching. Those constraints, while considerable, can become justifications for not embarking on more imaginative teaching. Hargreaves notes that: 'Those who focus only on teaching techniques and curriculum standards and who do not also engage teachers in the greater social and moral questions of their time, promote a diminished view of teaching and teacher professionalism that has no place in a sophisticated knowledge society' (Hargreaves, 2003: 151).

These discussions prompt research on teachers, teacher trainers and learners about what their thoughts might be on global citizenship as a cross curricular theme in schools and colleges. They also raise questions about how useful it is to construct a curriculum around artificially manufactured divisions between subject disciplines.

Remember, teachers are learners too!

Studying at M level provides an opportunity to immerse yourself in some key and powerful debates around education, schooling and classroom practice. Better informed teachers are better teachers! All through your professional role, remember that the best teachers fully admit to still learning themselves. This learning can focus upon both practice and theory – and, most importantly, the interplay between the two. You might like to revisit some of the evaluation skills we suggested in Chapter 17 as many of these will help you in your M-level writing.

Throughout this text we have presented a number of key ideas as relevant for M-level thinking – they offer an opportunity to engage critically with some key ideas in teaching and teacher education.

Chapter 1	Chapter 2	Chapter 3	Chapter 4
Situatedness – page7 The reflective practitioner – page 8 Professionalism – page 10	Crisis of masculinity – page 15 The role of education – page 16 The marketisation of education – page 21	The postmodern condition and education – page 32 Policy epidemic – page 32	Narrowing the academic/vocational divide – page 44 14–19 Competition *and* collaboration? – page 48
Chapter 5	Chapter 6	Chapter 7	Chapter 9
Critical theory – page 63 Values and education – page 64	Double thinking – page 73 Discourses of teaching – page 74	Presentation of self – page 86 Situated learning – page 86	Neuroscience versus learning styles – page 122 Pedagogy before technology! – page 124
Chapter 10	Chapter 12	Chapter 19	
The 'burden of assessment'? – page 134	The impact of cultural capital on educational achievement – page 162 The feasibility of 'inclusion' – page 170	Making a case for reflection? – page 270 The two worlds page 272	

Figure19.1   Overview of M-level thinking

Chapter links →

Themes and ideas explored in this chapter link to corresponding ideas in Chapters 2, 3, 4, 9, 12 and 20.

Suggested further reading 📖

Sewell, K. (ed.) (2008) *Doing Your PGCE at M Level: A Guide for Learners.* London: Sage.

References

Angus, L. (2004) 'Globalisation and educational change: bringing about the reshaping and reforming of practice', *Journal of Educational Policy*, 19(1): 43–56.

Ball, S.J. (1999) 'Global trends in educational reform and the struggle for the soul of the teacher', paper presented at the British Educational Research Association Annual Conference, University of Sussex at Brighton, 2–5 September. London: Centre for Public Policy Research, Kings College.

Bottery, M. and Wright, N. (2000) *Teachers and the State – Towards a Directed Profession*. London: Routledge.

Burden, P.R. (1982) 'Professional development as a stressor', paper presented at the annual meeting of the Association of Teacher Educators – Phoenix, in M.L Holly and McLoughlin. C. (eds) (1989) *Perspectives on Teacher Professional Development*. Have: Falmer Press.

Carter, M. (2000) 'Beginning teachers and workplace learning: an exploration of the process of becoming a teacher', paper presented at the 13th Annual International Congress for School Effectiveness and Improvement (ICSEI 2000), New South Wales Department of Education and Training.

Department of Employment and Skills (DfES) (2004) *Every Child Matters: Change for Children in Schools*. London: Department for Education and Skills.

Ecclestone, K. and Hayes, D. (2009) *The Dangerous Rise of Therapeutic Education*. London: Routledge.

Ereaut, G. and Whiting, R. (2008) *What Do We Mean by 'Wellbeing'? And Why Might It Matter?* London: Linguistic Landscapes, DCSF.

European Commission (2005) *Testing Conference on the Common European Principles for Teacher Competences and Qualifications 20th–21st June 2005*. Brussels: European Commission.

Fielding, M. (2001) 'Students as radical agents of change' *Journal of Educational Change* 2(3): 123–41.

Furlong, J. and Maynard, T. (1995) *Mentoring Student Teachers: The Growth of Professional Knowledge*. London: Routledge.

Furlong, J., Borton, L., Miles, S. and Whitty, G. (2000) *Teacher Eduction in Transistion*. Buckingham: Open University Press.

Ginns, I., Heirdsfield, A., Atweh, B. and Watters, J.J. (2001) 'Beginning teachers becoming professional through action research', *Educational Action Research*, 9(1): 111–33.

Green, A., Wolf, A. and Leney, T. (1999) *Convergence and Divergence in European Education and Training Systems*. London: University of London Institute of Education.

Halsey, K., Murfield, J., Harland, J. and Lord, P. (2008) *The Voice of Young People: an Engine for improvement? Scoping the Evidence*. London: National Foundation for Educational Research.

Hargreaves, A. (1994) *Changing Teachers, Changing Times*. London: Cassell.

Hargreaves, A. (2003) *Teaching in the Knowledge Society*. New York: Teachers College Press.

Hatch, J.A. (1999) 'What pre-service teachers can learn from studies of teachers work', *Teaching and Teacher Education*, 15: 229–42.

Hirst, P. and Thompson, G. (2002) 'The future of globalisation', *Cooperation and Conflict*, 37(3): 247–65.

Husbands, C. (2007) 'Does every child matter? Education, social care and the new agenda for children's services', in V. Brooks., I. Abbot. and L. Bills (eds), *Preparing to Teach in Secondary Schools*. London: McGraw-Hill.

Kelchtermans, G. and Ballet, K. (2002) 'The micropolitics of teacher induction – a narrative-biographical study on teacher socialisation', *Teaching and Teacher Education*, 18: 105–20.

Lacey, C. (1977) *The Socialisation of Teachers*. London: Methuen.

Lodge, C. (2008) 'Research matters – student voice and learning-focussed school improvement' *INSI*, no. 32.

McMahon, B. and Portelli, J.P. (2004) 'Encouragement for what? Beyond popular discourses of student engagement', *Leadership and Policy in Schools*, 3: 59–76.

MORI (2006) 'School inspections. A research study for Ofsted by Iposs', HMI 20060001. Ofsted:

Organisation for Economic Co-operation and Development (OECD) (2001) 'Knowledge and skills for life: first results from PISA 2000', OECD.

Organisation for Economic Co-operation and Development (OECD) (2003) 'Tomorrow's World: First Results from PISA 2003: OECD.

Pring, R. (2005) 'Labour government policy 14–19', *Oxford Review of Education*, 31(1): 71–85.

Ritzer, G. (1993) *The McDonaldization of Society*. London: Sage.

Shindler, J., Jones, A., Taylor, C. and Cadenas, H. (2004) *Don't Smile till Christmas: Examining the Immersion of New Teachers into Existing Urban School Climates*. Los Angeles, CA: Charter College of Education.

Stephens P., Egil Tonnessen, F. and Kyriacou, C. (2001) 'Teacher training and teacher education in England and Norway: competent managers and reflective carers', paper presented at the annual international seminar, Department of Educational Studies, University of York, 16 June.

Tickle, L. (2000) *Teacher Induction: The Way Ahead*. Buckingham: Open University Press.

Tickle, L. (2003) 'New directions in teachers' working and learning environment', paper presented at 2003 ISATT, Leiden, Netherlands.

Veenman, S. (1984) 'Perceived problems of beginning teachers', *Review of Educational Research*, 54(2): 143–78.

Wenger, R. (1998) *Communities of Practice: Learning, Meaning and Identity*. Cambridge: Cambridge University Press.

CHAPTER 20

MOVING ON: PROFESSIONAL FORMATION AND CONTINUING PROFESSIONAL DEVELOPMENT

Objectives

By the end of this chapter the reader will be able to:

1. understand the importance of professional identity;
2. reflect upon the training year as a basis for future professional development;
3. comprehend the role that practitioner research can play in continuing professional development;
4. possess a range of tools ready for interview and application processes;
5. understand the pivotal importance of continuing professional development for the years ahead.

Moving on ... one step at a time

The point of training to be a teacher is to enter the profession. But then again, it is not this simple. You are best advised to enter the profession seeing it as another step along a continuous process of learning, rather than simply an end goal of a programme or course of study. Like all professional learning, you will certainly find out a great deal more in the years to come, but the foundation should be what you have learnt on your training programme.

We often make a distinction between teacher education, which is a lifelong process, and initial teacher education, which covers the programmes that this book is designed to support. Teacher education does not end, and it is worth considering as you enter your first post what sort of teacher you think you are becoming and what challenges you think you might end up facing.

Who are you becoming?

Try to see your teacher education as a continuous process. It is always ongoing in terms of the professional identity you are forming – and will change from year to year, post to post and position to position. However, at the start of your first post this professional identity is probably at its most unstable.

Consider the following questions, based upon your reflective practice to date:

- What strategies have you tended to adopt the most?
- Why do you teach in this way and not others?
- Are there other ways to go about teaching the same learners that you have not tried?
- What might you learn from other colleagues and how can you accommodate their practice into your own?
- How do you know if an idea for classroom practice is worth trying?
- Against what measurements do you hold your own performance in the classroom?
- How do you judge the impact of your practice?

To summmarise these points – the single key question is 'who are you becoming?' – decide on what type of teacher you are.

Action research and practitioner research

In recent years action research for educational practitioners has risen to the fore as a means through which teachers can investigate and explore their own practice (see Baumfield et al., 2008). This development is often linked in the literature to the emphasis within the professional field to reflective practice. The idea that schools and colleges are places or communities of learning at every level and that, therefore, teachers within the same learning institutions are members of a 'community of practice' (Lave and Wenger, 1991; Wenger, 1998).

According to McNiff and Whitehead (2006) and Koshy (2005) action research is a distinctive approach to the practitioner research. Since it is 'action' and 'research' at the same time, this sort of research is often carried out by practitioners into their own practice. Thus, the classroom teacher, usually through experimentation and reflection, is both a researcher and a practitioner at the same time. In occupying both roles in this way, the outcome of action research is practical knowledge which can then lead to further change in one's own practice. To do this, practice–observation–reflection–experimentation–change–reflection and so on, many proponents of an action research paradigm within educational research cite Kolb and Fry (1975) and the notion of a 'learning cycle' (see Chapter 5).

The process of action research, as with any research processes, involves the identification of a research problem or question – something practitioners have noticed that they think warrants further consideration and investigation. The practitioner identifies the procedures for capturing data and documenting their analysis of this data and their reflections on the process. This commitment to practitioner research is a very powerful tool for encouraging teacher autonomy and continuing reflective practice, as well as offering something of tremendous value to colleagues within and outside your institution. This is an excellent means through which to continue your professional development, which is why we spend some time here looking at educational research practices that teachers can adopt to further their own professional understandings.

Writing as a researcher

Writing up your own M-level research can be an exciting, creative and fulfilling pastime. It is also extremely time-consuming and, at times, a painful experience. There can be nothing scarier (or more exciting) than starting your period of writing, confronting a blank page! Phillips and Pugh (2000) recommend the following strategies to help increase productivity when writing:

1. Make a rough plan (which you need not necessarily stick to but can revise).
2. Complete sections one at a time.
3. Revise and re-draft at least twice (and build this into your plan).
4. Find quiet conditions in which to write and, if possible, always write in the same place.
5. Set goals and targets for yourself (make these small and 'doable' rather than large and insurmountable).
6. Get 'critical friends' to comment on early drafts.

Remember that you are not aiming for perfection in your research but rather offering something that is of use to you, your colleagues and the professional communities of practice with which you engage.

Research strategies

When embarking on research for the first time it is helpful to consider that two methodological traditions – positivism and interpretivism – span opposite ends of a methodological rainbow. Positivists, drawing on the traditions of the natural sciences in their research methodologies, tend to adopt methods involving the use and analysis of quantitative data (for example, questionnaires, surveys). Associated with positivism is the belief that researchers, should, wherever possible, attempt to be as 'value neutral' and as 'scientific' as possible. Seen from this perspective the job of research is to collect data that points towards the creation of laws, theories and generalisations. Interpretivists, on the other hand, believe that it is more appropriate to use qualitative data such as interviews and observation, to study the social world. This 'value-laden' approach to research welcomes the idea of small-scale research and embraces the fact that researchers carry with them their biases, values, expectations and experiences into the research process. Seen from this perspective the researchers' job is to get inside the heads of the people they are researching to see how they interpret their world. Between these two approaches lie a range of different methodologies (for example, realism and feminism) that can inform and guide the researcher, not only in the planning and executing of their research but also in the analysis, interpretation and evaluation of any outcome generated.

Some methods used in educational research

- Experiments.
- Social surveys.
- Interviews (structured, semi-structured and unstructured)
- Focus groups.
- Observation (for example, participant, non-participant, covert and overt).
- Case studies.
- Analysis of official/unofficial statistics.
- Analysis of personal documents (for example, diaries, letters, confiscated class notes).
- Analysis of contemporary documents (for example, policy documents, reports and speeches).
- Podcasts.
- Analysis of virtual 'chat' communities.

It is possible to combine the use of both quantitative and qualitative methods when carrying out research (depending on how this is done, this is sometimes referred to as 'methodological pluralism' or 'triangulation'). It is perhaps worth mentioning, however, that the more research methods you adopt the more analysis and justification you will need to provide for your methodological choices. Simplicity is often the best advice when choosing a method of research. Remember that one method (for example, interviews) will still provide enormous amounts of data to sit through and analyse!

A few words on sampling strategies

Sampling refers to the processes of selecting those who you will study in your research. The 'sample' refers to the people or things who actually take part. How you chose this sample may well depend on which particular methodological approach you adopt. It will also depend on the sort of sampling frame (for example, a list of people in the relevant population from which the sample may be drawn). The following are just some of the sampling strategies that are commonly used by educational researchers:

- Random sampling: everyone or everything has an equal chance of being chosen for the research (for example, names chosen at random from a sampling frame; via a computer programme designed to generate random numbers).
- Systematic sampling: names are chosen at regular intervals from a sampling frame (for example, every tenth name from a telephone directory).
- Quota sampling: people are chosen according to specific characteristics but the way they actually get chosen is still random (for example, 20 males under the age of 30).
- Stratified sampling: this method of sampling divides people from the relevant population into layers or groups and then specific names are chosen from those groups.
- Snowball sampling: this method is quite often favoured by qualitative researchers carrying out small-scale research. Here the purpose is not to generalise but to get in-depth knowledge on issues that might be sensitive. Using this method, each respondent introduces the researcher to somebody they know that might wish to be involved in the research. As such the sample can be described as a 'self-selected sample'.

There are many more ways of sampling the particular items or people that you wish to carry out your research on. Remember, when choosing your particular sampling strategy, to consider any practical, ethical, theoretical and sensitive issues related to your research and those your research affects.

Changing professional identities

By 'teacher identity' we refer to how teachers view themselves as teachers; how teachers view others that they professionally engage with; and how teachers believe they are perceived by those 'others'. Teachers' identities are 'social identities' in that they are a fusion of both the individual identity of the teacher, that is, the image of the teacher's own qualifications, characteristics and values, and a collective identity, that is, the experience of being an integrated part of a group (Ulriksen, 1995). Teachers learn to be teachers through interaction and communication with others. There may be a host of working and other relationships that have an influence upon this learning process (Brown, 1997).

While teachers are significant actors in the construction of their identities and values, they are also partly constrained by the processes and structures of the 'communities of practice' (Wenger, 1998) in which they operate. Wenger (1998) draws attention to 'communities of practice' that contribute to identity formation. These include the immediate work group/department, the institution and the occupation itself, and can have the effect of structuring the work that teachers do as well as influencing their attitudes and values about the work they do. The existence of these communities of practice also means that any impact of national policies on education is not easy to specify or predict. This is because particular work groups or departments may have their own distinctive community of practice that might be resistant to any form of outside interference.

The construction of teacher identities as a set of processes varies from institution to institution. Teachers' identities and the institutional settings in which these identities are activated are mutually constitutive. For example, Twiselton (2004) has argued that teacher identity construction is a process that is not only individualistic but reliant on social interaction in a range of sociocultural groupings. Teachers can therefore express their identities in terms of the relationships they possess with colleagues they work with, while at the same time identifying themselves symbolically as 'teachers', subject specialists, 'managers', 'union representatives', and so on.

The construction of teacher identities also varies from country to country. Different combinations of 'others' combine to provide different internalised pictures of the world of teaching that teachers can both differentiate themselves from and identify with. In some countries, for example, schools are not as hierarchical or possess as many managerial positions, making teaching a far more isolated experience than that found in Britain. This can also mean that opportunities to move jobs within education are restricted as there are fewer positions to which a teacher can be promoted. Distinctions can be made between the interpersonal relationships with 'specific' or 'significant' others (for example, mentors, line managers, individual colleagues) and those that derive from membership of larger, more 'generalised' others (for example, membership in impersonal collectives such as subject associations or unions). The nature of these collectives is very much contingent on the networks and communities of practice that exist in different national settings.

Ibarra (2003) stresses how important it is for the successful development of 'working' identities that employees are able to break out of their existing network of colleagues so that new role models and new values can be developed. She stresses the importance of 'people who can give you glimpses of what you might become' (Ibarra, 2003: 169). To be 'reflective' about the type of teacher you become requires a variety of 'others' onto whom you can project your reflection. This raises all sorts of questions about the nature of professional identities and how important (or not) it is to move from one institution to another.

Continuing professional development

If you are reading this and you happen to have learnt how to drive a car, you will appreciate that passing your test, while no doubt a joyous occasion, did not instantly mean that you became a better driver. In fact it will have taken you a lengthy period of time before you felt both confident and competent to negotiate those busy roads on your own. The process of learning never ends and that is true once you have gained your teacher qualification. Continuing professional development (CPD) in. whatever form it takes, builds up your skills, supports career progression and should be focused on raising the standards of your teaching and student learning. Sufficient research literature demonstrates that CPD has a positive impact on curriculum, pedagogy, teachers' sense of commitment and their relationships with learners (Muijs et al., 2004).

There is no right time to embark on CPD, although most secondary trained teachers will experience elements of CPD during their induction year. Some teachers wish, after qualification, to keep their heads down in that first 'induction' year and hone their skills, developing resources and gaining a broad understanding of how their school functions and their place within it. Others wish immediately to consider career paths and the myriad of possibilities for professional development that most schools and colleges in Britain offer. Whatever you choose consider the following factors:

- What are your own strengths and weaknesses as a teacher?
- What opportunities exist within and outside your teaching institution to address those strengths and weaknesses?
- What opportunities exist in your own institution for career development?
- What sources of funding (if any) are you likely to need in order to pursue your CPD?
- What available time have you got outside of teaching that you can use to devote to CPD?

It would be worth noting all of the above bullet points when seeking out potential institutions for employment, and it is definitely worth asking about CPD as you come to the end of any job interview. Alternatively, you could do this in advance of your interview by requesting a copy of the school/college staff development policy. Try to talk to the CPD coordinator and ask about the way in which the school/college uses its in-service training days.

Teachers employed in the lifelong sector (sixth form colleges, FE colleges and other 'adult' learning centres) are required to undertake 30 hours' CPD per academic year. This is a professional requirement and is logged with the Institute for Learning (IfL). The institute is responsible for overseeing professional standards within this sector. In addition to where you work there are a variety of other possibilities for CPD. These include:

- subject associations;
- unions;
- local authorities;
- examination boards;
- Excellence in Cities groupings;
- universities (including your own ITT provider);
- partnership schools and colleges;
- the General Teaching Council for England (GTCE).

Talk to colleagues during your training and look at the university prospectuses. Continuing professional development has become big business now for many universities who are only too keen to cultivate your ambitions, and those of the schools in which you work. Many universities tie in the CPD needs of teachers to those of the schools or the colleges' strategic plans, producing a variety of opportunities for teachers to extend their professional knowledge.

Preparing for Interviews

If dealing with the rigours of your training and the demands of working in your school/college is not enough, at some stage you will have to broach the inevitable – searching for a job. We cannot begin to emphasise the importance you must give preparing for the interview. Before the day of the interview research the institution thoroughly. Check out Ofsted/Estyn reports, the institution's own website and if possible go to the location well in advance of your interview. If possible, try to visit the institution and talk to staff and learners as well as checking out noticeboards, libraries and so on. This will allow you to get a 'feel' for the place as well as estimate travel times and so on.

On the actual day you will almost certainly be required to prepare a short presentation. This could be in front of a number of staff at the school or college you are applying for. In some cases you might be required to 'teach' a short (usually about 20 minutes) section of a lesson to a class. Make sure you 'look the part'. While schools and colleges do have their own dress code, be it formal or informal, at interview it is expected that you dress smartly. Come armed with your teaching portfolio – even if you are not required to show it. There is something particularly impressive about interview candidates who can confidently offer you examples of resources, lesson plans, and so on. Make sure that you prepare enough copies of resources/lesson plans so that you can again, confidently, hand these to the interview/presentation panel. Make sure they are clearly labelled and in plastic wallets. Remember, the presentation is a chance for you to highlight how professional you are in all aspects of your work. Stick exactly to the time they give you to present (in the days leading up to the interview, time your presentation down to the minute). Under no circumstances read from anything that you have brought to the presentation. Your panel will be looking to see what your presentation skills are like and there is nothing worse than a candidate who reads from their lesson plan. Always finish your presentation by asking your panel if they have any questions and make sure that you hold eye contact with them throughout.

After your presentation you are likely to be called for interview. We have included below a range of possible questions that you might find useful in preparation for your interview:

- Could you tell us a little about yourself and your teaching experience?
- How do you think your sample lesson went?
- Apart from your formal qualifications, what special qualities are you offering that we would be interested in?
- What do you consider to be the key qualities of a good teacher of X?
- What relevant skills and experience do you feel you could bring to this post?
- What do you consider to be your strengths and weaknesses?

- In what ways do ICT/blended learning inform your teaching?
- Can you tell us what makes you suitable for this post?
- What are some of the teaching strategies you have used successfully?
- What attracted you to this post?
- Why do you want to teach in this kind of school?
- Tell us about an occasion when a pupil misbehaved in your lesson, and how you dealt with it.
- Choose a successful lesson that you have taught. Describe it briefly and explain why it was successful.
- How would a commitment to equal opportunities manifest itself in your work as a teacher?
- What do you think about the proposed reforms on 14–19 education?
- How can your subject contribute to citizenship?
- How have you catered for gender differences in your teaching?
- Tell us about mistakes that you have learned from in your teaching experience.
- How important do you think examinations are as a performance indicator?
- Choose one recent educational reform and explain how it affects your subject.
- What do you think are the characteristics of a good tutor?
- Tell us about different learning styles and how you have tried to cater for them in your teaching.
- How do you feel your training and teaching experience has prepared you for this position?
- How does this position lend itself to your career development?
- Why is the pastoral role of the teacher important?
- Tell us about the ways in which you differentiate your lessons.
- If a parent complained of political bias in one of your lessons, how would you deal with it?
- How do you see your role within the department/school/college?
- What is the role of your subject within the whole school curriculum?
- How would you develop a departmental area such as . . . ?
- In which areas would you like to gain more experience?
- How would you deal with a complaint or concern from a parent.
- A question related to the new National Curriculum and your own subject.
- A subject-specific question, for example, How would you teach ... (probability, grammar, spreadsheets)?
- What would you do to motivate reluctant learners?
- What strategies would you employ to manage new arrivals to the school who have very little or no English? Would you be happy to contribute to this work?
- Have you had any experience of coursework? How would you best prepare learners?
- Would you be prepared to take part in extra-curricular activities such as clubs and trips?
- What sorts of trips would you like to take your learners on that are relevant to your own subject?

- Have you had any experience of student/pupil voice? How has this informed your own practice?
- In what ways do you adapt your teaching for vocational as well as academic subjects?
- How have both ECM and AfL informed the strategies you deploy in the classroom?

We cannot guarantee that these questions will come up in exactly the form they take here, but by preparing for all of them you should be in a very strong position to answer anything that is thrown at you. Remember that everybody on that panel will have gone through interviews themselves and therefore will be sympathetic to you on the day. It is almost certain that the panel will, at the end of the interview, ask you if you have anything you wish to ask them. Have a couple of questions ready based on the research you have done prior to interview. Good luck!

Endnote: who will you become?

We started this chapter by asking you 'who are you becoming?' Now think about who you will become. It is probably true to say that if you are reading this at the end of your training you have changed in a whole variety of ways. If you are the sort of person who reads the end of a book before the beginning then think about how and why you might change – prepare yourself to develop as your own professional learning develops.

On a number of occasions in this book we have made the point that teachers are learners too! This is certainly true for the first year of teaching. For many the first year is both an exciting journey and an exhausting one: you will truly now 'own' your classes – a huge responsibility. Equally, you will work even longer hours than at present – and along with this increase in your workload comes the pressures of keeping on top of the work, ensuring all classes are well catered for and that all learners are as well supported as possible.

The subtitle for this book is 'theory, practice and reflection' and as we have said in the opening chapters, it is the interplay between these elements which makes teaching so powerful and which truly defines what it means to be a professional in our field of practice. We have said that this book was a combination of different elements:

- part training manual;
- part introduction to academic debates around education and teaching and learning;
- part teaching techniques, hints and tips

These are the elements needed of a good professional – to be able to juggle the need for theoretically informed teaching against seeing what works and asking yourself why? Have the insight to seek out why things are working as much as why things are not. To experiment and learn and show your own learners that you are as open to suggestions and change as you would like them to be.

We have enjoyed our lives as teachers and are sure that you will too.

Chapter links →

Themes and ideas explored in this chapter link to corresponding ideas in Chapters 1 and 5.

Suggested further reading 📖

Baumfield, V., Hall, E. and Wall, K. (2008) *Action Research in the Classroom*. London: Sage.

References

Baumfield, V., Hall, E. and Wall, K. (2008) *Action Research in the Classroom*. London: Sage.

Brown, A. (1997) 'A dynamic model of occupational identity formation', symposium paper presented at the *Journal of Vocational Education and Training* Second International Conference, 16–18 July, 'Policy and practice in vocational education and training', University of Huddersfield.

Ibarra, H. (2003) *Working Identities*. Cambridge, MA: Harvard Business School Press.

Kolb, D.A. and Fry, R. (1975) 'Toward an applied theory of experiential learning', in C. Cooper (ed.), *Theories of Group Process*. London: John Wiley.

Koshy, V. (2005) *Action Research for Improving Practice: A Practical Guide*. London: Sage.

Lave, J. and Wenger, E. (1991) *Situated Learning: Legitimate Peripheral Participation*. Cambridge: Cambridge University Press.

McNiff, J. and Whitehead, J. (2006) *All You Need to Know about Action Research*. London: Sage.

Muijs, D., Day, C., Harris, A. and Lindsay, G. (2004) 'Evaluating CPD: an overview', in C. Day and J. Sachs (eds), *International Handbook on the Continuing Professional Development of Teachers*. Maidenhead: Open University Press.

Phillips, E. and Pugh, D.S. (2000) *How to Get a PhD: A Handbook for Students and their Supervisors*, 3rd edn. Buckingham: Open University Press.

Twiselton, S. (2004) 'The role of teacher identities in learning to teach primary literacy', *Educational Review*, 56(2): 157–64.

Ulriksen, L. (1995) 'General qualification and teacher qualification in the vocational training system', Adult Education Research Group, Roskilde University.

Wenger, E. (1998) *Communities of Practice: Learning, Meaning, and Identity*. Cambridge: Cambridge University Press.

GLOSSARY

Academies A private sponsor is given control of these types of school, which may be an existing institution, or a newly built one and usually located in 'inner-city' areas. The remainder of the capital and running costs are met by the state.

Achievement What learners obtain as a final measurable outcome (often based on national examination).

Action research Practitioner (teacher)-based research where the researcher adopts transformative actions – often based on reflection and experimentation – with a view to developing aspects of their practice further.

Andragogy In contrast to the term 'pedagogy' this implies that adults learn in different ways from children and that teachers 'facilitate' more with adults than child learners. The assumption being that good teachers should be 'adragogic' in their approach to children.

Assessment for learning The view that assessment practices (especially formative) should be structured in order to enable learners to extend their learning in the future.

Behaviour for Learning Underpinning the 'Behaviour for Learning' approach is a commitment by the teacher to establishing positive relationships and a learning climate that enthuses and supports all learners, thereby diminishing the need for more pejorative strategies from the teacher.

Behaviour management The strategies teachers adopt to ensure learners are demonstrating approved behaviour.

Behaviourism A school of psychology that has influenced educational approaches to teaching and learning. In particular it focuses on the variety of ways teachers can transfer knowledge to learners.

Blended learning The merging of 'traditional' and digital means of teaching and learning where emergent technologies exist alongside and interwoven into other types of methods and approaches.

BTEC The initials stand for Business and Technology Education Council and refer to the body that awards a variety of vocational qualifications. Vocational qualifications come and go but BTECs have managed to retain a high status with learners, employers and teachers.

Building schools for the future (BSF) A New Labour policy that aims to renovate or rebuild all secondary schools throughout the UK.

Classroom management The strategies used to manipulate the learning environment to ensure learning takes place with the maximum efficiency, including behaviour management strategies.

Cognition Thinking.

Cognitive growth Refers to any sort of change in thinking that is brought about by events either internally within the brain (for example, the development of the frontal lobe) or externally (for example, certain forms of interaction, life events).

Communities of practice Learning groups within organisations which develop mutual learning and support practices among members performing similar practices.

Competencies Competencies are general descriptions of the abilities needed to perform a role in a profession. Applied to teaching they are often used to refer to the national standards expected to be achieved if a teacher is to become professionally qualified.

Consortia These are the bodies (made up of employers, schools, colleges, training providers, and so on) that the government uses to roll out the Diploma programme. Based on a competitive system, successful consortia gain funding to offer specific Diploma pathways.

Continuing professional development (CPD) Support, training and skills enhancement undertaken by professionals to keep in good standing with the development of their profession and their own professional expertise.

Cross-curricular The variety of ways in which formal learning can extend beyond traditional subject disciplines (for example, through the teaching of functional skills, citizenship).

Cultural capital The norms and values associated with a particular cultural group.

Differentiation Accommodating difference in learners and learning; ensuring that all learners are supported and developed.

Dual-professionalism The view that many teachers in further education (FE) are both a teacher and another (vocational) professional at the same time – thus giving them a dual professional identity.

Economic capital The financial means (money, property, and so on) associated with a particular cultural group that can be used (in education) to increase the educational attainment of learners.

e-learning The adoption of new (and increasingly digital) methods to enhance learning.

Emotional intelligence A term associated with American psychologist Daniel Goleman to create a wider understanding of what intelligence means. In particular he argues that self-awareness, self-regulation, motivation, empathy and social skills are as valid indicators of intelligence as more traditional understandings that tend to privilege logic and rationality.

Exclusion A contested term used to refer to the removal of learners from their learning environment. The term can refer to the temporary exclusion of a child from a lesson up to the permanent exclusion of the learner from a school/college.

Formal curriculum This refers to everything that is formally taught in the school or college, that is, the range of subjects on offer. It is often contrasted with the term 'hidden curriculum' used to refer to the informal ways that teachers and institutions 'teach' certain norms and values (for example, lining up, putting hands up, use of the term 'miss').

Formative assessment Regular assessment designed to help support learners with the next steps in their learning journey.

Further education (FE) The term that is used for any education beyond secondary education up to, but not including, degree-level studies.

Higher education (HE) Refers to adult education that offers degree-level studies.

Gifted and talented A contested term that many institutions use to describe the top 10 per cent of pupils who perform academically better than their counterparts.

Globalisation Global forces and patterns that interconnect and lead to a spread of influences across and between nations, continents and political and geographical regions.

Habitus Regular pattern and routine: the shape culture and norms give to practices.

Humanism An approach to education that embraces among others the works of Abraham Maslow, Carl Rogers, and Rudolf Steiner. Priority is given to the development of the whole person and not just the intellect.

Hyperactivism Rapid and continuous expansion (and flood) of political policy.

Identity Who you think you are.

Institutional racism The unintentional ways in which schools, colleges and other institutions marginalise learners as a result of their ethnicity, race and culture, etc.

Ipsative assessment Learner assessment of their own learning, illustrating through reflection directions to take to increase learning further.

Labelling The ways in which learners perceive themselves and how others perceive them based on a particular identity marker, for example, 'stupid', 'boffin', and so on. Often used to explain the process in which teachers attribute educational potential based on class, gender or ethnicity.

The marketisation of education The marketisation of education involves the belief that competition at all levels should provide a higher standard of education. By adapting business principles to education the idea embraces the notion that the market should allocate resources where required.

Meta-cognition Thinking about thinking, or, learning about learning.

Methods Tools adopted; in this case, it could be tools to aid teaching and learning (strategies) or assessment practices or, even, research tools.

Methodology The underlying and underpinning way of going about a practice; in this case, the practice of teaching and learning or the practice of educational research.

M-learning Branch of 'e-learning' adopting mobile technology and portable devices.

Motivation for learning Phrase associated with the Assessment Reform Group denoting the preconditions needed to enthuse learners to enable effective learning to take place.

Multiple intelligences An idea most famously associated with American psychologist Howard Gardner. In contrast to the nineteenth-century conception of intelligence as singular, logical and rational, Gardner argues that we have a variety of 'intelligences' that include mathematical, musical and intrapersonal.

Neurolinguistic programming (NLP) Bandler and Grinder's (1981) complex sets of beliefs, skills and behaviours revolve around the notions of: 'neuro' referring to, what they argue to be, a nervous system where experience is received through the five senses; 'linguistic' representing innate verbal and non-verbal language capabilities and 'programming' referring to the ways in which people can be 'trained' to think, speak and act in new ways.

Neuroscience This emerging field of interdisciplinary study owes much to the leaps in medical technology over the past 20 years and offers new understandings related to how the brain functions in relation to learning. This biological understanding and its application to educational theorising is problematic for teaching as it challenges many existing theories (for example, accelerated learning). It is nevertheless a welcome addition to educational studies.

NEET This acronym stands for 'not in education, employment or training' and is often used pejoratively to refer to the 250,000 British 16–19-year-olds who for a variety of reasons find themselves outside of mainstream education and training.

Pedagogy Pedagogy refers to a science of teaching embodying both curriculum and methodology.

PISA The OECD Programme for International Student Assessment (PISA), through its surveys of 15-year-olds in the principal industrialised countries, assesses how far students near the end of compulsory education have acquired some of the knowledge and skills essential for full participation in society. Their surveys are carried out every three years.

Plenary The activity at the close of a teaching session allowing learners to draw together the main points from the lesson.

Profession A body based upon codes, regulation and standards drawn together by virtue of offering an expertise and a specialism in knowledge and its production.

Professional identity Professional identity refers to how teachers view themselves as teachers; how teachers, view others that they professionally engage with and how teachers believe they are perceived by those 'others'.

Professional socialization This refers to the variety of ways that teachers become teachers. It acknowledges the many different processes, for example, learning the norms and values associated with a particular department, institution and subject discipline. It can take place both within and outside the institution the teacher is employed in (for example, by joining a teacher association and/or trade union).

Psychometric testing This has its origins in the nineteenth century and, drawing on psychological traditions, it refers to the ways in which intelligence and aptitude can be diagnosed through tests. One example being the 11+ test that some children sit to determine the type of schooling they might receive.

Pupil referral unit (PRU) These are educational institutions run by specialist staff who deal with learners with emotional and social difficulties. Many of these learners have been excluded from mainstream education. In most cases learners spend a short period of time (for example, two terms) in PRUs before being integrated back into mainstream schooling.

Reflection The act of thinking about one's practice with a view to developing it further.

Reflective practitioner The view that good teachers are constantly engaged with the self-assessment and evaluation of their own practice as a key aspect of their ongoing professionalism.

Scaffolding The building of layers of support to enable learning to take place. Slowly this support is reduced and may be completely taken away, leaving learners more independent.

Streaming This refers to the ways in which schools group learners based on ability. In contrast to 'setting', groups of learners study the same subjects together but are grouped into 'streams' (for example, high-ability streams, low-ability streams).

Setting Similar to 'streaming' but students are grouped together depending on how well or badly they perform in a particular subject discipline. This means that it is possible to be in a 'top set' for French and a 'bottom set' for history.

Summative assessment Assessment and testing that summarises the learning that has taken place.

Underachievement What an individual obtains in education relative to others of the same age cohort to indicate a lower rate and level of obtainment.

Vocational education In Britain, historically, a dividing line tends to exist between 'academic' subjects and 'vocational' subjects, the latter referring to more 'work'-related subjects (for example, hairdressing, business, design and technology). However the lack of parity of esteem in Britain between the 'vocational' and the 'academic' is often associated with hierarchies in the social background of learners.

Widening participation A commitment and drive to include more and more individuals and groups within educational settings and processes drawn from previously excluded or marginalised groups.

Zone of proximal development A term associated with Vygotsky, which refers to the zone between what pupils' level of development is (their actual level) and the level of development they could reach with suitable teaching (their potential level).

SWINDON COLLEGE

LEARNING RESOURCE CENTRE

INDEX

Added to a page number 'f' denotes a figure and 't' denotes a table.